ANTITRUST

AND TRADE

REGULATION

TODAY : 1969

MORE SELECTED ANALYSES FROM BNA'S ANTITRUST AND TRADE REGULATION REPORT

Prepared with the assistance of the ATRR Advisory Board
Edwin S. Rockefeller, Chairman
and the editorial staff of The Bureau of National Affairs, Inc.

by John C. Scott

BNA
BOOK

published by
THE BUREAU OF NATIONAL AFFAIRS, INC., WASHINGTON, D.C.

PRINTED IN THE UNITED STATES OF AMERICA
Standard Book Number 87179–086–6
Library of Congress Catalog Card No.: 67–25856

TABLE OF CONTENTS

i

70-02557

TABLE OF CONTENTS – (Contd.)

PREFACE

Each of the articles in this book is a reprint of an analysis published earlier in the regular weekly issues of BNA's Antitrust & Trade Regulation Report. Since they are reproduced here with few changes other than the addition of Federal Reporter citations, the date or original publication is given at the beginning of each analysis to help the reader relate the decisions and events described to the time of publication. In the judgment of BNA's editorial staff, however, all of the items reproduced here remain of current interest.

These analyses were selected from the ATRR issues published between April 11, 1967, and April 30, 1969. Earlier analyses that remain of current interest are collected in Antitrust and Trade Regulation Today: 1967, copies of which can still be purchased from BNA BOOKS, a division of The Bureau of National Affairs, Inc.

The members of the ATRR Advisory Board, whose judgment was relied on substantially in the evaluation of the developments analyzed, are listed below.

ADVISORY BOARD

Edwin S. Rockefeller, *Chairman*
Wald, Harkrader & Rockefeller
Washington, D. C.

Cyrus V. Anderson
PPG Industries, Inc.
Pittsburgh, Pennsylvania

H. Thomas Austern
Covington & Burling
Washington, D. C.

David Berger
Philadelphia, Pennsylvania

John Bodner, Jr.
Howrey, Simon, Baker & Murchison
Washington, D. C.

Leonard J. Emmerglick
Washington, D. C.

Ephraim Jacobs
Hollabaugh & Jacobs
Washington, D. C.

Earl W. Kintner
Arent, Fox, Kintner, Plotkin & Kahn
Washington, D. C.

Robert P. Knapp, Jr.
Windels, Merritt & Ingraham
New York, New York

Victor H. Kramer
Arnold and Porter
Washington, D. C.

Robert A. Longman
Celanese Corp.
New York, New York

Ira M. Millstein
Weil, Gotshal & Manges
New York, New York

Robert A. Nitschke
General Motors Corp.
Detroit, Michigan

S. Chesterfield Oppenheim
Washington, D. C.

Edwin H. Pewett
Glassie, Pewett, Beebe & Shanks
Washington, D. C.

Earl E. Pollock
Sonnenschein, Levinson, Carlin,
Nath & Rosenthal
Chicago, Illinois

George D. Reycraft
Cadwalader, Wickersham & Taft
New York, New York

Frederick M. Rowe
Kirkland, Ellis, Hodson, Chaffetz,
Masters & Rowe
Washington, D. C.

Worth Rowley
Washington, D.C.

Louis B. Schwartz
University of Pennsylvania
Philadelphia, Pennsylvania

Joseph E. Sheehy
Washington, D.C.

Richard A. Solomon
General Mills, Inc.
Minneapolis, Minn.

Gordon B. Spivak
Yale Law School
New Haven, Connecticut

Sigmund Timberg
Washington, D. C.

F. Gerald Toye
General Electric Company
Washington, D. C.

Jerrold G. Van Cise
Cahill, Gordon, Sonnett, Reindel
& Ohl
New York, New York

Malcolm Richard Wilkey
Kennecott Copper Co.
New York, New York

Larry L. Williams
Clifford, Warnke, Glass,
McIlwain & Finney
Washington, D. C.

PART I — COMBINATIONS AND CONSPIRACIES

<u>Subject:</u> "Combinations" in Restraint of Trade   (Published 10/22/68)

<u>Question</u>

Does the word "combination" in Section 1 of the Sherman Act connote a concept different from a contract, agreement, or conspiracy in restraint of trade?

<u>References</u>

Albrecht v. Herald Co., 390 U.S. 145, 36 LW 4171 (pp. A-1, X-1, ATRR No. 347, 3/5/68)
U.S. v. Parke, Davis, & Co., 362 U.S. 29 (1960)
Panel Discussion on New Theories of Price Conspiracy, 24 ABA Antitrust L.J. 76 (p. A-4, ATRR No. 145, 4/21/64)

<u>Background</u>

Section 1 of the Sherman Act outlaws "every contract, combination in the form of trust or otherwise, or conspiracy, in restraint of trade." Obviously, Section 1 prohibits actions by two or more persons. As the Supreme Court once put it: "An act harmless when done by one may become a public wrong when done by many acting in concert, for it then takes on the form of a conspiracy * * *." Eastern States Retail Lumber Dealers' Assn. v. U.S., 234 U.S. 600 (1914).

Some courts have drawn a distinction between contracts on the one hand and combinations or conspiracies on the other. Rice v. Standard Oil Co., 134 F. 464 (C.C. N.J. 1905); U.S. v. American Linen Supply Co., 1956 Trade Cases Para. 68,337 (N.D. Ill. 1956). At least indirectly, the Supreme Court has drawn a distinction between contracts and conspiracies. Several times the Court has held that an express agreement need not be shown to establish an unlawful conspiracy. American Tobacco v. U.S., 328 U.S. 781, 809 (1946); Interstate Circuit, Inc., v. U.S., 306 U.S. 208, 227 (1939); and U.S. v. Paramount Pictures, Inc., 334 U.S. 131, 142 (1948).

At least until recently, however, it was not customary to make a distinction between combinations and conspiracies. For instance, in U.S. v. Baumgartner, April 10, 1929, the Federal District Court for Northern Illinois charged a jury that "a combination is, in the nature of things, like any other agreement or conspiracy." ABA Antitrust Section, "Jury Instructions in Criminal Antitrust Cases," 22, 24 (1965). When the district judge instructed the jury in the American Tobacco case, 328 U.S. 781 (1946), he stated: "Thus you will see then an indispensable ingredient of each of the offenses charged in the information is a combination or conspiracy. Now, these terms as used in the Sherman Act have the same legal effect. I shall use them in these instructions interchangeably, without intending any distinction in their meaning." "Jury Instructions in Criminal Antitrust Cases," 161, 169. To the same effect is the jury charge in U.S. v. Local 36 of International Fishermen (245, 247). Indeed, a widely used antitrust case book begins a chapter with the statement: "The concept of conspiracy, which is of ancient lineage in the law, is a chief concept under the Sherman Act. Apparently, not much legal significance has been attributed to any distinction which might inhere in the use of the different terms 'combination' or 'conspiracy' as used in Section 1 of the Sherman Act, and it seems clear that the element basic to both, is some concert of action between two or more parties." Oppenheim and Weston, "Federal Antitrust Laws, Cases and Comments," 178 (1968). After the Supreme Court handed down its opinion in the Parke, Davis case listed in the references, however, there was some thought that the "combination" language of that opinion "indicates that you can prove a combination with little less evidence than you can a

1

conspiracy." 24 ABA Antitrust Law Journal at 100. Parke, Davis was found to have violated Section 1 of the Sherman Act by enlisting the aid of wholesalers, through refusal-to-deal threats, in enforcement of a resale-price-maintenance program and by using some retailers' willingness to cooperate as a means of persuading other retailers to comply with the pricing policy. Parke, Davis was held to have "created a combination with the retailers and the wholesalers." Through-out the opinion, the Court relied more on the word "combination" than on the word "conspiracy." "An unlawful combination is not just such as arises from a price maintenance agreement, ex-press or implied; such a combination is also organized if the producer secures adherence to his suggested prices by means which go beyond his mere declination to sell to a customer who will not observe his announced policy. * * * When the manufacturer's actions, as here, go beyond mere announcement of his policy in the simple refusal to deal, and he employs other means which affect adherence to his resale prices, this countervailing consideration is not present and therefore he has put together a combination in violation of the Sherman Act. * * * Thus, whether an unlawful combination or conspiracy is proved is to be judged by what the parties actually did rather than by the words they used." 362 U.S. at 43, 44.

The Parke, Davis opinion reversed a district court that had dismissed the government's complaint on the authority of U.S. v. Colgate & Co., 250 U.S. 300 (1919). But the Supreme Court insisted that it had already, in U.S. v. Bausch & Lomb Co., 321 U.S. 707 (1944) and FTC v. Beechnut Packing Co., 257 U.S. 441 (1922), limited the Colgate Doctrine to mean "no more than that a simple refusal to sell to customers who will not resell at prices suggested by the seller is permissible under the Sherman Act." Here, the opinion went on, it would have been perfectly lawful for Parke, Davis to announce a "simple refusal without more to deal with wholesalers who did not observe the wholesalers' net price selling schedule." But that policy became "tainted with the vice of illegality * * * when Parke, Davis used it as the vehicle to gain the wholesalers' participation in the program to effectuate the retailers' adherence to the suggested retail prices."

The Beechnut decision referred to in Parke, Davis did not involve the significance of the Sherman Act's word "combination," for it upheld an FTC order issued under Section 5 of the FTC Act, which does not require proof of a conspiracy, agreement, or combination. And the Bausch & Lomb opinion referred to seems to use "conspiracy" and "combination" inter-changeably when it says: "whether this conspiracy and combination was achieved by agreement or by acquiescence of the wholesalers coupled with assistance in effectuating its purpose is immaterial."

Then last term, in Albrecht v. Herald Co., cited in the references, the Supreme Court seemed to go all the way in separating the concept of a combination from that of a contract or conspiracy. "Section 1 of the Sherman Act * * * covers combinations in addition to contracts and conspiracies, express or implied. The Court made this quite clear in United States v. Parke, Davis & Co., 362 U.S. 29 (1960), where it held that * * * a combination arose when Parke, Davis threatened its wholesalers with termination unless they put pressure on their re-tail customers."

Conclusions

On the question posed at the outset of this Analysis, the Antitrust Bar seems to be sharply divided. At the 1968 spring meeting of the American Bar Association's Antitrust Sec-tion, 37 ABA Antitrust Law Journal 300, former Assistant Attorney General Donald F. Turner expressed confusion as to precisely what the Supreme Court had in mind when it indicated in Albrecht and Parke, Davis that a combination is something different from a conspiracy. But he made it clear he does not believe that the Court read the element of consent or agreement out of the word combination. During Mr. Turner's service as its chief, the Antitrust Division probably never tried to give Section 1 of the Sherman Act any broader scope than it did in footnote 31 to its brief in U.S. v. Arnold, Schwinn & Co., 388 U.S. 365 (pp. A-1, X-1, ATRR No. 309, 6/13/67). In a muted attack on the Colgate Doctrine, that footnote said: "The announce-ment plus the threat of cancellation would appear to create a tacit agreement with those distrib-utors and dealers who comply -- all Section 1 requires." Soon afterwards the question whether there must be compliance or tacit agreement before a Section 1 violation can be found divided the judges of the Court of Appeals for the First Circuit. Quinn v. Mobil Oil Co., 375 F. 2d 273 (pp. A-5, X-1, ATRR No. 299, 4/4/67).

Other antitrust lawyers, looking at the facts of the Albrecht, Beechnut, Bausch & Lomb, and Parke, Davis cases, insist that there was ample basis in each of those records to support a finding of a conspiracy and that therefore the emphasis those opinions placed on combination is not significant. True, they go on, there are situations in which the conspiring parties are not equally at fault -- where one imposes his will upon the other. Yet the word conspiracy fits that situation, they say; there must still be proof of concerted activity, and it is not possible to establish a combination with any less evidence of concerted activity than is necessary to establish a conspiracy.

Even accepting the proposition that the "combination" language in the Supreme Court's opinion appears in dicta, there is support in the Antitrust Bar for taking at face value the Supreme Court's statement that the Sherman Act "covers combinations in addition to contracts and conspiracies, express or implied." If a "combination" arose "when Parke, Davis threatened its wholesalers with termination unless they put pressure on their retail customers," then the unilateral action of a single party can create a combination between him and others who do not share his business interests or motives but are simply used to effect his unilateral policies. Surely the word conspiracy connotes a common purpose, intent, or design.

Treatment of a combination as something different from and less difficult to prove than an agreement or conspiracy could open important new avenues for expanding application of the Sherman Act. In our complex society, it is easy to conceive of two companies drifting into a relationship that has all the elements of a conspiracy except an agreement or a common design or purpose. (For example, see ANALYSIS, "Reciprocal-Buying Practices," p. B-1, ATRR No. 203, 6/1/65, reprinted at p. 16, Antitrust and Trade Regulation Today: 1967.) Indeed, the Court of Appeals for the Second Circuit has recently used the word "combination," without statutory basis, to describe and condemn, as "joint" action of affiliated companies in violation of Section 17 (d) of the 1940 Investment Company Act, parallel conduct of two companies that could not be shown to have acted by agreement. SEC v. Talley Industries, Inc., 399 F. 2d 396, (1968).

If the unwilling acquiescence of a customer or supplier is enough to create a "combination" between him and the enterprise putting pressure on him, may the unwilling acquiescence of smaller members of an industry in a price change by that industry's dominant company also create a combination? In U.S. v. Waltham Watch Co., 47 F. Supp. 524, 533 (S.D. N.Y. 1942), there is reasoning that implies antitrust responsibility on the part of an unwilling participant if he knows his action promotes the purposes of a conspiracy. See also U.S. v. National Lead Co., 63 F. Supp. 513, 525-6 (1945).

Is it possible that a large multi-division corporation or a single family of commonly-owned corporations might in and of itself be labeled a combination? After all, Standard Oil of New Jersey was deemed a "combination" in Standard Oil Co. v. U.S., 221 U.S. 1, 75 (1911). The immediate past Assistant Attorney General in charge of the Antitrust Division has indicated a preference for the "bathtub conspiracy" theory of proceeding against multi-corporation enterprises, even in reciprocal-dealing situations. 34 ABA Antitrust L.J. 122-123. Indeed, there are antitrust practitioners who believe there is no meaningful distinction between combination and conspiracy and that, even if there is, the Justice Department will never bring a case based on the distinction.

- 0 -

<u>Subject: Bathtub Conspiracies</u>   (Published 10/3/67)

<u>Question</u>

Under what circumstances does a corporation's dealings with its subsidiaries or divisions subject it to antitrust liability?

<u>References</u>

Hawaiian Oke & Liquors, Ltd., v. Joseph E. Seagram & Sons, Inc. (D. Hawaii) (pp. A-13, X-1, ATRR No. 317, 8/8/67).

Report of the Attorney General's National Committee to Study the Antitrust Laws, 1955, pp. 30-36.

<u>Background</u>

The proscription in Section 1 of the Sherman Act against "every contract, combination * * * or conspiracy, in restraint of trade" necessarily presupposes the existence of two or more contracting, combining or conspiring parties. In Section 1 cases involving corporations, their officials, their agents, their divisions and their subsidiaries, the courts have often been troubled by difficulties in ascertaining who and what are separate parties capable of contracting or conspiring with each other. In contrast with Section 2, which makes monopolization an offense even when it is the act of a single person or entity, Section 1 does not forbid a single person or entity to impose a restraint on trade.

Consequently, while employees of a single corporation have been convicted under indictments including Section 2 charges (Patterson v. U.S., 222 Fed. 599 (6th Cir. 1915); White Bear Theatre Corp. v. State Theatre Corp., 129 F. 2d 600 (8th Cir. 1942)), it has been held that a Section 1 charge, standing alone, cannot be sustained by proving joint action on the part of only a corporation and officers acting on its behalf (Nelson Radio & Supply Co. v. Motorola, 200 F. 2d 911 (5th Cir. 1952); Marion County Co-Op Assn. v. Carnation Co., 114 F. Supp. 58 (W.D. Ark. 1953)). The rationale of Nelson Radio is that "a corporation cannot conspire with itself any more than a private individual can, and it is the general rule that the acts of the agent are the acts of the corporation."

To be considered an agent incapable of forming a Section 1 conspiracy with his corporation, an individual must be completely free of any separable personal interest in the outcome of the activity being attacked. Poller v. CBS, 368 U.S. 464, 489 (1962). Moreover, individuals cannot insulate a conspiracy from Sherman Act attack by organizing a corporation as the instrumentality for carrying out their purpose. Bascom Launder Corp. v. Farny, 1950-51 Trade Cases 62,706 (S.D. N.Y. 1950); Beacon Fruit & Produce Co. v. H. Harris & Co. 152 F. Supp. 702 (D. Mass. 1957). "Any affiliation or integration flowing from an illegal conspiracy cannot insulate the conspirators from the sanctions which Congress has imposed." U.S. v. Yellow Cab Co. 332 U.S. 218 (1947).

When a single business enterprise is operated by a complex of related corporate entities or when several incorporated businesses are operated and controlled through the same ownership, though, the courts have decided that the separate corporate entities are capable of making a Section 1 conspiracy with each other. The Yellow Cab case involved six corporations controlled by a single majority stockholder.

In the Supreme Court's view, "an unreasonable restraint of interstate commerce * * * may result as readily from a conspiracy among those who are affiliated or integrated under common ownership as from a conspiracy among those who are otherwise independent. * * * The corporate inter-relationships of the conspirators, in other words, are not determinative of the applicability of the Sherman Act." In U.S. v. Timken Roller Bearing Co., 83 F. Supp. 284 (N.D. Ohio 1949), aff'd 341 U.S. 593 (1951), corporations affiliated through controlling stockholdings were held to have conspired with each other in violation of Section 1.

When the Attorney General's Committee reviewed the Yellow Cab and Timken decisions in 1955, it concluded that they applied Section 1 to combinations and conspiracies among commonly owned or controlled corporations only when their purpose or effect is "coercion or unreasonable restraint on the trade of strangers to those acting in concert *** Where such concerted action restrains no trade and is designed to restrain no trade other than that of the parent and its subsidiaries, Section 1 is not violated."

For example, a parent corporation's determination or approval of the prices to be charged by a subsidiary has been held not to be illegal price fixing. U. S. v. Arkansas Fuel Oil Corp., 1960 Trade Cases 69,619 (N.D. Okla. 1960). And intra-enterprise conspiracy claims have been rejected when the existence of separate corporations has no real economic or competitive significance. Syracuse Broadcasting Corp. v. Newhouse, 319 F.2d 683 (2d Cir. 1963); Sunkist Growers, Inc. v. Wickler & Smith Citrus Products Co., 370 U.S. 19 (1962). On the other hand, a parent corporation's directions to its subsidiary may create a Sherman Act conspiracy when the directions require the subsidiary to interfere with competition from the parent's rival. Aerojet-General Corp. v. Aero-Jet Products Corp. 235 F. Supp. 341 (N.D. Ohio 1963).

Unincorporated Divisions

Some members of the Attorney General's Committee felt that there are no circumstances under which a parent and its separately incorporated subsidiary should be held guilty "of an offense that must be committed by more than one person." But everyone agreed that "there would concededly be no liability under Section 1, if a company does business through unincorporated branches, divisions or departments."

The Committee's statement about unincorporated branches or divisions is supported by subsequent opinions on the capacity of unincorporated divisions to join with the "parent" corporation in a Section 1 conspiracy. Poller v. CBS, 284 F.2d 599 (D.C. Cir. 1960); Deterjet Corp. v. United Aircraft, 211 F. Supp. 348 (D. Del. 1962); Kemwel Automotive Corp. v. Ford Motor Co., 1966 Trade Cases 71,882 (S.D. N.Y. 1966); Johnny Maddox Motor Co. v. Ford Motor Co., 202 F. Supp. 103 (W.D. Tex. 1960); Nelson Radio & Supply Co. v. Motorola, 200 F.2d 911 (5th Cir. 1952). In the Poller case, a charge that CBS had conspired with one of its divisions was characterized by the court as "in reality a charge that CBS conspired with itself."

Each of those decisions on corporation-division conspiracies was distinguished on its facts by the first recorded opinion dealing with charges of a horizontal Section 1 conspiracy among unincorporated divisions of a single corporation. In the case listed in the references, Judge Martin Pence of the Hawaii Federal District Court instructed a jury that it could find a Section 1 Sherman Act violation in a conspiracy among Calvert Distilling Co., Four Roses Distilling Co., and Frankfort Distilling Co. to eliminate a wholesale distributor, even though each of those three companies is an unincorporated division of House of Seagram, Inc. Stressing the three divisions' use of separate and "pretty autonomous" sales organizations, Judge Pence saw a clear distinction between a "vertical" conspiracy involving a corporation and one of its divisions and a "horizontal" conspiracy among corporate divisions that otherwise act "entirely independently."

In Seagram's setup, he emphasized, each division was responsible for establishing a distribution system for its brand of whisky--a responsibility that included the choice of one or more wholesale distributors for every geographical area. Moreover, Seagram's conversion of Calvert, Four Roses, and Frankfort from incorporated subsidiaries into mere divisions came shortly after, and "apparently resulted from," the Supreme Court's decision in Kiefer-Stewart Co. v. Seagram, 340 U.S. 211 (1951). In refusing to attribute antitrust significance to the divisions' new "label," Judge Pence relied on the statement in Simpson v. Union Oil Co., 377 U.S. 13 (1964), that "differences in form often do not represent 'differences in substance.'"

Conclusions

The key to Judge Pence's decision in the Hawaiian liquor case would appear to be his reference to the Supreme Court's statement that substance is to prevail over form. The decisions applying Section 1 to "bathtub conspiracies" suggest that the courts tend to rely on that doctrine whenever they would otherwise be prevented from taking action against a flag-

rant violation of the spirit of the Sherman Act. Therefore, in addition to the Seagram divisions'
use of separate and independent sales organizations, the key facts in the Hawaiian liquor case
are the use of apparently rival brands and Seagram's previous unhappy experience with antitrust litigation predicated on the existence of separately incorporated enterprises.

At least some members of the antitrust bar are confident that not all federal judges
will accept Judge Pence's concept that a single corporation can encompass a number of business
entities capable of conspiring with each other. Many courts are expected to feel that his
approach ignores the practicalities of operating businesses under the corporate form. And
some judges may view the use of autonomous divisions and rival brands as bona fide attempts
to maintain additional competition and will refuse to condemn a single corporation for stopping
short of inter-division competition that is 100% pure. They may refuse to find it a matter of
substance rather than form that the House of Seagram was built with three roofs instead of one.

The issue whether autonomous divisions of a single corporation are capable of making
a Section 1 Sherman Act conspiracy with each other is not likely to be clearly resolved until
there are lower-court decisions the Supreme Court can review. And it would appear that the
decisions are most likely to be handed down in private damage litigation, for there is some
question whether the Justice Department's Antitrust Division will make any use of Judge Pence's
theory. At the April meeting of the American Bar Association's Antitrust Section (p. A-3,
ATRR No. 301, 4/18/67), Assistant Attorney General Donald F. Turner characterized the
"bathtub-conspiracy" theory as "not the happiest of legal doctrines" but one he would apply to
related companies "whenever predatory or coercive conduct is directed against outsiders."
His recent complaint against General Tire and three subsidiaries (pp. A-1, X-1, ATRR No.
295, 3/7/67) did charge a combination of purchasing power to coerce outsiders into reciprocal-
dealing commitments.

Mr. Turner's attitude as well as the tenor of the decisions suggest that there is no
trend toward changing the rule that a parent can direct the activities of a subsidiary without
incurring Sherman Act liability as long as those activities do not involve any predatory or
coercive conduct against outsiders. Judge Pence's opinion can be squared with that rule,
since he was dealing with conduct aimed at an independent wholesale distributor.

When subordinate branches or divisions--whether incorporated or unincorporated--
are involved, the key may well lie in the attitude manifested by the enterprise itself toward
the subordinate branches--whether they are treated, in the operation of their businesses, as
separate enterprises. If, as Judge Pence thought was true in the Seagram organization, the
separate divisions walk like competitors, look like competitors, and sound like competitors,
they will be treated as competitors forbidden to make agreements among themselves to limit
competition. Judge Pence carefully excluded from his ruling a "vertical" direction by Seagram
that each of its three "pretty autonomous" divisions simultaneously stop dealing with a
designated wholesaler. The point has been made by some antitrust experts that, if Judge
Pence would permit "vertical" intro-corporate collusion, a company in Seagram's position
might safely accomplish the same anticompetitive result by putting the divisions under the
direct control of a single executive. Again, it is suggested, form prevails over substance.
But other specialists counter with the observation that Judge Pence's rationale does not grant
Section 1 immunity on the basis of a mere formal shift of job titles. The three divisions
become a unified business enterprise for Section 1 purposes only if the single parent company
executive and his staff in fact make marketing decisions for the divisions. Consequently,
they reason, the parent corporation does give up something of substance when it centralizes.
It loses the flexibility its divisions previously had in responding to immediate competitive
situations and any other advantages that originally led it to use decentralized control.

- 0 -

Subject: Territorial Allocations   (Published 7/4/67)

Question

Is an agreement among competitors to allocate sales territories a per se violation of the Sherman Act when not ancillary to exploitation of a trademark and not accompanied by any other restraint on competition?

Reference

U.S. v. Sealy, Inc., 388 U.S. 350, 35 LW 4571 (pp. A-3, X-9, ATRR No. 309, 6/13/67)

Background

"There are certain agreements or practices which because of their pernicious effect on competition and lack of any redeeming virtue are conclusively presumed to be unreasonable and therefore illegal without elaborate inquiry as to the precise harm they have caused or the business excuse for their use. This principle of per se unreasonableness not only makes the type of restraints which are proscribed by the Sherman Act more certain to the benefit of everyone concerned, but it also avoids the necessity for an incredibly complicated and prolonged economic investigation * * *. Among the practices which the courts have heretofore deemed to be unlawful in and of themselves are price fixing * * * division of markets, * * * group boycotts, * * * and tying arrangements." Northern Pacific R. Co. v. U.S., 356 U.S. 1 (1958).

In White Motor Co., v. U.S., 372 U.S. 253 (pp. A-1, X-1, ATRR No. 86, 3/5/63), the Supreme Court did not think it had enough competitive-effect information to make up its mind whether "vertical" territorial exclusives--restrictions imposed by a manufacturer on his distributors -- should be declared illegal per se. But it had no reservations about "horizontal" divisions of territories by which competitors split up markets among themselves; they "are naked restraints of trade with no purpose except stifling of competition."

On the basis of such declarations by the Supreme Court and lower court decisions in cases like Johnson v. Joseph Schlitz Brewing Co., 33 F. Supp. 176 (E.D. Tenn. 1940), and U.S. v. General Dyestuff Corp., 57 F. Supp. 642 (S.D. N.Y. 1944), antitrust writers have generally listed horizontal divisions of territories among the restraints of trade that must be considered per se violations of the Sherman Act. S. Chesterfield Oppenheim, "Antitrust Booms and Boomerangs," 59 Northwestern Univ. L.R. 33, 35; Phillip Areeda, "Antitrust Analysis," Little Brown & Co., 1967, p. 207; Jerrold G. Van Cise, "Understanding the Antitrust Laws," Practising Law Institute, 1966, p. 118; Simon H. Rifkind, "Hoffman's Antitrust Law and Techniques," Mathew Bender & Co., 1963, Vol. 2, p. 57. In fact, Professor Oppenheim and Judge Rifkind have described market splitting as more anticompetitive than price fixing. After all, competitors who agree only to charge identical prices are not foreclosed from competing in the quality of their products, the services provided for customers, and the volume and ingenuity of their advertising.

In U.S. v. Sealy, the Supreme Court dealt specifically with a horizontal market-splitting agreement. Sealy is the owner of a nationally advertised trade name used in marketing mattresses and bedding products. It does not manufacture these products itself but licenses bedding manufacturers to make and sell their products under the Sealy name and trademarks. Each licensee agrees to limit his sales of Sealy-brand items to an assigned territory. Substantially all of Sealy's stock is owned by the manufacturer-licensees, and Sealy's board of directors and executive committee are composed entirely of licensee-stockholders or their nominees. Looking "at substance rather than form," Mr. Justice Fortas, for a 6-1 majority, found that "the territorial arrangements must be regarded as the creature of horizontal action by the licensees."

Having found horizontal market splitting, however, the Court did not take the next logical step and declare the arrangement illegal per se. Rather, the Court looked for further factual support for finding a Section 1 Sherman Act violation and found it in Sealy's fixing, and the licensee-manufacturers' policing, of retail prices. At that point, Mr. Justice Fortas decided he was faced with an "aggregation of trade restraints" like that involved in Timken Roller Bearing Co. v. U.S., 341 U.S. 593 (1951). "This unlawful resale price-fixing activity refutes [Sealy's] claim that the territorial restraints were mere incidents of a lawful program of trademark licensing."

Near the close of his opinion, Mr. Justice Fortas does make it clear that he is applying a rule of per se illegality to this "aggregation of trade restraints." In doing so, he rejects Sealy's attempt to draw an analogy between its territorial allocations and an agreement among "a number of small grocers" to "allocate territory among themselves on an exclusive basis as incident to the use of a common name and common advertisements." Mr. Justice Fortas does not think that the condemnation of Sealy's territorial arrangements requires the Court to also condemn such an arrangement among small grocers. He does not say that territorial allocations by small grocers would not be condemned as per se Sherman Act violations but rather simply reserves judgment on them. In a footnote to that portion of his opinion, he makes the statement that "an alleged market division, * * * like price fixing, group boycotts, and tying arrangements, has been held to be a per se violation of the Sherman Act," citing the Northern Pacific case.

In a dissenting opinion, Mr. Justice Harlan agreed "that the division of territories is illegal per se," if it is in fact horizontal. But he does not go along with the majority either that the arrangement is horizontal or that the territorial restraints "were part of the unlawful price fixing and policing." He would find Sealy's territorial limitations to be vertical in nature and therefore to be reasonable restrictions on intrabrand competition in the interest of more effective interbrand competition. Consistently with that view, he dissented from the Court's ruling the same day that a manufacturer's vertical territorial restrictions on wholesalers who obtain title to the manufacturer's products and resell them are illegal per se. U.S. v. Arnold, Schwinn & Co., 388 U.S. 365, 35 L.W. 4563 (pp. A-1, X-1, ATRR No. 309, 6/13/67).

Conclusions

The simple fact is that every statement the Supreme Court has ever made to the effect that a horizontal market division, standing alone, is a per se Sherman Act violation was a statement not really necessary to the decision reached in the particular litigation. Every Supreme Court decision directing or affirming the entry of an injunction against a market-splitting arrangement has been rendered in a context of related price fixing or other restraint. Even the two district judges who decided Johnson v. Schlitz and U.S. v. General Dyestuffs, mentioned above, wrote in a context of monopolistic or oligopolistic market control by the participating competitors.

On the other hand, the Sealy opinion certainly cannot be read as an application of the rule of reason to horizontal market splitting. The territorial restrictions in Sealy's trademark licenses were declared illegal per se because they were tied to the fixing of uniform resale prices. The question remains whether, when actually faced with a horizontal market division without more, the Supreme Court would say, "illegal per se." In Northern Pacific, White Motor, and now in the Sealy footnote, it has said it would, and Mr. Justice Harlan seems clearly to think it would. For the dissenting Justice, classification of the Sealy territorial arrangements as horizontal is enough to establish per se illegality despite the connection with trademark licensing and without regard to price fixing.

The Sealy opinion's reliance on the tie to price fixing and its failure to state flatly a per se rule for unattached market splitting should please those who have criticized the Court for announcing unnecessarily broad antitrust rules. But the presence of price fixing was apparently relied on because of two elements in the case that are not present in every horizontal

division of markets. First, the Sealy restrictions were written into licenses under a trademark that Sealy is entitled to exploit. Perhaps the Court is saying that, in the absence of
other related restraints, territorial allocations like Sealy's and Timken's are reasonably
ancillary to the trademark-licensing program. Otherwise, there would seem to be little point
in stressing the "horizontal" nature of the arrangements, since the traditional form of vertical territorial restraint was declared illegal per se in the Schwinn case.

Second, the participating manufacturers are relatively small operators combining
forces to compete on a nationwide basis with much larger competitors. If small merchants
are to be allowed, absent price fixing or other restraints, to make defensive divisions of sales
territories, then obviously such agreements are not illegal per se. If it is ever presented
with such a case, however, the Court is not likely to overlook the writings of those who point
out that market splitting has more anticompetitive consequences than price fixing. The Court
might also see in such arrangements a commitment by every participant except one to refuse
to deal with buyers located in that one participant's territory. And the Court has flatly declared commercial group boycotts illegal per se. Klor's, Inc., v. Broadway-Hale Stores,
Inc., 359 U.S. 207 (1959).

The Court's explicit reservation of judgment on whether "a group of small grocers"
might justify an allocation of territories may not be significant. Among small retailers who
advertise in common, a territorial allocation will generally work only as a restraint on store
locations, not as a complete ban on sales to consumers living outside an assigned area. Therefore, such an arrangement would not be likely to impose as great a restraint on competition
as sales-territory allocations among manufacturers. A territorial restriction on salesroom
locations was upheld in Boro Hall Corp. v. General Motors, 124 F. 2d 822 & 130 F. 2d 196
(2d Cir. 1942).

- 0 -

Subject: Agreements to Exchange Price Data   (Published 3/18/69)

Question

What price information can competitors exchange without running afoul of the
Sherman Act?

Reference

U.S. v. Container Corp. of America, 393 U.S. 333, 37 LW 4077 (pp. A-19, X-21,
ATRR No. 392, 1/14/69)

Background

Agreements among competitors on prices were first declared to be Section 1 Sherman
Act violations in U.S. v. Trans-Missouri Freight Association, 171 U.S. 505 (1897). Since
then a variety of price-monitoring and price-supervising programs -- most of them adminis-
tered by trade associations -- have been tested in the Supreme Court.

The collection and dissemination of price, sales, inventory, and customer data were
enjoined in American Column & Lumber Co. v. U.S., 257 U.S. 377 (1921). Emphasis was
placed in that opinion on evidence that the trade association had made a systematic effort,
along with the distribution of the data, to have members cut production and raise prices.
An even more elaborate program of sales-data distribution, coupled with a penalty-backed
agreement to adhere to announced price schedules, was outlawed in U.S. v. American Lin-
seed Oil Co., 262 U.S. 371 (1923). Similarly in Sugar Institute v. U.S., 297 U.S. 553 (1936),
and U.S. v. Socony-Vacuum Oil Co., 310 U.S.150 (1940), there were not only programs for the
exchange of price information but also commitments to adhere to announced price schedules.

In the Maple Flooring Manufacturers' case, 268 U.S. 563 (1925), the Court declared
that ". . . trade associations or combinations of persons or corporations which openly and
fairly gather and disseminate information as to the cost of their product, the volume of production, the actual price which the product has brought in past transactions, stocks of merchandise on hand, approximate cost of transportation from the principal point of shipment to
the points of consumption as did these defendants and who, as they did, meet and discuss such
information and statistics without however reaching or attempting to reach any agreement or
any concerted action with respect to prices or production or restraining competition, do not
thereby engage in unlawful restraint of commerce." The Maple Flooring Manufacturers'
Association did not, in its statistical reports to members, identify the parties to specific
transactions. See also Cement Manufacturers Protective Assn. v. U.S., 268 U.S. 588 (1925),
where prices to specific customers were exchanged. The Supreme Court upheld the exchange
program after noting that its purpose was protection against fraudulent inducement to deliver
more cement than needed for a specific job.

The Container Corporation case listed as the reference, "is unlike any of the other
price decisions we have rendered," according to Mr. Justice Douglas, who wrote the majority opinion. The Supreme Court reinstated a Justice Department suit to enjoin a price-data
exchange program that was accompanied neither by a systematic trade-association effort to
boost prices nor by a commitment to adhere to a price schedule. On the other hand, there was
an exchange of information concerning specific sales to identified customers , not a statistical
report on the average cost to all members. And the exchange was not claimed to be motivated
by fraud-avoidance reasons such as those involved in the Cement Manufacturers' case.

The district judge had dismissed the government's complaint (273 F. Supp. 18 (M.D.
N.C.), p. A-4, ATRR No. 322, 9/12/67) on the basis of findings that were left undisturbed
on appeal. First, competitive price information was sought by the sellers, manufacturers
of corrugated paper containers, in order "to compete effectively for the business of a purchaser." Ordinarily, the prices most recently charged or quoted by competing suppliers
were available from the purchasers themselves. Infrequently and irregularly, however, a
seller found it necessary to get or verify the price information through direct contact with

his competitor. While there was no express assurance that any seller who furnished such price information to a competitor was entitled to reciprocity when he needed similar information, the requested price information was "usually" furnished. These circumstances did not convince the district judge that the government had proven a basis for inferring an agreement to exchange price information.

Moreover, the trial court did not think that, assuming the existence of an agreement, its purpose or effect was to inhibit price competition. Among the market factors he cited as negating any impairment of price competition were: (1) a downward trend in price despite increasing manufacturing costs; (2) buyers' frequent changes of suppliers on the basis of price consideration; (3) industry statistics showing an absence of price uniformity or price stability; (4) evidence that sellers' pricing decisions were based not only on price data obtained from competitors but also upon plant production load, availability of needed materials, size of order, customer's credit rating, and similar factors; and (5) failure of the government to produce any evidence from customers to show price stabilization.

In argument before the Supreme Court, the government disclaimed any attack on exchange of composite price information through a trade association. Rather, it charged "that defendants through a combination have become too precise, and that precision inhibits competition" (p. A-13, ATRR No. 384, 11/19/68). The Supreme Court found both a "combination or conspiracy" and an unlawful anticompetitive result. "Concerted action * * * sufficient to establish the combination or conspiracy" was found in evidence that "each defendant on receiving that request usually furnished the data with the expectation that he would be furnished reciprocal information when he wanted it."

The prohibited result was "to stabilize prices though at a downward level." To support its finding of price stabilization, the Supreme Court relied on findings of the trial judge that: (1) while the containers vary as to dimensions, weight, and color, they are substantially identical, no matter who produces them, when made to the customer's specifications; (2) therefore, price was the medium of competition; (3) knowledge of a competitor's price usually meant that the seller matched that price or undercut it only slightly; (4) despite the industry's excess plant capacity and the downward trend of prices, it expanded during the year covered by the complaint from 30 manufacturers with 49 plants to 51 manufacturers with 98 plants; and (4) the industry was dominated by relatively few manufacturers -- 18 defendants accounted for 90% of the shipments.

From these facts "the inferences are irresistible," Mr. Justice Douglas declared, "that the exchange of price information has had an anticompetitive effect in the industry, chilling the vigor of price competition." True, price competition was not eliminated entirely, but "the limitation or reduction of price competition brings the case within the ban, for as we held in United States v. Socony Vacuum Oil Co., 310 U.S. 150, 224, n. 59, interference with the setting of price by free market forces is unlawful per se."

There may be some markets, Mr. Justice Douglas acknowledged, where such exchange of price information would have no effect on a truly competitive price. However, when the market for a fungible product is dominated by relatively few sellers, when "the competition for sales is price, and when the demand is inelastic (since the buyers placed orders for only immediate, short-run needs), a lower price does not mean a larger share of the available business but a sharing of the existing business at a lower return." Therefore, the exchange of price data tends toward price uniformity, the Court reasoned.

In a separate concurring opinion, Mr. Justice Fortas stated his understanding that the majority opinion does not hold price-exchange arrangements to be illegal per se. But the exchange of prices did make it possible "for individual defendants confidently to name a price equal to that which their competitors were asking. The obvious effect was to 'stabilize' prices by joint arrangement."

In a dissenting opinion joined by Justices Harlan and Stewart, Mr. Justice Marshall stressed evidence that the defendants, while they account for 90% of the sales, are only 18 of 51 producers in their market, that market entry is easy, that the number of sellers increased from 30 to 51 during the eight-year period covered by the complaint, that increasing demand almost doubled the size of the market during the same period, and that some excess capacity is present in the industry. In such a market, he maintained, it is logical to assume that the smaller and newer sellers will cut prices to capture a larger market share rather than acquiesce in oligopolistic behavior. Finally, he does not think there is any evidence in the record of the case in support of the majority's "irresistible" inference of anticompetitive effect.

Conclusions

Many antitrust lawyers find it necessary or useful to view from two separate standpoints the practice of exchanging price information among competitors. As counselors they have long advised their clients to avoid price discussions with competitors as they would the plague. As advocates defending a client who has not been inclined or able to avoid price discussions, however, they press the argument that exchange of price information is a Sherman Act violation only when it is shown to have a purpose or effect of curtailing competition.

The Container Corporation decision appears to vindicate both these positions. As Mr. Justice Fortas observed, the majority opinion did not find a per se Sherman Act violation in the exchange of specific information as to price charged individual customers. But any such exchange is unlawful per se if, in Mr. Justice Douglas' terms, it interferes "with the setting of price by free market forces." In a market experiencing declining prices, absence of price uniformity, and much switching of suppliers, the majority of the Court nevertheless found that exchange of price quotations had a forbidden price-stabilizing effect. Indeed, "the inferences are irresistible that the exchange of price information has had an anticompetitive effect." If the inferences were irresistible in this industry, some lawyers believe, every program among competitors for exchanging prices charged by identified sellers to identified buyers is a Sherman Act violation. And the majority's per se rule of illegality for price-exchanging arrangements that "interfere" with free price competition necessarily means that justifications such as that asserted in the Cement Manufacturers' case will no longer save such arrangements.

With regard to the bearing of Mr. Justice Douglas' opinion on the precedents sustaining trade-association programs for collecting and disseminating price statistics that do not identify specific transactions or parties, opinions are divided. Some experts feel that a good industry-statistics reporting program can have a greater stabilizing effect on prices than the occasional and irregular exchange of price quotes that occurred among the corrugated container manufacturers. Therefore, they believe, the curse of per se illegality falls on such programs as well. Other lawyers are just as convinced, however, that a distinction must be made between trade-association reporting of pricing statistics and exchange of price quotes. They feel the Maple Flooring Manufacturers' case is still good law -- at least for any industry that has not developed an oligopolistic structure. Operating a trade-association statistical reporting program under the protection of the Maple Flooring decision is not a simple task. Even assuming an industry has a perfectly lawful and reasonable purpose for reporting its sales statistics and gets an FTC advisory opinion clearing its program, the program will often be tainted by one or two instances of illegal exchanges by individual industry members. The trade association must be diligent in educating its members as to the importance of avoiding price discussions of any kind. Even if a seller's only motive in seeking his competitor's price is to avoid a Robinson-Patman Act violation, it may be that his only recourse is a look at the customer's invoice from the competing supplier.

- 0 -

Subject: Commercial Codes of Ethics   (Published 1/30/68)

Question

What antitrust risks does an industry run when it attempts to regulate trade practices of its members?

References

State v. National Funeral Directors Association, Wisconsin Circuit Court, Milwaukee County, November 29, 1967 (p. A-9, ATRR No. 336, 12/12/67)

U.S. v. National Funeral Directors Association, Complaint, E.D. Wis., November 24, 1967 (p. A-1, ATRR No. 334, 12/5/67)

FTC Advisory Opinion, File 673 7038 (pp. A-1, X-1, ATRR No. 307, 5/30/67)

FTC Advisory Opinion Digest 152 (p. A-7, ATRR No. 336, 12/19/67)

Background

By the time the Sherman Act was enacted in 1890, there were already a number of industries whose members had become sufficiently apprehensive about "unethical," "unfair," and "unconscionable" conduct in the market place to draft, and promise observance of, standards of conduct. That era's businessman was probably more apt than today's to include in the "unethical" or "unconscionable" categories activities or practices that are now regarded by the antitrust enforcement agencies as laudable techniques of hard competition. Yet even today trade association codes are a common subject of negative advice from the FTC and a frequent target of the Antitrust Division's court actions.

There is now no doubt that efforts to achieve price uniformity -- or even stability (U.S. v. Gasoline Retailers Assn., 285 F.2d 688 (7th Cir. 1961)) -- are per se violations of the Sherman Act. Yet the trade associations that have been proceeded against for price fixing are legion and increase in number every year. The most recent example is the National Funeral Directors Association, which was sued by the Justice Department last month for an injunction against its code provisions for expelling any member who does any price advertising. See also U.S. v. Utah Pharmaceutical Association, 201 F. Supp. 29 (D. Utah 1962), aff'd per curiam, 371 U.S. 24 (1962); and Northern Calif. Pharmaceutical Association v. U.S., 306 F. 2d 379 (9th Cir. 1962). "Price tampering" was the condemnatory label used by the federal district court for Southern California in U.S. v. Bakersfield Associated Plumbing Contractors, 1958 Trade Cases Par. 69,087, when it enjoined a group of associations of construction subcontractors from enforcing bid-depository rules that prohibited a discount on "combination" bids from exceeding 5% and imposed large bid fees and bid-withdrawal fees. In recent advisory opinions, the FTC has had to inform trade associations that they cannot discuss a policy of requiring suppliers to give firm price quotations (Advisory Opinion Digest 137, p. A-4, ATRR No. 320, 8/29/67), agree upon fair profit levels (Advisory Opinion Digest 115, p. A-4, ATRR No. 296, 3/14/67), set the prices members are to be paid for used assemblies returned for rebuilding (Advisory Opinion Digest 15, p. A-19, ATRR No. 243, 3/8/66), or distribute a standard service-pricing manual for electronics servicemen (Advisory Opinion Digest 158, p. A - 4, ATRR No. 339, 1/9/68). Product standardization is another widespread trade-association activity that has a bearing on the degree of price competition that is to prevail in the industry. Sometimes the government gets involved in the promulgation of product standards. Congress has provided for automobile safety standards in the National Traffic and Motor Vehicle Safety Act of 1966, 15 U. S. Code, 1391 et seq., and the Commerce Department regularly publishes product standards that have been accepted as the consensus of an industry. An industry member hurt by such standards was recently unsuccessful in a suit attacking the standards as a Section 1 Sherman Act conspiracy. Structural Laminates, Inc. v. Douglas Fir Plywood Assn., 261 F. Supp. 154 (D. Ore. 1966). He lost his suit because he did not prove that the defendant trade association's failure to obtain a change in the standards was motivated by a desire to suppress competition. And in U.S. v. Johns-Manville Corp., 259 F. Supp. 440 (E.D. Pa. 1966), industry product tests were upheld as "scientifically justified" even if they tended to eliminate some competition.

In Radiant Burners, Inc. v. Peoples Gas Light & Coke Co., 364 U.S. 656 (1961), on the other hand, allegations of arbitrary and capricious denial of a seal of approval under trade association product standards were held to describe a violation of Section 1 of the Sherman Act. And, in C-O-Two Fire Equipment Co. v. U.S., 197 F. 2d 489, 493 (9th Cir. 1952), product standardization was held illegal under the Sherman Act because it facilitated noncompetitive pricing. The FTC saw a quality-competition-eliminating purpose or result in macaroni man- ufacturers' rule reducing the percentage of durum-wheat flour used in their product (National Macaroni Manufacturers' Assn., Docket 8524, p. A-1, ATRR No. 150, 5/26/64, aff'd 345 F. 2d 421 (7th Cir. 1965)) but advised another trade association that it had no objections to its publication of product standards "as industry goals" (Advisory Opinion Digest 4, p. A-7, ATRR No. 223, 10/19/65).

More recently (Advisory Opinion Digest 152, p. A-7, ATRR No. 336, 12/19/67), the Commission refused to approve a trade association's product-standards program that made membership a condition of using the association's quality-certification mark. However, the Commission also said nonmembers could be charged a higher fee for use of the mark, pro- vided the differential merely insured that nonmembers "pay an equal share of the costs neces- sary to support the program."

Among the other trade association code sections that have been disapproved are pro- visions for one-year requirements contracts and uniform delivery and credit terms (Advisory Opinion Digest 97, p. A-9, ATRR No. 277, 11/1/66); prohibitions against advertising that one's service is better or faster (Advisory Opinion Digest 80, p. A-9, ATRR No. 265, 8/9/66); a construction contractors' rule requiring use of a bid depository and barring the submission of "split" bids -- e.g., bids for only plumbing or only electrical work -- (Mechanical Contractors' Bid Depository v. Christiansen, 352 F. 2d 817 (10th Cir. 1965)); and a "no switching" rule for key employees (Union Circulation Co., 51 FTC 647, affirmed 241 F. 2d 652 (2d Cir. 1957). The FTC has approved, though, a trade association's plan to require members to pledge com- pliance with trade practice rules (Advisory Opinion Digest 64, p. A-2, ATRR No. 259, 6/28/66).

Enforcement Provisions

There are precedents indicating that not only the substantive rules but also the enforce- ment provisions of an ethics code must be free of anticompetitive purpose or result. For ex- ample, one of the elements the Supreme Court stressed in reversing dismissal of the Sherman Act charge in the Radiant Burners case was the industry procedure for boycotting any product that wasn't awarded a seal of approval. Boycotts or "blacklists" have been major factors in many of the landmark cases condemning industry procedures for self-regulation. Standard Sanitary Mfg. v. U.S., 226 U.S. 20 (1912); Eastern States Lumber Assn. v. U.S., 234 U.S. 600 (1914); Fashion Originators' Guild v. FTC, 312 U.S. 457 (1941). The Standard Sanitary and Fashion Originators cases suggest that the good motives of the industry or its trade asso- ciation are irrelevant. "The law is its own measure of right and wrong, of what it permits, or forbids" (226 U.S. at 49). In such situations, the trade association is "in reality an extra- governmental agency, which prescribes rules for the regulation and restraint of interstate commerce, and provides extra-judicial tribunals for determination and punishment of violations, and thus 'trenches upon the power of the national legislature and violates the statute' " (312 U.S. at 465). Cf. Sugar Institute v. U.S., 297 U.S. 553, 598-599 (1936).

Concern about creation of "an extra-governmental agency" was also expressed by Federal Trade Commissioner Elman when he dissented last Spring from an advisory opinion clearing a provision in an industry code of ethics for the imposition of limited fines on vio- lators. (Advisory Opinion File 673 7038, pp. A-1, X-1, ATRR No. 307, 5/30/67). An or- ganization of magazine publishers and subscription sales agencies formed to halt deceptive sales practices was told that the Commission had no objections to provisions authorizing the code's "administrator" to assess amounts of money to be paid by code violators "as liqui- dated damages, not as a penalty." The advisory opinion assumed "that there will be no co- ercion of any agency to subscribe to the plan, no coercion of any agency to remain in it after it has subscribed." Actually, the code obligated a participating agency to give six months' notice of withdrawal. Similar "liquidated damages" provisions were written into a cigarette advertising code the tobacco industry submitted to the Justice Department for clearance in

1964 (p. A-14, ATRR No. 147, 5/5/64). Because Congress and the FTC were considering advertising and labeling standards for the industry, the Antitrust Division declined to clear "permanent establishment" of the advertising controls but did agree "in the meantime" to bring no criminal prosecution based on adherence to the code (pp. A-22, X-23, ATRR No. 154, 6/23/64).

In its advice to the subscription sales agencies, the FTC balked at sanctioning a plan to recommend that salesmen be suspended from their jobs for willful disobedience of the code. It did clear, though, provisions authorizing the code administrator to hold hearings and maintain a public list of willful violators. Later (Advisory Opinion Digest 133, p. A-3, ATRR No. 314, 7/18/67) the Commission advised a trade association that it could discuss an agreement to comply with a labeling ruling of a federal agency but could not take steps to enforce any such agreement. This ruling conforms to the approach the Commission takes in the administration of trade practice rules, which are generally developed by the affected industry under FTC supervision. Each set of trade practice rules contains a standard provision that the industry "may, at its option, form a trade practice committee." That committee may publicize the trade practice rules and related FTC rules and may meet with the Commission to discuss administration and revision of the trade practice rules. But it may not "(1) interpret the rules; (2) attempt to correct alleged rule violations; (3) make determinations or express opinions as to whether practices are violative of the rules; (4) receive or screen complaints of violations of the rules; or (5) perform any other act or acts within the authority of the Federal Trade Commission or any other governmental agency or department."

Last year, at a bar association meeting, Assistant Attorney General Donald F. Turner questioned both the adequacy and appropriateness of any joint industry efforts toward consumer protection as to quality or even safety. 1967 New York State Bar Association Symposium 36. One of the points he made is that businessmen often act arbitrarily or discriminatorily when policing the activities of their competitors. The necessity for fair play among competitors in self-regulation situations was stressed by the Supreme Court in Silver v. New York Stock Exchange, 373 U.S. 341 (1963) (pp. A-8, X-1, ATRR No. 97, 5/21/63).

Conclusions

Most of the uncertainty that exists today concerning application of the antitrust laws to industry codes relates to enforcement provisions included in those codes. Language in some advisory opinions (such as Digest 133) seems to indicate a reluctance on the part of the FTC to clear provisions for private sanctions against industry code violations, even when the conduct to be punished is forbidden by law. Its reasoning in those opinions appears consistent with that of the Standard Sanitary and Fashion Originators cases. But in the Commission's clearance of the subscription sales agencies' "liquidated damages" agreement many antitrust lawyers see a reversion to the approach taken by the Supreme Court in the Sugar Institute case. That 1936 opinion praised voluntary self-regulation by industry as sometimes "more effective than legal processes" and even recognized that such self-regulation "may appropriately have wider objectives than merely the removal of evils which are infractions of positive law."

The key to the Commission's advice to the subscription sales agencies is probably to be found in its observation that its conclusion "is a tentative one since there is little recorded experience upon which to predicate such a judgment." The real test of an industry code is the manner of its operation. Since the subscription sales agencies' code does provide for the imposition of sanctions, anticompetitive consequences are clearly possible. If the trade association widely publicizes its activity, membership could become too important for a competitor to abandon in order to avoid discriminatory or anticompetitive penalties. It was only "in view of the magnitude of the problems which confront the industry" in the form of widespread deceptive selling practices that the Commission agreed to take the risk of industry self-regulation. Even then it gave only temporary three-year clearance, with instructions that the plan be resubmitted for new approval after three years, during which all enforcement proceedings must be reported to the Commission.

After all, it was actual anticompetitive "effects" that led to the outlawing of industry self-regulation in the Standard Sanitary, Eastern States Lumber, Fashion Originators, and

Sugar Institute cases. None of the court decisions finding Sherman Act violations have dealt with code provisions that merely could be anticompetitive if improperly used. Either they were anticompetitive on their face or they were in fact used in an anticompetitive manner. Even the Radiant Burner and Silver complaints contained allegations of discriminatory or anticompetitive application. Despite the Assistant Attorney General's lack of confidence in the good faith of self-regulating businessmen, even he would probably not move against an industry code that in fact does not operate to inhibit competition.

A question remaining is whether an industry code that never inhibits competition is worth the trouble. The answer seems to be yes in industries plagued with Section 5 FTC Act violations that the Commission does not have the resources to deal with. And there are other industries in which a code of ethics that does nothing more than establish rules against clear violations of the law proves valuable because it gives industry members confidence to adopt trade-policy changes they would not have the courage to initiate individually.

- 0 -

Subject: Concerted Choice of Supplier   (Published 11/5/68)

Question

Is an agreement by several competitors to buy exclusively from a single supplier a per se violation of the Sherman Act?

Reference

Instant Delivery Corp. v. City Stores Co., 1968 Trade Cases Para. 72,454 (E.D.Penn.)

Background

For some time prior to April 1967, four of Philadelphia's largest department stores had been using a consolidated package-delivery service furnished by a single company. They found a consolidated delivery service to be the most efficient and economical method of delivering packages because that arrangement made possible a greater concentration of deliveries to any given area of the city. When labor difficulties stopped the delivery company's operations in April 1967, the department stores were forced to make other arrangements with a number of independent delivery services. Eventually two of them worked out arrangements with one delivery service, and the other two with a second delivery service.

In December, 1967, one of the delivery firms informed its two clients that, once the Christmas rush had passed, it would be unable to maintain efficient service at existing contract rates. The four stores then invited the two carriers to compete for a consolidated package service. The carriers were asked to present their respective capabilities and contract rates at a meeting of representatives from all four stores. After that meeting, the two largest stores chose one of the carriers and then tried to persuade representatives of the other two stores to use the same carrier, arguing that it was more financially stable and enjoyed better labor relations. A third store, having been influenced by the action of the first two, went along with their choice. Soon thereafter at a meeting of representatives of all four stores, the fourth store joined in reestablishing a consolidated delivery service and in the selection of the carrier already chosen by the other three.

The second delivery service that had been doing business with two of the stores sued all four stores and their chosen delivery service for treble damages and an injunction under the antitrust laws, charging a concerted refusal to deal. In the decision given as reference, the Federal District Court for Eastern Pennsylvania denied the complaining carrier's motion for a preliminary injunction.

The district court did not deny the existence of an agreement among the four department stores, but it viewed that agreement as not one to refuse to deal with the complaining carrier. "Their agreement was limited to the reestablishment of a consolidated delivery service with which they had earlier enjoyed a long and satisfactory experience, and to the selection of one of two competing carriers to perform that service." The complaining carrier "is a disappointed competitor, not the object of an illegal boycott."

Cases like Klor's, Inc. v. Broadway-Hale Stores, 359 U.S. 207 (1959), holding that group boycotts or concerted refusals to deal are per se violations of Section 1 of the Sherman Act, were distinguished by the court. In each of those cases, it was noted, the aim and purpose of the refusal to deal was either to force a change in the boycotted businessman's trade practices or to exclude him from competition. Here, on the other hand, there was no intent to discriminate against or exclude the complaining carrier. Indeed, the complaining carrier "was invited to compete, and did so vigorously, for selection as the carrier to perform the consolidated delivery. * * * The decision that each of the stores made was to select [the successful carrier], not to exclude [the complaining carrier]." Exclusion of the complaining carrier was a mere "by-product of the decision to reinstitute consolidated delivery which necessarily involves the use of one carrier."

In its refusal to find a boycott in per se violation of the Sherman Act, the court relied on two precedents: Interborough News Co. v. Curtiss Publishing Co., 225 F. 2d 289 (2nd Cir. 1955), and Parmelee Transportation Co. v. Keeshin, 186 F. Supp. 533 (N.D. Ill. 1960), affirmed, 292 F. 2d 794 (7th Cir. 1961), review denied, 368 U.S. 944 (1961). In the Interborough News case, magazine publishers were charged with combining to eliminate one wholesaler in favor of several new wholesalers. The trial judge found there had been no combination or conspiracy between any of the defendants. But it apparently was not disputed that one of the publishers had initiated dealings with the new wholesalers and had then sent other publishers communications stressing the advantages of doing business with the new wholesalers.

In the words of the Second Circuit, that publisher "had a legal right to break away from a wholesaler whose service it considered unsatisfactory and to set up and encourage by subsidy new competing wholesalers; and there is no reason apparent to us why [the publisher] should not use every reasonable effort to influence and persuade other national distributors to patronize the new competing wholesalers." The court of appeals stressed a finding that "each defendant independently negotiated its agreements with its respective wholesalers."

The Parmelee opinion sustained the joint selection of an inter-terminal transfer service by a group of railroads using the terminals. Both the district court and court of appeals opinions stressed that in Chicago v. Atchison T. & S.F. Ry. Co., 357 U.S. 77 (1958), the Supreme Court recognized the right of railroads under the Interstate Commerce Act to act as a group in selecting a transfer operator to provide inter-station service.

Having put aside the rule of per se illegality in the Instant Delivery case, the Philadelphia Federal District Court announced that the question whether consolidated delivery constitutes an unreasonable restraint of trade "can only be resolved at the trial * * *, after the parties have had an opportunity to develop fully the factual setting out of which consolidated delivery emerged." In view of the greater efficiencies made possible by a consolidated delivery service and in view of the widespread use of consolidated delivery by retail business establishments, the court did not feel that the complaining carrier had demonstrated a substantial probability that it will ultimately prevail on the issue of reasonableness.

On appeal to the Court of Appeals for the Third Circuit, the complaining carrier's brief pressed the theory of per se illegality, but the case was settled prior to argument.

Conclusions

Some of the accepted principles of antitrust law can be fitted together to support a conclusion that an agreement by several competitors to buy exclusively from a single supplier -- either a product or, as in Instant Delivery, a service -- is a per se Section 1 Sherman Act violation. Business enterprises are as obligated to compete when they do their buying as they are when they do their selling. Los Angeles Meat & Provision Drivers Union v. U.S., 371 U.S. 94 (1962); Union Carbide & Carbon Corp. v. Nisley, 300 F. 2d 561 (10th Cir. 1962). And competing sellers cannot lawfully combine in their decisions as to whom they will accept as customers. U.S. v. General Motors Corp., 384 U.S. 127 (pp. A-1, X-1, ATRR No. 251, 5/3/66).

Even an agreement by a single buyer to buy exclusively from one seller, while not illegal per se, does violate Section 1 of the Sherman Act and Section 3 of the Clayton Act if shown to be anticompetitive. Standard Fashion Co. v. Magrane-Houston Co., 258 U.S. 346 (1923). When several enterprises combine in such an arrangement, the risk of monopolization or restraint of trade, it is arguable, may be great enough to obviate the need of specifically exploring anticompetitive effect. "An act harmless when done by one may become a public wrong when done by many acting in concert." Eastern States Retail Lumber Dealers Assn. v. U.S., 234 U.S. 600, 614 (1914).

Use of common buying agencies by groups of competitors has been held lawful. Arkansas Brokerage Co. v. Dunn & Powell, 173 Fed. 899 (8th Cir. 1909); Associated Greeting Card Distributors of America, 50 FTC 631 (1954). In neither of those cases, however, was the buying agency restricted to dealing with a single source of supply. Nor was there an agreement among the competing buyers that they would rely exclusively on the common buying agency. In the Arkansas Brokerage case, each member of the parent group, acting on his own, did refuse to buy from any other firm unless it would match the price available through the common buying agency. "Whether a similar situation would be countenanced today," though "is open to question." Lamb & Kittelle, "Trade Association Law and Practice," Little, Brown & Co. (1956).

In any event, application of a rule of per se illegality to the concerted choice of an exclusive supplier by four of the largest enterprises in a market may not mean that every group selection of an exclusive supplier is a Sherman Act violation. As articulated by the Supreme Court, a "per se" rule is merely a "principle of per se unreasonableness" designed to bypass "incredibly complicated and prolonged economic investigation * * * to determine at large whether a particular restraint has been unreasonable." Northern Pacific R. Co. v. U.S., 356 U.S. 1, 5 (1958). Even in Northern Pacific "tying agreements" were held unreasonable per se only when the seller has control or dominance over the tying product and a "not insubstantial" amount of commerce is affected by his tying practice. In U.S. v. Sealy, 388 U.S. 350 (pp. A-3, X-9, ATRR No. 309, 6/13/67), moreover, after citing the statement in White Motor Co. v. U.S., 372 U.S. 253 (pp. A-1, X-1, ATRR No. 86, 3/5/63) that horizontal territorial agreements are illegal per se, the Supreme Court reserved judgment on whether "a number of small grocers might allocate territory among themselves * * * as incident to the use of a common name and common advertisements" (the very practice the Justice Department seems to be attacking in U.S. v. Topco Associates, Inc., Civil Action 68 C 76, filed January 15, 1968, in N.D. Ill. (p. A-14, ATRR No. 340, 1/16/68). Apparently, therefore, conduct must do more than fit a particular label like "horizontal territorial agreement," "concerted refusal to deal," or even "price fixing" (See Chicago Board of Trade v. U.S., 246 U.S. 231 (1918)) before it will be held unreasonable per se.

Suppose, then, the Instant Delivery case had gone to trial and the four department stores had been able to prove (1) that it is not economically feasible for them to supply delivery service for their customers unless they choose a single supplier and (2) that they made their choice after giving every available carrier a full and fair opportunity to compete for their contract. Some antitrust experts believe these two factors would take this concerted choice of a supplier outside the category of per se violations. They feel addition of these two factors would create the type of situation Federal Trade Commissioner Philip Elman had in mind when he said: "A realistic analysis of competitive practices is necessary, therefore, not only when the question is whether the practice is illegal under the rule of reason, but equally (if not more so) when the question is whether one of the existing per se categories should be extended to embrace the practice. The categories are not self-defining; their bounds cannot be ascertained by reference to the semantic overtones of the verbal formula in which the rule is capsuled. To fix the rule's outer limits requires, above all, attention to its underlining rationale, which may be far narrower than the form of words in which the rule is expressed, and an understanding of the factual situation to which the rule is sought to be applied." Elman, "Petrified Opinions' and Competitive Penalties," 66 Col. L. Rev. 625, 626-7 (1966).

In making an economic analysis of the "factual situation" presented by concerted choice of a single delivery service--or even, for that matter, in applying the rule of reason to it--should one consider the effect of a consolidated delivery service upon only the market in buying and selling delivery services? Visible in that market are important consumer benefits in the economies that are apparently available in a single package delivery--economic benefits that might well outweigh the benefits of insisting on continuing competition among several delivery companies.

Or must one also look at the effect of these economies on competition among retail stores for the custom of consumers? Are four of the largest department stores in a metropolitan market to be permitted to join forces in order to offer a service their competitors cannot match? Could any two or more retailers combine to gain such an economic advantage over their competitors? Even assuming the rule of reason is applicable, are the economies of a consolidated delivery service properly to be weighed in the balance? "Our inquiry is whether, assuming nonpredatory motives and business purposes and the incentive of profit and volume considerations, the effect upon competition in the market place is substantially adverse." U.S. v. Arnold, Schwinn & Co., 388 U.S. 365, 375 (pp. A-1, X-1, ATRR No. 309, 6/13/67).

Subject: Labor Exemption--Union Initiation of Minimum Pricing   (Published 10/29/68)

Question

Does labor's antitrust exemption protect efforts to preserve job and wage structures by bargaining for restrictions on employers' pricing of their products or services?

References

American Federation of Musicians v. Carroll, 391 U.S. 99, 36 LW 4441 (pp. A-13, X-28, ATRR No. 358, 5/21/68)
International Brotherhood of Treamsters v. Oliver, 358 U.S. 283 (1960)
Amalgamated Meat Cutters v. Jewel Tea Co., 381 U.S. 676 (pp. A-1, X-6, ATRR No. 204, 6/8/65)
Analysis, "Labor Unions and the Antitrust Laws," p. 39, Antitrust and Trade Regulation Today: 1967

Background

A retail marketing-hours restriction imposed by a butchers' union through multi-employer bargaining was approved by the Supreme Court in Amalgamated Meat Cutters v. Jewel Tea Co. Although the Court could not muster a majority to support any one of the three opinions filed in the case, six justices did agree that marketing hours are necessarily tied to working hours and hence are a mandatory subject of bargaining and within the antitrust exemption granted organized labor by the Norris-LaGuardia Act and Sections 6 and 20 of the Clayton Act. But three of these justices "seriously doubt that either the union or Jewel could claim immunity" for an agreement between them establishing a schedule of meat prices. 381 U.S. at 689.

Subsequently, in American Federation of Musicians v. Carroll, the court concluded that a union's minimum price list for orchestra engagements was in substance a control of musicians' wages and therefore a proper subject of union interest. Several orchestra leaders sued the Federation for treble damages and an injunction. The orchestra leaders attacked the legality of membership rules placing restrictions on the "club date" engagements of union members. "Club dates" are one-time engagements at such social events as weddings, fashion shows, and commencements. There are no collective-bargaining agreements in the field; club-date engagements are rigidly regulated by the union's bylaws and regulations. Orchestra leaders were pressured into becoming union members and were required to engage a minimum number of "sidemen" for club-date engagements to charge prices set out in a "price list booklet." Each price is a total of (1) the minimum wage scales for sidemen, (2) a "leader's fee," which is double the sideman's scale when four or more musicians are used, and (3) an additional 8% to cover social security, unemployment insurance and other expenses. If the leader does not personally appear but designates a sub-leader, then he must pay the sub-leader one and one half times the wage scale whenever four or more musicians perform.

The Federal District Court for Southern New York had dismissed the complaint, finding all the union's practices to be within the definition of "labor dispute" in the Norris-LaGuardia Act. The Court of Appeals for the Second Circuit had reversed on the ground that the fixing of minimum prices even by a union is illegal. In reversing the court of appeals, the Supreme Court agreed with both lower courts that, even though the orchestra leaders are employers and independent contractors, they constitute not a "non-labor" group but a "labor" group. The Court approved the criterion applied by the district court -- the "presence of a job or wage competition or some other economic interrelationship affecting legitimate union interests between the union members and the independent contractors." When that "economic interrelationship" exists, there is a "labor dispute" outside the reach of the Sherman Act; "the allowable area of union activity was not to be restricted to an immediate employer-employee relation."

Two possible qualifications of the rule stated by the Court may be inferred from footnote 10 to the opinion, which points out that "the 'price list' establishes only a minimum charge; there is no attempt to set a maximum. Nor does the union attempt by its minimum charge to assure the leader a profit above the fair value of his labor services." The footnote also quotes a statement by a dissenting judge in the court of appeals that "a different result might be warranted if the floor were set so high as to cover not merely compensation for the additional services rendered by a leader but entrepreneurial profit as well."

The price list was considered to be "indistinguishable in * * * [its] effect from the collective bargaining provisions" in Local 24, International Brotherhood of Teamsters v. Oliver, 358 U. S. 283 (1960). The Oliver opinion approved a negotiated requirement that rentals charged for use of owner-operated trucks be held up to a minimum level to preserve prevailing wage standards. The minimum-rental provision there was "narrowly restricted * * * to the times when the owner drives his leased vehicle for the carrier, and to the adverse effects upon the negotiated wage scale which might result when the rental for the use of the leased vehicle was unregulated." In Musicians v. Carroll the price list was similarly designed to protect sidemen and subleaders from job and wage competition of the leaders. It did apply to non-performing leaders.

Justices White and Black, dissenting, viewed application of the Musicians' price list to nonperforming leaders as a significant shift of power to the unions, enabling them to impose industry-wide prices, a result these two justices regarded as distinguishable from the Oliver decision. When the leader does not lead but functions only as an entrepreneur and hires a subleader, he must nevertheless charge a price higher than his total wage bill. This, observed Mr. Justice White, means that the price covered managing and administering a business, which are not "labor-group work." A more flexible rule that would extend immunity only to matters that specifically affect union members was urged.

Conclusions

It is not always easy to draw the line between union price-influencing activities that are legitimate wage-boosting efforts and those that are "nonlabor" activities subject to the Sherman Act. If all members of the organization claiming union status are independent contractors or entrepreneurs rather than employees, apparently it is a Sherman Act violation for such an organization to maintain a standard of prices. Columbia River Packers Association v. Hinton, 315 U.S. 143 (1942); U.S. v. Women's Sportswear Manufacturers Association, 336 U.S. 460 (1949); Taylor v. International Union of Journeymen Horseshoers, 353 F.2d 593 (4th Cir. 1965). In Musicians v. Carroll, on the other hand, most of the union members were apparently mere "sidemen" whose economic interests were so closely tied to those of the orchestra leaders, who were also union members, that the union was permitted to set price minimums for the leaders. Likewise, in the Oliver case, employee truck drivers' wages were necessarily affected by the rentals collected by owner-operators of trucks.

The key issue in cases like Carroll and Oliver relates to the existence of the "economic interrelationship" between the "employee" union members and the "independent contractors" or "entrepreneurs," for that "interrelationship" is essential to "labor group" status for the "entrepreneurs." The FTC may shed some light on that matter when it decides a case argued October 15. National Association of Women's and Children's Apparel Salesmen, Inc., Docket 8691. The Commission's staff has argued that the interests of "traveling salesmen" and "resident salesmen" in the apparel industry are not sufficiently interrelated to justify antitrust exemption for the trade-show activities conducted by their national association solely, the staff maintains, for the benefit of the traveling salesmen. The Commission was told that the traveling salesmen, unlike the resident salesmen, are independent contractors rather than employees of the clothing manufacturers. The staff's position had been sustained by the hearing examiner (p. A-11, ATRR No. 358, 5/21/68).

The statement by three justices in Amalgamated Meat Cutters v. Jewel Tea Co. questioning whether "either the union or Jewel could claim immunity" for an agreement establishing a schedule of meat prices raises another "economic interrelationship" problem — the relationship that must exist between prices and wages before a labor group consisting entirely of employees and facing no competition from "independent contractors" may negotiate for a contract setting a minimum price schedule. A couple of dozen cases decided recently by the

National Labor Relations Board indicate that just such an issue may arise in the field of automobile marketing. Chicago-area automobile dealers sought review of the NLRB regional director's orders scheduling representation elections among their salesmen. The NLRB was told that the election petitions were filed by an organization that had forfeited its right to represent employees by openly stating its purpose to effect a criminal price-fixing conspiracy. A feature of the "program" announced by the American Federation of Professional Salesmen was to add to the factory-invoice price of an automobile (1) fixed percentages for a union health and welfare program, a retirement program, a sales commission, and certain expenses and (2) a 3% minimum profit for dealers. The Board did not rule on the question whether a union can properly insist upon such contract terms once it becomes a certified or recognized bargaining agent. Instead, the Board merely sustained without opinion the regional director's ruling that the minimum-markup demand does not affect the labor union's qualifications as such for purposes of a representation election.

The automobile salesmen's cases are factually distinguishable from Musicians v. Carroll and Teamsters v. Oliver in one important respect -- it is a product, not a service, on which price cutting would be restricted. All the cases in which the Supreme Court has applied the labor exemption to activities designed or found to have a direct influence on pricing involve prices charged chiefly for services. In Oliver, for example, it was recognized that the truck rentals were made up in large part of pay for the owner-driver's services. When the three-justice opinion in the Jewel Tea case made its gratuitous statement of doubt as to the legality of a price restriction, on the other hand, it spoke of the price of meat. It is "the labor of a human being" that Section 6 of the Clayton Act excludes from the "article[s] of commerce" subject to the antitrust laws.

- 0 -

Subject: Resale Price Fixing Through Refusal to Deal   (Published 5/7/68)

Question

In view of the Supreme Court's decision in Albrecht v. Herald, what can a supplier lawfully do to control resale prices of his dealers?

References

Quinn v. Mobil Oil Co., 375 F.2d 273 (1st Cir.) (pp. A-5, X-1, ATRR No. 299, 4/4/67)

Albrecht v. Herald Co., 390 U.S. 145, 36 LW 4171 (pp. A-1, X-1, ATRR No. 347, 3/5/68)

Analysis, "Resale Price Maintenance Through Refusals To Deal--II," (p. B-1, ATRR No. 125, 12/3/63), reprinted at p. 88, "Antitrust and Trade Regulation Today: 1967"

Background

Generally, a manufacturer or distributor who wishes to set his customers' resale price must get the concurrence -- and police the performance -- of all or most of his customers. Except in states with effective fair-trade laws, the means he may lawfully use to impose his resale-pricing policy on his customers are limited by such decisions as U.S. v. A. Schraeder's Sons, 252 U.S. 85 (1920), and U.S. v. Parke, Davis & Co., 362 U.S. 29 (1960). Apparently he is still safe, under the Colgate Doctrine, 250 U.S. 300 (1919), if he does nothing more than announce suggested prices and follow a policy of refusing to continue to sell to those who don't stay within the pricing limits he suggests.

Occasionally, a manufacturer or distributor may have cause for concern about the pricing practices of only one of his customers. Efforts to persuade that single customer to reform his pricing policies would appear to be subject to the same Sherman Act restrictions as any other resale-price-fixing program. But what if all the "persuasion" is unsuccessful and the manufacturer or distributor stops dealing with the recalcitrant dealer without ever winning his cooperation. The Court of Appeals for the First Circuit dealt with that problem in Quinn v. Mobil Oil and decided that there could be no violation of Section 1 of the Sherman Act, since there was no actual resale-price agreement. Unlike the monopolization ban in Section 2 of the Sherman Act, the court reasoned, Section 1's proscription of contracts, combinations, or conspiracies in restraint of trade does not outlaw unilateral attempts to violate its provisions.

The First Circuit's ruling affirmed dismissal of a treble-damage complaint for failure to allege an antitrust violation. A former operator of a Mobil gas station had alleged that, when his station lease came up for renewal in 1963, he was orally informed by Mobil that, unless he reduced the retail price of gasoline by one cent a gallon, his rent would be substantially increased.

Although his one-year lease was renewed at only a slight increase in rent, Mobil began pressuring him a few months later, he charged, to reduce his price or terminate his lease. It delayed payments to him, attempted to unload consignments of tires, batteries, and accessories, and attempted to apply the money owed him to payment for this unwanted merchandise. The former station operator said he resisted these pressures, however, and was then denied renewal of his lease in 1964.

"From these facts," it was clear to the First Circuit "that the only provision of the federal antitrust laws that need be considered here is Section 1 of the Sherman Act." The court agreed that the complaint set out more than a simple refusal to deal but nevertheless found the facts alleged to be distinguishable from those involved in U.S. v. Parke, Davis; Simpson v. Union Oil Co., 377 U.S. 13 (1964); and Broussard v. Socony Mobil Oil Co., 350

F.2d 346 (5th Cir. 1965). In each of these cases, there was a combination or conspiracy either by virtue of the manufacturer's use of its wholesalers and other retailers to maintain resale prices or through the complaining retailer's temporary compliance with, or agreement to, the manufacturer's resale-price-fixing policy.

In a concurring opinion Judge Coffin joined in the majority holding that allegation of conspiracy is essential, but he said he would go further and find no pleading of a Section 1 violation even if the complaint alleged a completed vertical price-fixing agreement. He distinguished between the anticompetitive effects of minimum-resale-price maintenance and the anticompetitive effects of maximum-resale-price maintenance, "as practiced by a single manufacturer or supplier."

Chief Judge Aldrich disagreed with both views. He found vertical price fixing illegal per se, whether maximum or minimum prices are set. And he saw "no difference in substance between pressure to induce the making of an unlawful agreement and pressure to reinstate one that has been broken. * * * This would not only be an unfortunate distinction, since any future 'Quinn' could establish rights for himself simply by making the requested agreement one day and breaking it the next, but also, it seems to me, an illogical one."

Albrecht Decision

The Albrecht case also involved a price ceiling. The St. Louis Globe Democrat advertises a suggested retail price for its papers, and its carriers have exclusive territories subject to termination if prices they charge exceed the suggested maximum. One carrier raised his delivery price. The Globe objected and advised the carrier that, because of the paper's reserved right to compete in such a situation, it was informing his subscribers that the Globe itself would deliver at a lower price. In addition, the Globe hired a circulation company to solicit the carrier's subscribers. About 300 of the 1200 subscribers on the carrier's route switched to direct delivery by the Globe. Meanwhile, the Globe continued to sell papers to the carrier but warned him that he would be cut off if he continued selling at the higher price. Since the Globe did not want to deliver its own papers, it gave the 300 customers to another carrier who knew the Globe would not tolerate overcharging and understood he would have to return the route if the first carrier discontinued his pricing practice. The Globe then informed the first carrier he could have his customers back if he would charge the suggested price. When the carrier brought a treble-damage suit, the Globe stopped all deliveries to the carrier.

The jury returned a verdict for the Globe, and the U.S. Court of Appeals for the Eighth Circuit affirmed the district judge's denial of the former carrier's motion for judgment notwithstanding the verdict. The Supreme Court reversed and remanded. It held, citing Parke, Davis, there was a combination within the meaning of Section 1 of the Sherman Act among the Globe, the circulation company, and the carrier who took over part of the treble-damage claimant's route.

The finding of combination is based on the circulation company's knowledge that the purpose of the solicitation campaign was to force the damage claimant to lower his price and on the replacement carrier's knowledge that he was getting the route as part of a program to obtain conformance to advertised prices. From its Parke, Davis opinion, the Court derived the proposition that a "combination," as that term is used in the Sherman Act, is a concept "in addition to contracts and conspiracies express or implied."

In footnote 6, the Court elaborated: "Under Parke, Davis petitioner could have claimed a combination between respondent and himself, at least of the day he unwillingly complied with respondent's advertised price. Likewise, he might successfully have claimed that respondent had combined with other carriers because the firmly enforced price policy applied to all carriers, most of whom acquiesced in it. * * * Petitioner's amended complaint did allege a combination between respondent and petitioner's customers. Because of our disposition of this case it is unnecessary to pass on this claim. It was not, however, a frivolous contention. See FTC v. Beechnut Packing Co., 257 U.S. 441 (1922)."

The majority quoted from Kiefer-Stewart Co. v. Seagram & Sons, Inc., 340 U.S. 211 (1951), that agreements to fix maximum prices "no less than those to fix minimum prices, cripple the freedom of traders and thereby restrain their ability to sell in accordance with their own judgment." Vertically fixed maximum prices were held to be illegal per se.

"Unpersuasive" is the Court's characterization of the Eighth Circuit's suggestion that the maximum resale price was necessary to protect the public from the anticompetitive impact of the carriers' exclusive territories. If the court of appeals was correct, "the entire scheme must fall under Section 1 of the Sherman Act."

Conclusions

Since price ceilings are per se illegal, the main issue in all resale price fixing cases is whether there is a contract, combination, or conspiracy within the meaning of Section 1 of the Sherman Act. The Albrecht opinion sets out so many possible combinations it is difficult to conceive of a resale price maintenance program that is both effective and lawful.

The Court's statement that the "[Globe] had combined with other distributors because the firmly enforced policy applied to all carriers, most of whom acquiesced in it," apparently carries the day for the government's reasoning in its amicus memorandum (p. A-9, ATRR No. 333, 11/28/67) in Amplex of Maryland, Inc., v. Outboard Marine Corp. The Antitrust Division urged the Supreme Court to accept the review petition of an outboard-motor franchisee who claimed he was terminated because he refused to acquiesce in a motor manufacturer's exclusive dealing arrangements. The government explained that the franchise proved or offered to prove that the manufacturer tried to persuade its dealers not to carry competing motors, that the manufacturer threatened with termination franchisees who failed to deal exclusively, and that most franchisees in fact deal exclusively. In addition, although the court of appeals (380 F.2d 112, p. A-5, ATRR No. 311, 6/27/67) did not reach the question, the government thought the record showed that the exclusive dealing produced a sufficiently serious foreclosure of outlets to competing motor manufacturers to establish the requisite anticompetitive effect. Finally, the franchisee's evidence showed that it was canceled because it carried a competing line of motors.

In those circumstances, the government saw exclusive-dealing arrangements and refusals to deal as merely two aspects of the same illegal design. The refusal to deal serves an integral function in maintaining an unlawful system of exclusive dealing and of preserving tacit acquiescence of other dealers in that system. Moreover, Section 4 of the Clayton Act permits any person "injured in his business or property by reason of anything forbidden in the antitrust laws" to maintain a treble-damage suit. Therefore, the Antitrust Division asserted, if a dealer is injured by the refusal to deal, then the injury is by reason of something forbidden in the antitrust laws--the illegal exclusive-dealing arrangements with other dealers.

The Antitrust Division explained that, were it not that a significant number of franchisees are willing to accede to exclusive dealing arrangements, a franchisor would not be able to refuse to deal with a recalcitrant distributor. In addition, the termination of a franchisee necessarily indicates to other dealers that threats of cancellation for handling competing products are to be taken seriously. In fact, the Antitrust Division urged the Court, if necessary, to further curtail "the limited dispensation" conferred on refusals to deal under the Colgate doctrine as qualified in Parke, Davis.

Yet, the government did rely on the existence of actual though "tacit," exclusive-dealing arrangements between the motor manufacturer and acquiescent dealers. (See, Lenox, Inc., Docket 8718, p. A-16, ATRR No. 355, 4/30/68) It did not venture to suggest a combination" concept distinguishable from "contract" or "conspiracy." In fact, the government may not be inclined to rely on the Albrecht opinion in its enforcement program. At the Spring meeting of the ABA's Antitrust Section (37 ABA Antitrust L.J. 300) the Assistant Attorney in charge of antitrust said he is "a little puzzled" as to what the Supreme Court meant when it said a combination is different from a conspiracy. Then he remarked, "I do not think the per se rule of illegality on resale price maintenance applied to minimum prices should be automatically extended to maximum price fixing."

The government's view of Albrecht, however, does not detract from its validity for use by a treble-damage claimant.

The plaguing question still remains: What is left of the Colgate doctrine? Several years ago ATRR suggested (p. B-1, ATRR No. 64, 10/2/62, reprinted at p. 84, "Antitrust and Trade Regulation Today: 1967") that Colgate allows a supplier to refuse to do business with price cutters -- and now price raisers -- provided he does not go beyond mere announcement of his policy and the simple refusal to deal. One of the conclusions reached was that, whatever view lawyers may take of the continuing validity of the Colgate doctrine, it is difficult, if not impossible, for the businessman to make any practical use of the doctrine as it now stands. Modern supplier-distributor relationships were characterized as so complex that there is always a danger that a tacit resale-price-fixing agreement violating the Sherman Act may be inferred from a manufacturer's unilateral announcement of, and some retailers' adherence to, specified resale prices.

The majority opinion in Albrecht makes no mention whatsoever of the Colgate case. However, in a dissent, Mr. Justice Harlan backtracked from his assertion in Parke, Davis, that the Parke, Davis decision overruled Colgate.

In any event, antitrust lawyers are still divided over the vitality of Colgate. If a supplier suggests a resale price, and then, when a distributor refuses to abide by it, the manufacturer simply writes the distributor and says "I no longer wish to do business with you," there would seem to be no antitrust liability. But, suppose a manufacturer has 100 distributors and the above sequence of events is repeated 10 times, it could be inferred that the "[manufacturer] had combined with other [distributors] because the firmly enforced price policy applied to all [distributors], most of whom acquiesced in it." n. 6, Albrecht v. Herald; But see Klein v. American Luggage Works, Inc., 323 F.2d 787 (3rd Cir.) (pp. A-1, X-1, ATRR No. 119, 10/22/63).

- 0 -

Subject: The Merger Guidelines   (Published 7/23/68)

Question

How will the Justice Department's Merger Guidelines affect enforcement of Section 7 of the Clayton Act?

Reference

"Merger Guidelines," Justice Department announcement, May 29, 1968 (pp. A-10, X-1, ATRR No. 360, 6/4/68).

Background

Merger standards were high on the list of "guidelines" former Assistant Attorney General Donald F. Turner decided to issue soon after he took charge of the Antitrust Division in mid-1965. At the American Bar Association Antitrust Section's 1966 Spring Meeting (p. A-1, ATRR No. 249, 4/19/66), Mr. Turner virtually promised to issue merger guidelines before October 1 of that year. They were finally issued on May 21 of this year, when Mr. Turner had only one working day left before the effective date of his resignation.

In the meantime, the FTC had stolen some of Mr. Turner's thunder. On January 17, 1967, the Commission released statements of its enforcement policies regarding mergers in the food-distribution industries (p. X-1, ATRR No. 289, 1/24/67) and acquisitions of ready-mixed concrete companies by cement manufacturers (p. X-4, ATRR No. 289, 1/24/67). (The Commission's policy statements are analyzed at p. B-1, ATRR No. 300, 4/11/67). Then earlier in May of this year the Commission issued a public statement of its enforcement policy on product-extension mergers for grocery-products manufacturers (p. X-1, ATRR No. 358, 5/21/68).

Unlike the FTC, the Antitrust Division made no attempt to establish guidelines for particular industries. Rather, it spelled out standards applicable to all industries. The Antitrust Division set out no new rules such as the FTC's requirement that cement companies and large food merchants give it 60 days' advance notice of their planned acquisitions. The Antitrust Division merely published "the standards currently being applied by the Department of Justice in determining whether to challenge corporate acquisitions and mergers under Section 7."

In a press release announcing the guidelines, Attorney General Ramsey Clark expressed hope that they will "provide a basis for a continuing dialogue between government and business concerning the role and scope of anti-merger enforcement in the maintenance of a free competitive economy." The Department anticipates that it will amend the guidelines from time to time * * * to reflect changes in enforcement policy that might result from subsequent court decisions, comments of interested parties, or Department reevaluations. Because changes in enforcement policy will be made as the occasion demands and will usually precede the issuance of amended guidelines, * * * the existence of unamended guidelines should not be regarded as barring [the Department] from taking any action it deems necessary to achieve the purposes of Section 7." At a press conference held in conjunction with announcement of the guidelines, a Justice Department spokesman reported that the guidelines were not cleared with the FTC and that the Commission's policy statements were not presented to the Justice Department in advance of publication.

At the outset, the Antitrust Division's guidelines focus on market structure "chiefly because the conduct of the individual firms in a market tends to be controlled by the structure of that market, i.e., by those market conditions which are fairly permanent or subject only to slow change (such as, principally, the number of substantial firms selling in the market, the relative sizes of their respective market shares, and the substantiality of barriers to the entry of new firms into the market)."

It is recognized in the guidelines that the first step in making an assessment of market structure is ascertainment of the relevant market. "A market is any grouping of sales (or other commercial transactions) in which each of the firms whose sales are included enjoy some advantage in competing with those firms whose sales are not included. The advantage need not be great, for so long as it is significant it defines an area of effective competition among the included sellers in which the competition of the excluded sellers is, ex hypothesi, less effective." This test of significant competitive advantage is observed by the guidelines in describing the product dimension of the relevant market ("line of commerce") and its geographic dimension ("section of the country"). Acknowledging that precise delineation of geographic markets is often impossible, the Antitrust Division says it will "challenge any merger which appears to be illegal in any reasonable geographic market, even though in another reasonable market it would not appear to be illegal."

Horizontal Mergers

Ordinarily, the Division's judgment on whether to attack a horizontal merger will be based on market shares. In a "market highly concentrated" -- one in which the four largest firms control "approximately 75 percent or more" of the business -- acquisition of a company with only 1 percent of the sales will be challenged if the acquiring firm has 15 percent or more; acquisition of a company with 2 percent of the sales will be challenged if the acquirer has 10 percent; and acquisition of a 4 percent element in the market will be challenged if the acquirer also has as much as 4 percent. In a market that is less highly concentrated, acquisition of a company making 1 percent of the sales will not be attacked unless the acquiring company has at least 25 percent of the market; acquisition of a company with 2 percent of the sales will be attacked if the acquirer has as much as 20 percent; acquisition of a company with 3 percent of the market will be challenged if the acquirer has 15 percent; acquisition of a company with 4 percent will not be left unmolested if the acquirer has 10 percent; and a company controlling 5 percent of the market will not be permitted to acquire one that has 5 percent or more of the sales.

The Department will apply stricter standards in a market showing a trend toward concentration. A concentration trend exists, in the Department's view, when the aggregate market share of any grouping of the largest firms in the market from the two largest to the eight largest had increased by 7 percent or more of the market since any base year five-ten years prior to the merger. In those circumstances, the Division will challenge the acquisition by any of those largest firms of any company with a market share of 2 percent or more.

In addition, the guidelines set out two nonmarket share standards that will cause the Justice Department to sue: (1) "acquisition of a competitor which is a particularly 'disturbing,' 'disruptive,' or otherwise unusually competitive factor in the market;" and (2) a merger involving a substantial company that, while it has an insubstantial market share, "possesses an unusual competitive potential or has an asset that confers an unusual competitive advantage."

Vertical Mergers

"With all vertical mergers it is necessary to consider the probable competitive consequences of the merger in both the market in which the supplying firm sells and the market in which the purchasing firm sells, although a significant adverse effect in either market will ordinarily result in a challenge by the Department." A vertical merger will be regarded as having an objectionable competitive impact on the supplying firm's market when a supplying firm with 10 percent or more of the sales in that market acquires one or more purchasing firms accounting in the aggregate for 6 percent or more of the total purchases in that market, "unless it clearly appears that there are no significant barriers to entry into the business of the purchasing firm or firms."

The guidelines express a view that this test with regard to effect on the supplying firm's market will normally result in challenges against most of the vertical mergers that may have adverse effect in the purchasing firm's market. There are additional situations set forth, however, in which vertical mergers will be regarded as raising entry barriers in the purchasing firm's market or as creating disadvantages for the purchasing firm's competitors and therefore will be found objectionable. The most common of these situations arises when the supplying firm and its competitors sell a complex product in which innovating charges have been taking place or a scarce raw material or other product whose supply cannot be readily expanded to meet increased demand. In that situation, the merged firm may have the power to use any temporary superiority, or any shortage, in the product of the supplying firm to put competitors of the purchasing firm at a disadvantage. Where such a product is a significant feature or ingredient of the end-product manufactured by the purchasing firm and its competitors, the Antitrust Division will ordinarily challenge a merger or series of mergers between a supplying firm accounting for 20 percent or more of the market sales and a purchasing firm or firms accounting in the aggregate for 10 percent or more of the sales in its market.

Even when those market-share figures are not involved, the Department will ordinarily challenge "acquisitions of suppliers or customers by major firms in an industry in which (i) there has been, or is developing, a significant trend toward vertical integration by merger such that the trend, if unchallenged, would probably raise barriers to entry or impose a competitive disadvantage on unintegrated or partly integrated firms, and (ii) it does not clearly appear that the particular acquisition will result in significant economies of production or distribution unrelated to advertising and other promotional economies." (The government's recent antimerger actions against the Mead Corp. and Hammermill Paper Co. (p. A-9, ATRR No. 365, 7/9/68) probably illustrate application of this rule.) Action will also be taken to stop acquisition of a customer or supplier for the purpose of increasing the difficulty of entry by potential competitors or putting competitors "at an unwarranted disadvantage."

Conglomerates

In the category of "conglomerate mergers," the guidelines put all "mergers that are neither horizontal nor vertical," so that the term includes market-extension mergers -- consolidation of companies selling the same product in different geographic markets -- and product-extension mergers -- consolidations of "sellers of functionally closely related products which are not, however, close substitutes," in the words of the FTC's Clorox opinion (pp. A-7, X-1, ATRR No. 127, 12/17/63). The guidelines deal with three categories of conglomerate mergers: (1) those eliminating potential entrants, (2) those creating a danger of reciprocal buying, and (3) those that threaten to entrench or enhance the market power of the acquired firm.

Recognizing that potential competition may often be the most significant competitive limitation on the exercise of market power by leading firms, the guidelines predict action against "any merger between one of the most likely entrants into the market" and (1) any firm with "approximately 25 percent or more" of the market; (2) one of the two largest firms in a market if their share therein amounts to "approximately 50 percent or more"; (3) one of the four largest firms in a market if the eight largest have "approximately 75 percent or more" of the market and the merging firm has "approximately 10 percent or more"; or (4) one of the eight largest firms in a market if their total share amounts to "approximately 75 percent or more" and either (a) the merging firm's share is "not insubstantial" and there are no more than one or two "likely entrants" or (b) the merging firm is a rapidly growing firm.
"Any merger which creates a significant danger of reciprocal buying" will "ordinarily" be challenged. And "a significant danger of reciprocal buying is present whenever approximately 15 percent or more of the total purchases in a market in which one of the merging firms ('the selling firm') sells are accounted for by firms which also make substantial sales in markets where the other merging firm ('the buying firm') is both a substantial buyer and a more substantial buyer than all or most of the competitors of the selling firm." Moreover, the Department will also ordinarily challenge any merger undertaken to facilitate the creation of reciprocal-buying arrangements, as well as any merger creating the possibility of substantial reciprocal buying by a company with a record of reciprocal buying. Except in "exceptional circumstances," the guidelines do not accept resulting economies as justification for a merger creating a significant danger of reciprocal buying.

Mergers involving potential competition and reciprocal buying are the only two types of conglomerates that the guidelines regard "as having sufficiently identifiable anticompetitive effects to be the subject of relatively specific structural guidelines." But "the Department will ordinarily investigate the possibility of anticompetitive consequences, and may in particular circumstances bring suit, where an acquisition of a leading firm in a relatively concentrated or rapidly concentrating market may serve to entrench or increase the market power of that firm or raise barriers to entry in that market."

(For a review of the guidelines' treatment of the failing-company defense, see p. 47.)

Conclusions

Antitrust experts see little, if anything, new in the general factors the Antitrust Division says it will take into account in enforcing Section 7 of the Clayton Act. But the guidelines do make a significant contribution to what has come to be known as "the numbers game" -- the use of market-share figures to show a merger's anticompetitive possibilities. Certainly the definition, for example, of a "concentration trend" in terms of a specific percentage increase in the shares of a definite number of firms is an important innovation. No effort seems to have been made to tighten antimerger enforcement, for the market-share figures given by the guidelines are probably higher in many instances than the Supreme Court's decisions would require them to be.

Unless the guidelines intend to include purchases when they define a market as "any grouping of sales (or other commercial transactions)," their reliance entirely upon sales figures leaves a gap in the standards, though it may be a small one. Serious anticompetitive results can follow from merger of two important buyers in a market who, however, use the purchased material in the production of two quite different products and therefore do not themselves sell in the same market or in competition with each other. Their merger might have no impact at all in either of the two markets in which they sell and yet give them complete domination of the market in which they buy their common raw material. For example, consider the merger of two companies that are the principal buyers of fruit pits and nut shells from a host of small food packers. One crushes the pits and shells for resale in the soft-abrasives market, but the other pulverizes them for sale to the oil fields as an additive to drilling mud. Can we assume the "sales" percentage figures set out in the guidelines will be applied here also? Or will buyers be looked upon as (1) generally less advantageously situated and therefore entitled to larger market shares or (2) generally more advantageously situated and hence restricted to smaller market shares?

One problem in publishing these numbers for everyone to see is that some business executives will view them as hard and fast, easily applied tests that will simplify expansion-by-merger decisions. For most mergers, however, the key to Section 7 lawfulness is the much more esoteric task of defining the relevant market. And the business executive's boundaries for the market in which market shares are to be computed might be quite different from the government's. Much extended litigation in the merger field has been occasioned by disputes over market definition. U.S. v. Pabst Brewing Co., 384 U.S. 546 (pp. A-4, X-23, ATRR No. 257, 6/14/66); U.S. v. Continental Can Co., 378 U.S. 441 (pp. A-11, X-1, ATRR No. 154, 6/23/64); U.S. v. Aluminum Co. of America, 377 U.S. 271 (pp. A-2, X-6, ATRR No. 151, 6/24/64); U.S. v. Philadelphia National Bank, 374 U.S. 321 (pp. A-9, X-7, ATRR No. 101, 6/18/63).

Generally, if it is reasonable to do so, the government selects the market definition that will give the merging companies the most impressive market shares. Once that propensity is recognized by the business community, the guidelines may well have a merger-deterring effect. Some businessmen have a horror of litigation, regardless of its probable eventual outcome and can therefore be expected to carefully limit their acquisitions to the areas left open by the guidelines. Marginal acquisitions will often be dropped to avoid any risk of litigation; or, perhaps, increased use will be made of the Department's Business Advisory Procedures. Nevertheless, for this type of business executive, it is good news that the standards are not as tough as the Supreme Court might have made them.

At the same time, publication of the guidelines could also have a noticeable case-generating effect. Even though the standards set out were already well known to the Antitrust Division's staff of attorneys, their publication will make them harder for the Division's staff to overlook or ignore in specific situations. Some lawyers believe, however, that this effect, like the deterrent effect on corporate executives, will be temporary and that in a few years the existence of the guidelines will be forgotten. The FTC may go its own way and not follow the guidelines; the courts won't follow them; and the key to the litigated cases will continue to be definition of the relevant market -- usually, definition of the product market.

- 0 -

References

FTC Enforcement Policy with Respect to Mergers in the Food-Distribution
Industries (p. X-1, ATRR No. 289, 1/24/67)
FTC Enforcement Policy with Respect to Vertical Mergers in the Cement
Industry (p. X-4, ATRR No. 289, 1/24/67)
Lehigh Portland Cement Co. et al., FTC Dockets 8680, 8685, and 8657,
February 6, 1967 (p. A-7, ATRR No. 292, 2/14/67)

Background

Some degree of certainty or predictability in the application of Section 7 of the Clayton
Act has long been the wishful dream of some elements in both the business community and the
enforcement agencies. Early in 1964, Federal Trade Commissioner Philip Elman proposed at
a Federal Bar Association briefing conference in Washington, D. C., that the Commission
study merger economics in particular industries and prepare rules or guidelines defining the
type or size of merger it would proceed against in each industry. And merger standards were
high on the list of "guidelines" Assistant Attorney General Donald F. Turner decided to issue
soon after he took charge of the Antitrust Division in mid-1965. A year ago at the American
Bar Association Antitrust Section's spring meeting (p. A-1, ATRR No. 249, 4/19/66), Mr.
Turner virtually promised to issue a merger guideline before last October 1.

It was the FTC that took action first, however. On January 17 of this year the Commission released statements of its enforcement policies regarding mergers in the food-distribution
industries and acquisitions of ready-mixed concrete companies by cement manufacturers.

In the food-distribution industries, the Commission promised to "focus particular attention on mergers or acquisitions by food retailing and wholesaling corporations with combined
annual sales in excess of $100 million." The greatest diligence, the Commission announced,
will be exercised when mergers result in combined annual food sales of more than $500 mil-
lion. Setting the background for its establishment of these standards, the Commission tells of
its observation of "very significant changes during the past decade and a half" in the structure of food retailing. Increasing concentration in both national and local markets and the
growing importance of grocery chains have forced the Commission to devote "much of the ***
merger enforcement activity *** to this sector of the economy." The Commission then went
on to describe briefly each of its complaint proceedings in this area, including pending litigation against Kroger Co. (Docket 7464) for five acquisitions made in the late 1950's.

With regard to vertical cement-industry mergers, the Commission stressed both the
size of the acquired ready-mixed-concrete producer and its relative position in its local
metropolitan market. The Commission promised to investigate any acquisition of a ready-
mixed concrete firm in a market to which the acquiring cement producer is either an actual or
potential supplier. Whenever such an investigation reveals an "acquisition of any ready-mixed-
concrete firm ranking among the leading four nonintegrated producers in any metropolitan market, or the acquisition of any ready-mixed-concrete company or other cement consumer which
regularly purchases 50,000 barrels of cement or more annually" the Commission will issue a
Section 7 complaint, "unless unusual circumstances in a particular case dictate the contrary."
The same procedure will be followed if a cement company acquires several smaller concrete
producers whose cumulative cement purchases meet that test or if a smaller concrete producer
is acquired by a cement producer already integrated forward into the ready-mixed-concrete
business in that market.

The Commission's policy statement as to the cement industry echoed some of the allegations made in its outstanding cement-industry complaints -- for example, that vertical mergers
"may set off a 'chain' reaction of acquisitions" and "may" inhibit new entrants. While the
background information set out in the statement does not relate to any specific complaint proceedings, it does list several specific metropolitan markets in which the ready-mixed-concrete
industry is regarded as "quite concentrated." The Commission flatly concludes "that vertical

mergers and acquisitions involving cement manufacturers and consumers of cement, particularly ready-mixed-concrete companies, can have substantial adverse effects on competition in the particular market areas where they occur." The Commission relies heavily on a report filed by its economics staff in April of last year (p. A-16, ATRR No. 250, 4/26/66) on "Mergers and Vertical Integration in the Cement Industry" and on the results of public hearings held by the Commission following publication of that report.

Having established guides to indicate when it will move against food and cement mergers, the Commission adopted a novel device for insuring that the guides will be applied throughout the two industries involved. It announced that each year it will serve every food retailer and wholesaler making annual sales in excess of $100 million and every portland-cement producer, regardless of size, with a Section 6(b) FTC Act order requiring each to give the Commission at least 60 days' advance notice of any proposed acquisition covered by the policy statements. In this particular aspect of the Commission's action, Chairman Dixon and Commissioner MacIntyre did not concur.

Both policy statements have been cited as prejudgments of pending merger cases. Companies in both industries have demanded dismissal of complaint proceedings against them. The Commission has already denied the dismissal motions of Lehigh Portland Cement Co. and two other cement producers, as well as Lehigh's novel motion to transfer its case to the Antitrust Division. The three cement producers objected to the Commission's conduct of industry-wide public hearings, investigation of the cement industry, and its release of an economic report while it was litigating complaint proceedings against them. These actions by the Commission were attacked as infringements of administrative due process of law in the pending complaint proceedings. The Commission rejected these contentions, holding that the policy statements merely set forth criteria for identifying acquisitions that warrant the Commission's immediate attention. In any specific proceeding, the Commission announced, the issues will still be decided on the basis of the record in that particular case. "Respondents are entitled to have their cases adjudicated by Commissioners with open minds, not empty ones." Still pending is a similar motion by Kroger Co., Cincinnati, (Docket 7464, p. A-8, ATRR No. 292, 2/14/67) based on the policy statement with respect to food-distribution mergers.

Conclusions

There does not seem to be any widespread doubt in the antitrust bar about the Commission's authority to issue the guidelines. The policy statements are nothing more than announcements of the circumstances under which the Commission will initiate an investigation or deem the issuance of a Section 7 Clayton Act complaint to be in the public interest. The Commission's declarations are not binding on anyone and do not constitute "rules" or "regulations" needing a base in a statutory grant of authority. The Commission has merely done what any law-enforcement agency, including the Antitrust Division, can clearly do.

In fact, some antitrust experts think the policy statements contain no information a businessman cannot get from any competent lawyer. In U.S. v. Von's Grocery Co., 384 U.S. 270, 34 LW 4425 (pp. A-11, X-1, ATRR No. 255, 5/31/66), the Supreme Court struck down a food-distribution merger that created a regional supermarket chain with annual sales of less than $175 million. And the Commission's own pending and completed proceedings against vertical cement-industry acquisitions have made it clear that it regards as suspect any cement-producer acquisition of a substantial ready-mix firm.

As indicated by developments in the Lehigh and Kroger cases, some antitrust lawyers see in the Commission's statements advance declarations or judgments that mergers of the types described in the two policy statements are indeed violations of the Clayton Act. In a sense, though, an element of prejudgment is built into the administrative system at the FTC, for under Section 11 of the Act the Commission must "have reason to believe" that an antitrust violation occurred each time it issues a Section 7 complaint.

Interesting legal problems could arise out of the unorthodox use the Commission made of its authority under section 6(b) of the FTC Act to require "special reports" from business enterprises. For some years the Commission and the Justice Department have unsuccessfully attempted to persuade Congress to enact a statute requiring companies to give advance notification of merger plans. Now the Commission is claiming that it had power to require pre-merger notification all along under the FTC Act.

Does Section 6 give the Commission power to require reports of planned future activity as opposed to records of past conduct? Although decisions like U. S. v. Morton Salt Co., 338 U. S. 632 (1950), are regarded as establishing that the Commission's Section 6 authority is a broad civil-investigative-demand power, there is language near the end of Justice Jackson's opinion to suggest that Section 6(b) may be more limited in scope. Even the Antitrust Division's civil-investigative-demand authority has been held not to include authority to inquire about possible future antitrust violations. In re Union Oil Co. of California, 225 F.Supp. 486 (S.D. Calif.) (pp. A-8, X-7, ATRR No. 129, 12/31/63). And in U.S. v. St. Regis Paper Co., 181 F.Supp. 862 (S.D. N. Y. 1960), the Federal District Court for Southern New York struck several questions from a Section 6 order on the theory that Section 6 was adopted as a convenience to the business community as well as to the Commission and that the Commission must be content with information recorded in the regular course of business and readily available.

Another interesting question arises as to the method the Commission might adopt in enforcing the Section 6 orders it issues pursuant to these two policy statements. Under Section 10 of the FTC Act, a corporation cannot be penalized for failure to comply with a Section 6 order until it has been served with a notice of default and 30 additional days have elapsed without compliance. If the Commission needs notification from the company as to an impending merger, how will it know when a company has failed to comply with one of these orders requiring notification? Once the merger is consummated, premerger notification is no longer possible and yet the company presumably would not have been served with the required default notice.

Finally, there may be situations in which compliance with the Commission's 60-day notice provision will in effect operate as a requirement that a merger be delayed. Mergers conspicuous enough to fall within the Commission's guideline will often take longer than 60 days to consummate. But it is conceivable that two companies might find themselves in a position to complete a merger within a few days after the idea first occurred to them. Presumably, they could not comply with the Commission's Section 6(b) order unless they delayed their merger until the 60-day notice period elapsed.

It has been pointed out by some members of the Antitrust Bar that the manner in which the Commission adopted the Section 6 order requirement suggests that it could peremptorily extend the requirement to all industries. But few expect the Commission to adopt a general requirement of pre-merger notification or even to adopt policy statements for nearly all industries. They feel such action is likely only in connection with the few industries in which the Commission has had a chance to conduct detailed economic surveys or to bring a number of complaint proceedings as a vehicle for gathering data and shaping policy.

- 0 -

Subject: **FTC Merger-Policy and its Consent Orders**   (Published 2/4/69)

Question

What is the relationship between FTC merger guidelines and its consent orders?

References

FTC Enforcement Policy with Respect to Mergers in the Textile Mill Products
Industry (p. X-1, ATRR No. 385, 11/26/68)
Burlington Industries, Inc., FTC Docket C-1473 (p. A-6, ATRR No. 385, 11/26/68;
p. A-1, ATRR No. 393, 1/21/69)

Background

When the Federal Trade Commission announced its Enforcement Policy with Respect to
Mergers in the Textile Mill Products Industry, Commissioner Jones dissented. She maintained
that the guidelines set out "are manifestly unfair to the industry when coupled with the simultaneously announced acceptance by the Commission of a consent order against Burlington
Industries legalizing in effect the same acquisitions which are clearly contrary to the guidelines."

The policy statement promised "examination" for possible Section 7 Clayton Act enforcement action of "any horizontal merger in a textile mill product submarket where (1) the
combined firms rank among the top four or (2) have a combined market share of 5% or more of
any submarket in which the four largest firms account for 35% or more of the market." According to Commissioner Jones, the Commission's consent order against Burlington "in effect
puts a stamp of approval on a series of preguideline acquisitions made by Burlington which has
enabled Burlington to move in the overall textile mill products industry from second to first
place and similarly to advance its industry ranking to within the top four grouping in several
product submarkets within this broader textile market. The Commission has been frequently
criticized for adopting a merger policy which ignores or leaves untouched the largest firms in
an industry and which concentrates its enforcement fire on the middle tier companies struggling
to compete with their larger industry rivals. * * * The Commission's action today for the
first time in my judgment gives some solid substance to this criticism."

When the Commission made final its consent order terminating the Burlington case, Commissioner Jones revoiced her dissent: "If the mergers described in the guidelines will give rise
to possible anticompetitive consequences in the future when engaged in by the rest of the industry, all of whom rank well below Burlington in asset and sales value, I cannot understand how
the Commission can conclude that identical mergers entered into by Burlington during the past
decade do not also give rise to anticompetitive consequences or to the likelihood of such consequences."

In the Commission's press release announcing the entry of the consent order, there was
a statement that "Commissioner MacIntyre noted for the attention of all concerned that the Commission's consideration of guidelines for the textile industry will receive further consideration
of the Commission on January 22, 1969." On that date the Commission met for two hours with
a six-man delegation from the American Textile Manufacturers Institute. While no further
pronouncements have come from the Commission, the ATMI issued a statement that the Commission was asked to reconsider its guidelines. The textile mill products industry is not the
only one in which the Commission's consent orders have allowed retention of acquired businesses
whose acquisition would be questioned by full-force application of merger-policy statements.
The Commission's willingness to settle for prohibitions against future acquisitions -- sometimes
with divestiture -- had produced, by the time its policy statement for the food-distribution industry was published (pp. A-1, X-1, ATRR No. 289, 1/24/67), a number of consent orders in
that industry appearing to sanction mergers frowned on by the policy statement.

In that policy statement, the Commission promised to give "attention and consideration"
to any merger by retail food chains that results in combined annual food store sales in excess
of $500 million. However, in two of the merger cases cited in the footnotes to the factual

background for its policy statement, the Commission issued orders requiring no divestiture by leading grocery chains. National Tea Co., Docket 7453 (pp. A-1, X-1, ATRR No. 245, 3/22/66); Winn-Dixie Stores, Docket C-110 (p. A-9, ATRR No. 271, 9/20/66). A third order-- in Grand Union Co., Docket 8458 (p. A-2, ATRR No. 206, 6/22/65) -- required divestiture of only ten of the 59 grocery stores whose acquisition was attacked in the complaint. And in its complaint against Kroger Co., Docket 7464 (p. A-15, ATRR No. 385, 11/26/68) was dropped after reference to "the longevity of the case," the further delays associated with additional hearings called for by a complaint amendment attacking a new grocery-chain acquisition by Kroger, and the Commission's policy-statement requirement that it be given 60 days' notice of any future acquisitions.

Similarly, the Commission's consent order in a proceeding against a major cement manufacturer's acquisitions of ready-mix concrete producers seem to fall well short of the standards subsequently set out in the Commission's Enforcement Policy with Respect to Vertical mergers in the Cement Industry (p. X-4, ATRR No. 289, 1/24/67). "Unless unusual circumstances in a particular case dictate to the contrary," the Commission threatened to issue a complaint challenging the acquisition by a cement manufacturer "of any ready-mixed concrete firm ranking among the leading four nonintegrated ready-mix producers in any metropolitan market." In Lone Star Cement Corp., Docket 8585 (p. A-12, ATRR No. 185, 1/26/65), the consent order required Lone Star to dispose of most of the ready-mix concrete plants of an acquired subsidiary that was the largest producer of ready-mixed concrete in the Norfolk and Richmond areas of Virginia. Having disposed of 16 of its 20 Norfolk-Richmond area plants in accordance with the terms of the order, however, the Lone Star subsidiary remained one of the top four producers, and it is probably still the largest.

Conclusions

To a degree, inconsistency between policy statements or guidelines and orders terminating litigation is explainable in terms of basic differences in the nature and goals of the two techniques of law enforcement. First, the Commission's guidelines are not restricted in their content, as are cease-and-desist orders, by any necessity for getting the approval of either a court or the merging companies. Since the Commission's staff and budget are limited, sometimes the most fruitful allocation of its resources requires settlement of litigation for something less in the way of relief than is obtainable as a matter of law. Second, guidelines or policy statements indicate that the Commission will investigate, or file complaints against, certain types of mergers; they give no commitment as to how the complaint proceedings will be terminated. The guidelines are designed to influence future business conduct, not to undo the past. Therefore, a consent order apparently sanctioning a merger condemned by guidelines but prohibiting future mergers may have a purpose quite consistent with that of guidelines -- to arrest a trend and thereby obtain greater compliance for the future. A merger may be attacked because it represents a good place to stop a developing trend rather than because it is a particularly anticompetitive one in and of itself. Cf. U.S. v. Von's Grocery Co., 384 U.S. 270 (pp. A-11, X-1, ATRR No. 255, 5/31/66).

Some lawyers feel the FTC majority made a mistake in not giving an explanation of the contrast between the textile mill guidelines and the Burlington consent order -- especially since the Commission is known to have simultaneously dropped investigations of other substantial textile-mill mergers the staff wanted to undo. These lawyers report that, in the absence of explanation, smaller mills have become resentful of the Commission's foreclosure to them of a means of growth their larger competitors have been allowed to take full advantage of. And the Commission's dismissal of the Kroger complaint is cited as proof to some expansion-minded grocery chains that the Commission can be outlasted in merger litigation.

Other experts insist, though, that the Commission has adopted the equitable course of changing the rules only prospectively and therefore took a step toward certainty in -- and more respect for -- the antitrust laws. They insist that the textile mill industry is aware of this Commission purpose. Moreover, the Commission's action is not unfair unless the prior mergers gave the merging companies a competitive advantage. Such an advantage is not always derived from a merger, although the Commission's policy statement on the cement industry described important advantages of vertical integration there.

Like the Antitrust Division's Merger Guidelines (p. X-1, ATRR No. 360, 6/4/68; analyzed, p. B-1, ATRR No. 367, 7/23/68), the FTC's policy statements may not go as far in outlawing mergers as would be possible under the Supreme Court's Section 7 Clayton Act opinions of recent years. Moreover, once it starts a complaint proceeding, the Commission has more control over termination of that proceeding than the Justice Department can exercise in ending its injunction suits. An FTC decision to accept a consent order is not appealable, whereas interested public agencies and other industry members may be able to intervene in the Justice Department's district court suits and fight for a stronger order. Cascade Natural Gas Corp. v. El Paso Natural Gas Co., 386 U.S. 129 (pp. A-18, X-1, ATRR No. 294, 2/28/67). But cf. U.S. v. Harper & Row Publishers, Inc. (N.D. Ill.) (p. A-15, ATRR No. 333, 11/28/67), affirmed sub nom. City of New York v. U.S., 390 U.S. 715 (p. A-6, ATRR No. 354, 4/23/68); U.S. v. Blue Chip Stamp Co., 272 F.Supp. 432 (C.D. Calif. 1967) affirmed sub nom. Thrifty Shoppers Scrip Co. v. U.S., 389 U.S. 580 (p. A-9, ATRR No. 340, 1/16/68); and U.S. v. Alcoa, 41 F.R.D. 342 (E.D. Mo.) (p. A-12, ATRR No. 289, 1/24/67) appeal dismissed sub nom. Lupton Mfg. Co. v. U.S., 388 U.S. 457 (p. A-7, ATRR No. 309, 6/13/67), where intervention was denied.

Someone hurt by an FTC consent order clearing a merger he thinks violates the guidelines seems to have no recourse as to the Commission's action. If he can prove injury, he may bring a treble-damage suit for his actual losses and seek injunctive protection against threatened or potential harm. But even in such a suit he must assume that the court will know the Commission has given its approval to the merger under attack.

- 0 -

Subject: Conglomerate Mergers   (Published 2/18/69)

Question

   To what extent do existing antitrust laws apply to conglomerate mergers?

References

   Study Paper No. 2, Studies by the Staff of the Cabinet Committee on Price Stability
      (Superintendent of Documents, GPO, $1.00) (p. A-2, ATRR No. 394, 1/28/69)
   Testimony of Assistant Attorney General Richard W. McLaren, Senate Judiciary
      Committee, January 29, 1969 (p. A-1, ATRR No. 395, 2/4/69)
   "Conglomerate Mergers and the Future," Panel Discussion, 37 ABA Antitrust Law
      Journal 318 (1968)
   FTC Resolution Directing Investigation of Acquisitions and Mergers, July 2, 1968
      (p. A-10, ATRR No. 365, 7/9/68)

Background

   At the Senate Judiciary Committee's hearing on confirmation of his appointment, new
Assistant Attorney General Richard M. McLaren announced that the Antitrust Division will
give "high priority" to antitrust action against conglomerate mergers. A conglomerate merger
is generally defined as one combining companies that were neither competitors (horizontal
merger) nor supplier and customer (vertical merger). The new Antitrust Division chief took
the position that court actions against conglomerate acquisitions should be attempted under
Section 7 of the Clayton Act before new legislation is sought.

   The views he expressed seem to inaugurate a change of policy at the Justice Department.
Former Assistant Attorney General Donald F. Turner remarked a number of times that he
thought new legislation is needed to deal with conglomerate mergers. "For example, *** Congress should pass a statute that would say to the top 50 or 100 companies 'any time you make
an acquisition in excess of a certain size you must peel off assets of comparable magnitude.'"
Senate Small Business Committee hearings, April 6, 1967 (p. A-11, ATRR No. 300, 4/11/67).
Mr. Turner's view won support recently from the staff of the Cabinet Committee on Price
Stability, which, in a report calling for vigorous antitrust enforcement to curb concentration,
said the Clayton Act appears inadequate to cope with conglomerate mergers (p. A-2, ATRR
No. 394, 1/28/69).

   The Antitrust Division filed a record number (24) of Clayton Act antimerger suits in
1968, of which nine can be regarded as involving conglomerate acquisitions. Five of those
nine were bank acquisitions that extended the acquiring bank's offices into a new geographic
market (market-extension merger). Each of the remaining four was a "product extension"
acquisition -- a term defined in Procter & Gamble Co., FTC Docket 6901 (pp. A-7, X-1, ATRR
No. 127, 12/17/63) as "the merger of sellers of functionally closely related products which are
not, however, close substitutes" -- "another variant of the conventional horizontal merger."
The FTC's annual merger reports have classified as conglomerates an overwhelming majority
of the mergers effected in recent years (p. A-11, ATRR No. 349, 3/19/68). Only ten antimerger complaints were filed by the FTC in 1968, and all except Kennecott Copper Corp.,
Docket 8765 (p. A-10, ATRR No. 370, 8/13/68), attacked mergers said to have significant
vertical or horizontal features. Early in 1968 (p. A-19, ATRR No. 349, 3/19/68), the Joint
Economic Committee of Congress expressed concern about the trend revealed in the Commissions' statistics and questioned whether the FTC and the Antitrust Division are being as vigorous and imaginative as they might be in applying the antitrust laws to conglomerate mergers.
The Committee described the enforcement agencies as "well equipped with legal authority" to
investigate and challenge such mergers.

Studies Planned

   Four months later (p. A-10, ATRR No. 365, 7/9/68), citing the "growing concern on the
part of * * * congressional committees," the FTC directed its staff to begin a broad "in depth"

investigation of conglomerate mergers. The investigation is "to cover not only the short-run anticompetitive aspects of such mergers, but also broader issues, including the relationship between conglomerate mergers and technical or business efficiencies, the economic performance of conglomerate firms in the market place, and the effect of conglomerate mergers on the competitive vigor of enterprises by their change in status from independent firms to subsidiaries or divisions of conglomerates, and the impact of such structural changes on long-run competitive activity." Upon completion of the staff investigation, the Commission announced, it will hold a public hearing.

In the 91st Congress, the House Antitrust Subcommittee has plans for "a comprehensive investigation of conglomerate mergers," and at least one senator is determined to push for similar action in the Senate (p. A-5, ATRR No. 379, 10/15/68). The House Subcommittee chairman believes "it may be that the traditional standards of the antitrust laws against mergers and combinations which 'may be substantially to lessen competition, or tend to create a monopoly' need reevaluation in the light of economic and political effects of conglomerate mergers." In addition, Chairman Wilbur Mills of the House Ways and Means Committee has undertaken a study of the financing of conglomerate takeovers with a view to reassessing the interest deductions and installment-reporting privilege accorded the debentures often exchanged for take-over stock.

There have been expressions of concern, too, about the entry of conglomerates into regulated industries. On February 7, 1969, the FCC announced its intention to investigate conglomerate ownership of broadcasting stations (p. A-11, ATRR No. 396, 2/11/69). Chairman Wright Patman of the House Banking Committee has introduced a bill to regulate "one-bank holding companies," and the administration's bill is expected to be introduced this week (p. A-1, ATRR No. 397, 2/18/69). It was once reported that a committee of antitrust specialists was preparing a report for the White House on conglomerate mergers (New York Times, March 22, 1968, p. 69), but the White House has a new tenant.

Clorox Case

The Supreme Court's only decision on conglomerate mergers is FTC v. Procter & Gamble Co., 386 U.S. 568 (pp. A-13, X-1, ATRR No. 300, 4/11/67). "All mergers are within the reach of Section 7 and all must be tested by the same standard, whether they are classified as horizontal, vertical, conglomerate or other." The P&G decision reinstated an FTC order outlawing a "product extension" merger. "The products of the acquired company are complementary to those of the acquiring company and may be produced with similar facilities, marketed through the same channels and in the same manner, and advertised by the same media." 386 U.S. at 577. This relationship between the products of P&G, the acquiring firm, and Clorox, the acquired company, gave that merger a quasi-horizontal element.

Nevertheless, the Supreme Court stressed three competitive factors that appear relevant as to mergers more conglomerate than the product-extension type: (1) the relative disparity in size and strength as between P&G and the largest firms in the liquid-bleach industry; (2) excessive concentration in the liquid-bleach industry and Clorox's dominant position in the industry; and (3) the elimination of P&G as a potential competitor in the liquid-bleach industry. (The relationship of the Court's rationale to purely conglomerate mergers is analyzed in the analysis following this one, p. 43.)

It was subsequently held in General Foods Co. v. FTC, 386 F.2d 936 (3d Cir.) (pp. A-14, X-2, ATRR No. 331, 11/14/67), review denied, 391 U.S. 919 (p. A-24, ATRR No. 358, 5/21/68), that proof of elimination of a potential competitor is not essential to establishing the illegality of a product-extension type of conglomerate merger. The anticompetitive effects attributed there to the entry of a giant parent into a market of smaller firms were deterrence of new entrants from the market and inducement of existing sellers to compete less vigorously for fear of retaliation.

Enforcement Policy

In U.S. v. Wilson Sporting Goods Co. (p. A-7, ATRR No. 351, 4/2/68) and U.S. v. Caterpillar Tractor Co. (p. A-3, ATRR No. 351, 4/2/68), the Justice Department used the

Procter & Gamble precedent to get temporary restraining orders against two product-extension mergers. Still pending are two more recent actions to enjoin product-extension mergers: U. S. v. Interpace Corp.; U. S. v. Combustion Engineering, Inc. (pp. A-7, A-12, ATRR No. 380, 10/22/68). In addition, Justice Department opposition before the Federal Communications Commission caused International Telephone & Telegraph Corp. to call off its agreement to acquire American Broadcasting Company, Inc. (p. A-2, ATRR No. 339, 1/9/68); Bethlehem Steel Corp. was induced to abandon plans to acquire Cerro Corp. (Wall Street Journal, March 21, 1968, p. 3); and Antitrust Division and FTC investigations may have been instrumental in persuading Gulf and Western, one of the largest conglomerates, to drop attempts to acquire Allis-Chalmers Co. (p. A-16, ATRR No. 365, 7/9/68) and Armour & Co. (p. A-17, ATRR No. 343, 2/6/68).

Although the P&G-Clorox case is generally regarded as the first specimen of conglomerate-merger litigation, the Supreme Court had earlier sustained an FTC order outlawing a merger of companies that were neither competitors nor supplier and customer. Resulting opportunity for reciprocal dealing (a practice whose antitrust status is analyzed at p. B-1, ATRR No. 203, 6/1/65, and p. B-1, ATRR No. 276, 10/25/66; reprinted at pp. 16-22, Antitrust & Trade Regulation Today: 1967) was a principal basis for the Supreme Court's finding of forbidden anticompetitive effect in FTC v. Consolidated Foods Corp., 380 U.S. 592 (pp. A-1, X-1, ATRR No. 199, 5/4/65).

The Justice Department has filed a number of Section 7 complaints grounded on the reciprocal-dealing theory of competitive effect. In U.S. v. General Dynamics Co., 258 F.Supp. 36 (S.D. N.Y.) (pp. A-1, X-1, ATRR No. 269, 9/6/66), the government obtained a decree requiring General Dynamics, a major government contractor, to divest itself of an industrial-gas producer whose products it had promoted through use of its purchasing power. A consent order entered in May, 1964 (p. A-18, ATRR No. 147, 4/7/64) forced Ingersoll-Rand Co., a big steel buyer, to give up plans to buy three producers of coal-mining equipment. Earlier, in granting a preliminary injunction against the acquisitions (218 F.Supp. 530, p. A-21, ATRR No. 194, 4/30/63), the Federal District Court for Western Pennsylvania observed that the acquisitions would increase Ingersoll-Rand's steel purchases to such an extent that the coal mines' purchase of mining equipment could be influenced by the mines' desire to retain the goodwill of the steel industry, one of their largest customers.

Still pending is a suit challenging the acquisition of Penick & Ford, a large corn-products manufacturer, by R. J. Reynolds Tobacco Co., an important user of paper packaging products in which corn starch is an ingredient. The New Jersey Federal District Court denied a preliminary injunction (242 F.Supp. 518, pp. A-1, X-1, ATRR No. 203, 6/1/65) for lack of evidence that Reynolds would go along with the corn starch industry's reciprocity practices.

Anticompetitive Effects

The Justice Department listed in its Merger Guidelines (p. X-5, ATRR No. 360, 6/4/68; analyzed at page 27, supra) only two types of conglomerate mergers "as having sufficiently identifiable anticompetitive effects to be subject of relatively specific structural guidelines": (1) those eliminating potential entrants to an industry and (2) those creating a danger of reciprocal buying. But "the Department will ordinarily investigate the possibility of anticompetitive consequences, and may in particular circumstances bring suit, where an acquisition of a leading firm in a relatively concentrated or rapidly concentrating market may serve to entrench or increase the market power of that firm or raise barriers to entry in that market."

In his widely discussed 1965 article, "Conglomerate Mergers and Section 7 of the Clayton Act," 78 Harvard L.R. 1313, Mr. Turner discussed four other possible anticompetitive results of conglomerate mergers: (1) Economies of scale in production, distribution, research, selling, management, or capital acquisition may reduce the conglomerate's costs to a point that it can drive smaller competitors out of a business. (2) A diversified firm may be able to drop its prices in one of its markets so low that competitors are wiped out in that market. (3) Substitution of a large wealthy conglomerate as owner of one of many small competitors may frighten the others into competing less vigorously for fear of provoking retaliation. (4) Entry of the large conglomerate may discourage entry of new competitors. But he did not rate the threat of these results as sufficiently serious to outweigh the advantages of encouraging economies of scale. His view that promotional economies should not be an affirmative ground for invalidating a merger under existing antitrust law was apparently rejected by the Supreme Court in the P&G-Clorox case.

Motivation

In all probability, there are conglomerate acquisitions made without a thought to acquiring market leverage through reciprocity or a "deep pocket." Some seem to be nothing more than empire building -- either out of a desire for power and publicity or a compulsion to compete with other expanding conglomerates. Sometimes the acquiring company has idle cash it must invest and merely intends to choose the best investment. Or it may want to diversify to smooth out seasonal peaks and valleys in its income or to reduce its dependence upon a line of business that has become more competitive, is losing out to technological advance in related product lines, or is becoming subject to increasing governmental regulation.

Other acquisitions are prompted by securities-market factors -- e.g., the acquired firm's capitalization, profit ratio, or rate of growth is such that amalgamation produces a stock-earnings ratio higher than the acquiring company's and therefore pushes up the price of the stock once the merger is consummated. Sometimes tax considerations are paramount: one company may have losses that can be set off against the other's taxable earnings. The acquired company may have plant sites, raw materials, cash, or management or technical know-how or personnel that the acquiring company needs.

The impetus for the merger may come even from the acquired company. It may seek to sell out to forestall a takeover by a company that is interested only in short-term capital gains or would make an undesirable parent for some other reason. Small one-man or family corporations are often forced to sell out because cash is needed to settle the leading stock-holder's estate or pay estate taxes or because the decedent was the guiding force whose loss crippled the management of the business. But the most common motive for the acquired company is the premium offered for its stock. Take-over prices rose to an all-time peak in 1968, according to a study released early in January by W. T. Grimm & Co., Chicago, financial consultants specializing in corporate mergers. The average price paid under successful tender offers in 1968 was 24.6 times earnings -- a 40% increase over the 17.6 ratio that prevailed in 1967. An average premium of 25% over market price was paid for take-over stock in 1968.

Conclusions

Many antitrust lawyers agree with the new Assistant Attorney General that there is much to be done about conglomerate mergers under existing antitrust law before a need for new legislation can be established or defined. In fact, some of them are already convinced that existing legislation is readily adaptable to deal with whatever economic problems conglomerate mergers create. Our antitrust laws, they point out, do not establish a set of frozen standards but a constitution-like set of flexible criteria under which judicial precedents have been developed that have relevance even for conglomerate enterprises. Appalachian Coals, Inc. v. U.S., 288 U.S. 344, 474-5 (1933).

The first step in assessing the status of conglomerate mergers under existing law is to segregate out those that have clear anticompetitive potentialities. Product-extension and market-extension mergers fall within that category, for they have a horizontal flavor, as Commissioner Elman pointed out in the FTC's P&G-Clorox opinion. In addition, court proceedings summarized above seem to establish a firm basis for attacking conglomerate acquisitions that eliminate potential competitors, for the presence of this element likewise gives a merger a quasi-horizontal character.

Even a "pure" conglomerate merger -- one uniting companies in businesses so unrelated that neither would have moved into the second field on its own -- is not necessarily untouchable. If the merger gives either company inordinate economic power or leverage in its market, there is a basis for attacking it. The Justice Department's and the FTC's successes in cases based on reciprocity illustrate this principle. So does the warning in the Antitrust Division's Merger Guidelines that "an acquisition of a leading firm in a relatively concentrated or rapidly concentrating market may serve to entrench or increase the market power of that firm or raise barriers to entry in that market." That warning seems justified by the Supreme Court's emphasis of size and strength factors in the P&G-Clorox opinion.

In some industries it may even be possible to establish anticompetitive effect on the basis of absolute, rather than relative, size. Some $40 million in annual advertising expenditures -- not a large amount to some of today's conglomerates -- has been characterized by the Supreme Court as "a powerful offensive and defensive weapon against new competition." American Tobacco Co. v. U.S., 328 U.S. 781, 797 (1946).

Is the residue of small or medium-sized "pure" conglomerate mergers, not amenable to control under existing law, large enough or does it create a serious enough problem to justify new legislation? It remains to be seen whether the planned FTC and congressional studies of conglomerates will produce data that will answer that question. These studies will also have to explore the advantages to be gained through conglomerate mergers: the corporate-income stability achieved by diversification; the enormous economies of scale in some industries; and the resulting availability of a market for small enterprises whose key management people have died or become ready to retire, their working capital inadequate, or their technology obsolete. Some lawyers suggest, therefore, that any drastic antitrust enforcement program against conglomerate mergers should await the outcome of the studies.

While studies of the conglomerate-merger trend generally delve into the motives for merging, intent or motive has been eliminated by the Supreme Court as a relevant consideration in applying antitrust principles. "Our inquiry is whether, assuming nonpredatory motives and business purposes and the incentive of profit and volume considerations, the effect upon competition in the marketplace is substantially adverse." U.S. v. Arnold, Schwinn & Co., 388 U.S. 365, 375 (pp. A-1, X-1, ATRR No. 309, 6/13/67).

If the studies now in progress produce statistics showing that conglomerate mergers have created a serious economic problem, it may turn out that what Congress must deal with in legislation is not the conglomerate mergers of the future but those of the past. The statistics may reveal an economic problem that can be solved only by a significant roll back of the merger trend -- a task that might be beyond the grasp of current antitrust law or, more likely, of the present staff and budget allowances of the FTC and Antitrust Division.

Conceivably, the statistics could reveal not so much an economic problem as a social or political one -- clusters of power that raise a threat to governmental flexibility and the exercise of the public will in government. It is here that the matter leaves the antitrust laws as they are now construed.

- 0 -

Subject: "Product Extension" Mergers   (Published 6/13/67)

Question

    What guidelines are provided by the Supreme Court's recent Clorox opinion?

Reference

    FTC v. Procter & Gamble Co., 386 U.S. 568, 35 LW 4329 (pp. A-13, X-1,
       ATRR No. 300, 4/11/67)

Background

    In its report on the 1950 Celler-Kefauver amendment, the House Judiciary Committee declared an intention to make Section 7 of the Clayton Act applicable to "all types of mergers and acquisitions, vertical and conglomerate as well as horizontal, which may have the specified effect." H.Rep. 1191, 81st Cong., 1st Sess. p. 11 (1949). When it reinstated the FTC order outlawing the acquisition of Clorox Chemical Co. by The Procter & Gamble Co., the Supreme Court put it this way: "All mergers are within the reach of Section 7 and all must be tested by the same standard, whether they are classified as horizontal, vertical, conglomerate or other."

    The need for the words "or other" promptly became apparent when the Court, like the FTC, labeled the P&G-Clorox combine a "product extension" merger. "The products of the acquired company are complementary to those of the acquiring company and may be produced with similar facilities, marketed through the same channels and in the same manner, and advertised by the same media." Previously, however, P&G, the nation's leading producer of household cleaning agents, had not produced, distributed, or used household liquid bleach, the product of which Clorox is the leading manufacturer.

    The FTC's opinion (Docket 6901, pp. A-7, X-1, ATRR No. 127, 12/17/63) stressed five competitive factors: "(1) the relative disparity in size and strength as between Procter and the largest firms of the bleach industry; (2) the excessive concentration in [the bleach] industry at the time of the merger and Clorox's dominant position in the industry; (3) the elimination of Procter as a potential competitor of Clorox; (4) the position of Procter in other markets; and (5) the nature of the 'economies' enabled by the merger."

    Mr. Justice Douglas, the Supreme Court's spokesman, thought the anticompetitive effects of the merger are quite apparent: "(1) The substitution of the powerful acquiring firm for the smaller, but already dominant, firm may substantially reduce the competitive structure of the industry by raising entry barriers and by dissuading the smaller firms from aggressively competing; (2) The acquisition eliminates the potential competition of the acquiring firm."

    It was not disputed that household liquid bleach is the relevant product market, and the relevant geographic markets are the entire country and a number of separate regional markets. The household-liquid-bleach industry is heavily concentrated, and bleach is a distinctive product with no close substitutes. High shipping costs, combined with low sales prices made it unprofitable to ship bleach more than 300 miles from the point of manufacture. Most manufacturers are limited to a single region because they have only one plant.

Acquired Company

    Clorox was described by Mr. Justice Douglas as the only manufacturer of household liquid bleach that sells nationally. At the time of the merger Clorox was making approximately 50 percent of national sales. Its nearest rival accounted for just under 16 percent of total industry sales and limited its distribution to areas west of the Mississippi. The six largest manufacturers of bleach controlled almost 80 percent of the market, and the remaining 20 percent was divided among more than 200 small producers.

    Moreover, territorial limitations on distribution were said to give Clorox greater dominance than is shown by figures of national sales. Clorox's seven principal competitors did no business in New England, the Middle Atlantic States, or metropolitan New York. In those areas its market share was 56 percent, 72 percent, and 64 percent respectively.

Mr. Justice Douglas stated that, since all liquid bleaches are chemically identical, advertising and sales promotion are vital. In 1957 Clorox spent almost $3.7 million on advertising. Another $1.7 million was spent for other promotional activities. The FTC found these heavy expenditures went far to explain why Clorox had secured so high a market share even though the retail price for its bleach was equal to or sometimes higher than those of its competitors.

Acquiring Company

P&G was characterized by the Court as a large, diversified manufacturer of low-price, high-turnover household products. At the time of the acquisition, P&G accounted for 54.4 percent of all packaged detergent sales. The three leading manufacturers in this market accounted for 80 percent of total sales. In 1957 P&G was the nation's largest advertiser, spending more than $80 million on advertising, and $47 million on sales promotion. According to the Court, P&G enjoyed substantial advantages in advertising and sales promotion as a result of its large sales volume and its ability to advertise its products jointly.

Mr. Justice Douglas was satisfied that the interjection of P&G into the liquid-bleach industry would lessen price competition, which he did not think is vigorous now. He thought "there is every reason to assume that the smaller firms would become more cautious in competing due to their fear of retaliation by Procter. It is probable that Procter would become the price leader and that oligopoly would become more rigid." The relatively limited resources available to Clorox and its resulting inability to obtain discounts restricted the amount it could spend on advertising. Even though P&G could not devote its entire budget to advertising Clorox, it could divert a large portion to meet the short-term threat of a new entrant. The Court specifically dismissed the argument that possible economies, including advertising economies, can be used as a defense to illegality.

Also dismissed as a consideration in determining the legality of the acquisition was evidence that Procter had not engaged in predatory practices and that other producers, subsequent to the merger, were selling more bleach for more money than ever before. The Court expressly noted that the Commission had placed no reliance on the post-acquisition activities of Procter in holding that the acquisition was unlawful. And the Court itself stated: "If the enforcement of Section 7 turned on the existence of actual anti-competitive practices, the congressional policy of thwarting such practices in their incipiency would be frustrated."

The Court agreed with the FTC's conclusion that the Clorox acquisition eliminated P&G as a potential additional competitor -- in fact, as the most likely new entrant -- in the liquid-bleach industry. P&G had recently launched a new abrasive cleaner in an industry similar to the liquid-bleach industry, and it had wrested leadership from a brand that had in that market an even larger share than Clorox had in its market. Liquid bleach is a natural avenue of diversification, the Court reasoned, since it is complementary to P&G's products, is sold to the same customers through the same channels, and is advertised and merchandised in the same manner.

Conclusions

A great deal of the interest manifested by the antitrust bar and the business community in the P&G case both before and after the decision was based on a belief that the case had an important bearing on the extent to which Section 7 of the Clayton Act would be applied to the current flood of conglomerate mergers. But the FTC and the Supreme Court took the P&G-Clorox combination out of the "conglomerate" classification, apparently agreeing with the definition of "conglomerates" set out by the House Judiciary Committee in 1949. House Report 1191, cited at the beginning of this article, defines a "conglomerate" merger as one "in which there is no discernible relationship in the nature of business between the acquiring and acquired firms." Neither the Antitrust Division nor the FTC has ever brought suit against such a merger.

Nevertheless, some antitrust experts read the opinion as establishing broad principles that could be relied upon by the enforcement agencies in Clayton Act proceedings against conglomerate mergers. The Federal Trade Commission's chairman has already made the statement, at the spring meeting of the American Bar Association's Antitrust Section (p. A-4, ATRR No. 301, 4/18/67), that the opinion "should cause corporate management to seriously reappraise their conglomerate-merger plans." He agreed that the Clorox opinion "does not answer all questions regarding conglomerate mergers," but "it does provide a sound foundation upon which to begin constructing rules of law in this area." At the same meeting, the Assistant Attorney General in charge of the Antitrust Division, on the other hand, said the decision "does not substantially alter my views on what to look for." He had assumed all along "that the FTC was right in that case."

The first aspect of the Supreme Court's opinion that the FTC might point to in support of a complaint against a purely "conglomerate" merger, as defined by the House Committee, is the emphasis it places on the elimination of P&G as a potential additional producer and marketer of household liquid bleach. Conceivably, it could be argued that any time a company acquires a going business in an entirely new industry it has demonstrated the existence of a desire to enter that industry -- even if its only purpose was to obtain a broader, more diversified, and therefore more stable base of operations.

Moreover, the anticompetitive dangers the Supreme Court saw for the household-bleach market in the entry by P&G with its "deep pocket" for advertising and promotion are matters that could also arise as the result of a purely conglomerate merger. There must be many industries in which the substitution of a huge, powerful outsider for one of the major competitors already in the industry could be said to "reduce the competitive structure of the industry by raising entry barriers and by dissuading the smaller firms from aggressively competing."

The opinion would seem to furnish the enforcement agencies with a particularly good precedent for proceeding against many market-extension mergers -- that is, mergers that expand the acquiring company's operations into a new geographic area without adding to the products it markets. It should be much easier, for instance, to convince a court that a West Coast carpet manufacturer is a potential entrant into the Gulf Coast market than that it is a potential competitor in the publishing industry.

It is clear that, with the Antitrust Division, at least, this element of eliminating potential competition is an important one in the decision whether to attack a market extension. Two of the four oil-company mergers Senator Wayne Morse (D-Ore) recently questioned Assistant Attorney General Donald F. Turner about were market extensions, and the Antitrust Division chief justified his inaction in both instances by assuring the senator that the acquiring firm "was probably not a significant potential competitor" in the acquired company's market area (p. A-11, ATRR No. 303, 5/2/67).

Limiting Factors

There are on the other hand, important limiting factors present in the Clorox case to give comfort and support to counsel defending conglomerate mergers. Mr. Justice Douglas does place considerable reliance on the close relationship between household bleach and the products already marketed by P&G. In effect, therefore, the Court saw in the merger a quasi-horizontal element that will not be present in a purely conglomerate merger.

Second, the Court was dealing not only with related products or markets but also with the largest firms in each of those two markets. Not only was Clorox the largest producer of liquid household bleach but it was described by the Court as the "dominant" firm in that market. There are few industries that can be said to have a single "dominant" firm, so most purely conglomerate acquisitions might be distinguished from P&G-Clorox on that ground.

Third, the product made and sold by Clorox has the same chemical formula as the product marketed by its competitors -- a factor of some significance in the Supreme Court's and the FTC's unfriendly attitude toward the "deep pocket" advertising P&G might engage in. Therefore, the Clorox opinion could be distinguished by counsel defending an acquisition of a leader in an industry whose members sell products that vary in style, quality, and usefulness.

Each of these three factors was stressed by the FTC majority when it struck down General Foods' acquisition of S.O.S. (Docket 8600, pp. A-7, X-20, ATRR No. 245, 3/22/66). The Commission's 4-1 majority stressed the structural similarity between the household-steel-wool market and the liquid-bleach market and rested its holding squarely on its P&G-Clorox decision. Like P&G, General Foods is engaged in the sale of a broad range of low-cost, high-turnover household consumer goods sold in groceries and supermarkets through massive advertising and sales promotion. And household steel wool, like liquid bleach, can be marketed by the same techniques and through the same distributional outlets and is purchased by the housewife at the same time as other products sold by General Foods. Advertising is a central factor in the marketing of steel-wool pads, and the various brands of pads are virtually indistinguishable from each other.

The Commission's order outlawing the General Foods-S.O.S. merger is awaiting review by the Third Circuit, which heard argument June 6. The court of appeals has been reminded that Commissioner Elman, who wrote the FTC's Clorox opinion, dissented in General Foods, emphasizing the absence of any suggestion that General Foods could be considered a potential competitor in the steel-wool soap-pad market.

The reliance the Supreme Court placed on the evidence that the Clorox acquisition eliminated P&G as a potential additional competitor in the household-bleach market could also be an important means of distinguishing that combination from most purely conglomerate mergers. The evidence cited by Mr. Justice Douglas for his finding that Procter was a likely entrant dealt with the close economic relationship between P&G's past activities and the production and marketing of household liquid bleach, with the ready availability of raw materials and equipment for bleach production, and with other similar economic factors. The Court's approach seems to lend support to the government's contention in its pending appeal attacking the Penn-Olin joint venture (U.S. v. Penn-Olin Chemical Co., No. 760, p. A-10, ATRR No. 292, 2/14/67) that potential competition is a matter to be decided, not on the basis of evidence of subjective intent, but on the basis of such objective factors as the acquiring company's capabilities, the structure of the market, and the economic forces governing the firms in the market. But these objective standards would scarcely carry the same weight -- or even be subject to proof -- in a purely conglomerate-merger case. Surely the government, in such a case, would have to come through with some sort of evidence of subjective intent to establish the possibility of entry.

Other experts see in the Supreme Court's decision another manifestation of the Court's conviction that any solidification in an oligopolistic situation is bad per se. They feel that the Court would have reached the same result if the Clorox acquisition had been accomplished by U.S. Steel, for example, instead of P&G. This line of thinking greatly minimizes the importance of many of the elements specifically mentioned by Mr. Justice Douglas -- the lack of quality differences in the industry's products, the close relationship between household bleach and P&G's regular line of products, and the elimination of a possible new competitor.

Such a discussion may be purely academic, anyway, for it seems doubtful that the enforcement agencies, presently, at least, have either the time or the inclination to mount an antimerger attack of that scope. The Assistant Attorney General's letter to Senator Morse explaining the Antitrust Division's failure to attack several rubber and oil mergers refutes the idea that an increase in oligopoly power will automatically trigger enforcement action against a merger. And a 3-2 FTC majority recently agreed to a consent order that let P&G keep most of the assets of the largest independent coffee company in the country, a firm about four times as big as Clorox (Docket C-1169, p. A-15, ATRR No. 293, 2/21/67).

- 0 -

Subject: The Failing-Company Doctrine   (Published 6/18/68)

Question

What is the present status of the failing-company defense for acquisitions attacked under Section 7 of the Clayton Act?

References

International Shoe Co. v. FTC, 280 U.S. 291 (1930)

U.S. v. Maryland and Virginia Milk Producers Assn., 167 F.Supp. 799 (D.D.C. 1958), affirmed, 362 U.S. 458 (1960)

Granader v. Public Bank, 281 F.Supp. 120 (E.D. Mich. 1967)

U.S. v. Third National Bank in Nashville, 390 U.S. 171, 36 LW 4178 (pp. A-3, X-8, ATRR No. 347, 3/5/68)

Merger Guidelines, Department of Justice announcement, May 19, 1968 (p. X-1, ATRR No. 360, 6/4/68)

U.S. v. Reed Roller Bit Co., 274 F.Supp. 573 (W.D. Okla. 1967) (p. A-1, ATRR No. 314, 7/18/67)

FTC Advisory Opinion Digests 165-170, 176-180, 182, 184-5, and 189, announced February 13, 1968 (p. A-13, ATRR No. 344, 2/13/68)

Background

"In the light of the case thus disclosed of a corporation with resources so depleted and the prospect of rehabilitation so remote that it faced the grave probability of a business failure with resulting loss to its stockholders and injury to the communities where its plants were operated, we hold that the purchase of its capital stock by a competitor (there being no other prospective purchaser), not with a purpose to lessen competition, but to facilitate the accumulated business of the purchaser and with the effect of mitigating seriously injurious consequences otherwise probable, is not in contemplation of law prejudicial to the public and does not substantially lessen competition or restrain commerce within the intent of the Clayton Act." This language in the International Shoe case has come to be known as the "failing company defense" in antimerger proceedings under Section 7 of the Clayton Act. The defense received explicit recognition in the legislative history of the 1950 amendments to Section 7. H. Rep. 1191, 81st Cong., 1st Sess., p. 6 (1949); S. Rep. 1775, 81st Cong., 2d Sess. p. 7 (1950).

It has been recognized as a valid defense in at least nine subsequent merger cases but has been sustained in only two. The defense succeeded in U.S. v. Maryland and Virginia Milk Producers Assn., which involved acquisition of two dairies "hopelessly insolvent and *** deeply in debt" (167 F.Supp. at 808), and in Granader v. Public Bank, 281 F.Supp. 120 (E.D. Mich. 1967), which involved acquisition of a bank, found by a state court to be "on the brink of bankruptcy with no possibility of recovery," by the competitor that made "the best offer" at a sale conducted by the Federal Deposit Insurance Corporation as court-appointed receiver. In the Granader case, the court acknowledged that application of the failing-company defense involves a determination of who else would or could purchase the failing business but its opinion does not indicate that it made such a determination. The court granted summary judgment sustaining the "failing company" defense on the basis of the evidence that the successful bidder "provided the best offer in light of the circumstances." Mere evidence that the former owners of the acquired business enterprise had made a firm and unqualified decision to liquidate it will not suffice to establish the defense. Erie Sand and Gravel Co. v. FTC, 291 F.2d 279 (3rd Cir. 1961). In that horizontal-merger case, there were other potential purchasers who would have guaranteed continuation of the acquired firm's business under new proprietorship, but they were outbid by the acquired firm's major competitor. The Third Circuit limited the International Shoe doctrine "to the acquisition of a competitor which is in such straits that the termination of the enterprise and the dispersal of its assets seems inevitable unless a rival proprietor shall acquire and continue the business." The Ninth Circuit took a similar attitude toward evidence that, upon the death of a key official in the midst of difficult rehabilitation efforts, the directors of a company decided to give up. Crown Zellerbach Corp. v. FTC, 296 F.2d 800 (9th Cir. 1961).

The Supreme Court has passed only once on the defense since International Shoe. In U.S. v. Diebold, Inc., 369 U.S. 654 (1962), it reversed a summary judgment against the government after finding a genuine factual controversy on the issue whether "Diebold was the only bona fide prospective purchaser" of the failing business. (The litigation eventually ended in a consent order, 1963 Trade Cas. 70,738.) In U.S. v. Philadelphia National Bank, 374 U.S. 321, 372, n. 46 (pp. A-9, X-7, ATRR No. 101, 6/18/63), the Supreme Court suggested that the failing-company defense "might have somewhat larger contours as applied to bank mergers because of the greater public impact of a bank failure." And in the Nashville Bank case listed in the references, the Court seemed to read the 1966 Bank Merger Act's concern for "the convenience and needs of the community" as permitting a competitor's acquisition of a bank that is in "stagnant and floundering" condition. Again, however, the Supreme Court stressed the need for eliminating other less anticompetitive methods of saving the "floundering" bank and satisfying the community's "convenience and needs." The district judge was instructed on remand to ascertain whether the bank's ownership had made "concrete efforts to recruit new management" and to assess the possibility of a sale of the bank to other owners who might be willing to face up to the management difficulties over a more extended period.

Merger Guidelines

The Justice Department gave its view of the defense in its merger guidelines as follows:

"A merger which the Department would otherwise challenge will ordinarily not be challenged if (i) the resources of one of the merging firms are so depleted and its prospects for rehabilitation so remote that the firm faces the clear probability of a business failure, and (ii) good faith efforts by the failing firm have failed to elicit a reasonable offer of acquisition more consistent with the purposes of Section 7 by a firm which intends to keep the failing firm in the market. The Department regards as failing only those firms with no reasonable prospect of remaining viable; it does not regard a firm as failing merely because the firm has been unprofitable for a period of time, has lost market position or failed to maintain its competitive position in some other respect, has poor management, or has not fully explored the possibility of overcoming its difficulties through self-help.

"In determining the applicability of the above standard to the acquisition of a failing division of a multi-market company, such factors as the difficulty in assessing the viability of a portion of a company, the possibility of arbitrary accounting practices, and the likelihood that an otherwise healthy company can rehabilitate one of its parts, will lead the Department to apply this standard only in the clearest of circumstances."

The guidelines also state that the Department will apply the failing-company defense to vertical mergers and to conglomerate mergers. In the last paragraph of its guidelines, however, the Antitrust Division indicates that it will not be strict in applying its definition of "failing" condition when certain types of conglomerate mergers are involved.

FTC Rulings

The FTC has defined the defense as "the notion that the challenged acquisition could not under any circumstances be regarded as having the probability of substantially lessening competition because the acquired company was in such financial condition that it could no longer be regarded as a competitor in any sense of the word, actual or potential." Dean Foods Co., Docket 8674 (p. A-10, ATRR No. 280, 11/22/66). In the Dean Foods case, the Commission reversed its hearing examiner's acceptance of the defense, citing his failure to take into account the "overall profit picture" of all operations of the company said to be failing, including profitable operations of its subsidiaries in other markets not affected by the merger and its nonoperating income from securities and real estate holdings.

This theory that the defense might be applicable to a financially healthy company's sale of a "failing" division or subsidiary was also rejected by the Commission earlier in Farm Journal, Inc., 53 FTC 26 (1956). A district judge said, in U.S. v. Reed Roller Bit Co., 274 F.Supp. 573, on the other hand, that the doctrine "would seem" to extend to the sale of an unprofitable subsidiary by a prosperous parent.

In its litigated cases, the Federal Trade Commission has never sustained the failing-company defense. But in 14 of 26 merger-clearance advisory opinions announced February 13 of this year, the Commission gave the acquired companies' usually "failing," but sometimes "unprofitable," "poor," or "distressed," condition as a major reason for its failure to oppose the transactions. Generally, the Commission also relied on indications that reasonable efforts had been made to find other buyers but had been unsuccessful. Often, too, an additional factor was cited as minimizing probable anticompetitive effects: ease of entry into the industry involved, declining state of the industry as a whole, or limited geographical or product scope of existing competition between the merging firms. In six instances, the acquiring company was seeking clearance under an outstanding FTC order prohibiting further acquisitions without advance Commission approval.

The proposed "Failing Newspaper Act" pending in Congress (S. 1312) also attributes a broad scope to the "failing" concept and seems to recognize "failing" status in subdivisions or subsidiaries of prosperous companies. Section 3(6) defined "failing newspaper" as "a newspaper publication which, regardless of its ownership or affiliations, appears unlikely to remain or become a financially sound publication."

Conclusions

The definition of the failing-company defense is well known; only its application is uncertain. The doctrine was originally adopted in a decision that permitted the largest company in an industry to acquire another of the giants in its industry, whose next financial statements would have disclosed "a condition of insolvency" under state law. The International Shoe opinion dismissed as "speculation" suggestions that the acquired manufacturer might have obtained "further help from the banks" or "might have availed itself of a receivership." The company's officers, stockholders, and creditors were deemed "more able than commission or court to foresee future contingencies" and choose the best course of action.

This line of thinking seems far removed from the current attitude reflected in the decisions summarized above, with the possible exception of the Granader case. The Supreme Court, at least, expects a great deal more today in the way of exhaustion of alternative remedies than it did in 1930. One reason for the chance is the 1950 revision of Section 7's competitive-injury test. It is no longer necessary to show that the effect of the acquisition "may be to substantially lessen competition between the corporation whose stock is so acquired and the corporation making the acquisition." As now written, Section 7 merely requires a showing that "the effect of such acquisition may be substantially to lessen competition." It is nevertheless clear, from the Supreme Court's action in U.S. v. Diebold, Inc., 369 U.S. 654 (1962), and a dictum in the Brown Shoe case, 370 U.S. 294, 319 (1962), that the defense still exists -- that it can still be assumed that no anticompetitive consequences will flow from the acquisition of a company that is out of the market anyway. In fact, the defense succeeds in saving many more mergers than the public record would indicate. Antitrust lawyers report that the enforcement staffs at both the Antitrust Division and the FTC often accept failing-company defenses that might not be sustained by the Commission or the courts.

Availability of the defense to a failing division or subsidiary of an otherwise thriving company is the subject of some disagreement among members of the antitrust bar. While some have no doubt that "failing" status depends on the condition of the entire business organization, others are shocked by the suggestion that a company must either continue a failing operation or scrap it without salvaging its value as an operating enterprise. Perhaps the FTC and the Antitrust Division do not quite see eye-to-eye on this matter either, for the merger guidelines seem to take a more lenient attitude toward sales of failing divisions than have the FTC decisions summarized above.

Further refinement of the FTC's views may be forthcoming in Crown Cork and Seal Co., Inc., Docket 8687. In the initial decision in that case (p. A-9, ATRR No. 346, 2/27/68), the hearing examiner rejected a "failing company" defense based on evidence that the acquired company was in financial trouble because of losses in divisional operations that were not related to the industry in which the Commission's complaint alleged anticompetitive effect resulting from the merger. The initial decision is now awaiting review by the Commission, which held in Dean Foods that "failing" status must be determined from the over-all finances of the corporation.

There may still be a question whether the failing-company doctrine applies to vertical acquisitions even though the Merger Guidelines indicate the Antitrust Division has no doubt about it. The issue has been raised in United States Steel Corp., FTC Docket 8655, and the hearing examiner rejected a suggestion by complaint counsel that the rationale of the International Shoe doctrine does not apply to vertical acquisitions (p. A-16, ATRR No. 256, 6/7/66). An argument can be made that the doctrine has greater merit for vertical than horizontal mergers. Acquisition of a financially troubled company by a supplier or by a customer will frequently revive the failing business as a factor in the market, whereas a horizontal merger always assures elimination of the "failing" company as a competitor.

Will the doctrine save an acquisition when other purchasers of the failing business are available but in each instance acquisition by the other purchaser would have greater anticompetitive effects? Some of the FTC's advisory opinions indicate that the Commission would answer yes.

- 0 -

Questions

Under what circumstances have orders terminating merger cases imposed prohibitions on classes of future mergers?

Do the federal courts and the FTC have the power to prohibit a class of future acquisitions?

References

U.S. v. Times Mirror Co., 274 F.Supp. 606 (D.C. Calif.) (pp. A-8, X-1, ATRR No. 327, 10/11/67)

Brief for Respondent on Appeal from the Initial Decision in American Brake Shoe Co., FTC Docket 8622 (p. A-8, ATRR No. 268, 8/30/66), October 26, 1966

Sections 11(b) and 15, Clayton Act, 15 U.S. Code 21(b) and 25

Section 5(b), FTC Act, 15 U.S. Code 45(b)

Background

By Section 15 of the Clayton Act, the federal district courts "are invested with jurisdiction to prevent and restrain violations" and the United States Attorneys, "under the direction of the Attorney General," are admonished "to institute proceedings in equity to prevent and restrain such violations." Section 11(b) of the Clayton Act provides that the administrative agencies to which it assigns enforcement responsibility, including the FTC, are to "issue * * * an order requiring such person to cease and desist from such violations, and divest itself of the stock, or other share capital, or assets, held * * * contrary to the provisions of Section 7." Section 5(b) of the FTC Act calls for "an order requiring such person * * * to cease and desist from using such method of competition or such act or practice."

A few weeks ago, in U.S. v. Times Mirror Co., the Federal District Court for Central California, having found a newspaper acquisition to be a "violation" of Section 7 of the Clayton Act, was asked by the Justice Department not only to require divestiture of the acquired enterprise but also to forbid the defendant to acquire any other daily newspaper in its metropolitan area. The Court refused to issue "a perpetual injunction" against mergers in a market whose future it "cannot prejudge with sufficient certainty." Its opinion cited the Supreme Court's statement in Brown Shoe Co. v. U.S., 370 U.S. 294, 319-20 (1962), that "legislative history illuminates congressional concern with the protection of competition not competitors, and its desire to restrain mergers only to the extent that such combinations may tend to lessen competition." The district court then denied the government's subsequent motion for a twelve-year requirement of advance Justice Department approval of any Times Mirror acquisition, subject to the court's review of any denial of approval (p. A-11, ATRR No. 333, 11/28/67).

The FTC's power to issue orders curbing future mergers -- at least when the complaint is based entirely on Section 7 of the Clayton Act -- has been questioned in an appeal from the initial decision in Docket 8622. American Brake Shoe Co. is contending that the only remedy the Commission has authority to grant in a Section 7 case is divestiture of the illegally acquired stock or assets. Since the Commission did not choose to add a Section 5 FTC Act count to its complaint against American Brake Shoe Co., the company's counsel insists that court decisions recognizing broad Section 5 remedial powers are "not in point." The appeal was argued February 1, 1967, but the Commission has not yet announced its decision. Yet, merger-decree clauses restricting defendants' future acquisitions have become quite fashionable; decrees lacking some sort of curb on future mergers are now the exception. Only four of the twenty-two orders issued during the last two years in FTC merger cases and only seven of the twenty-four antimerger decrees obtained within that period by the Antitrust Division fail to deal with future mergers. Furthermore, twelve of the FTC future-merger bans were imposed in proceedings based entirely on Section 7 of the Clayton Act. Three of those twelve orders were issued without consent after full hearings.

Three of the four FTC orders that lack provisions restricting future mergers are consent orders involving the cement industry, for which the Commission issued antimerger guidelines early this year (Enforcement Policy with Respect to Vertical Mergers in the Cement Industry, p. X-4, ATRR No. 289, 1/24/67). The fourth FTC order in that category is a litigated order outlawing a product-extension merger -- General Foods' attempted entry into the household-steel-wool market through acquisition of the S.O.S. Co. (Docket 8600, pp. A-7, X-20, ATRR No. 245, 3/22/66). (That order was recently affirmed by the Court of Appeals for the Third Circuit, pp. A-14, X-2, ATRR No. 331, 11/14/67.)

Among the Antitrust Division's seven decrees ignoring future mergers are two involving industries in which there are relatively few competitors (U.S. v. Eversharp, Inc., p. A-1, ATRR No. 324, 9/26/67; U.S. v. Alcoa, p. A-19, ATRR No. 251, 5/3/66); one enjoining an acquisition that was abandoned after it was delayed by preliminary injunction (U.S. v. Pennzoil Co., p. A-5, ATRR No. 240, 2/15/66); one outlawing a conglomerate merger only because of its "reciprocity" opportunities (U.S. v. General Dynamics Co., p. A-2, ATRR No. 283, 12/13/66); two containing no divestiture requirements (U.S. v. World Journal Tribune Corp., p. A-2, ATRR No. 274, 10/11/66; U.S. v. West Virginia Pulp & Paper Co., p. A-17, ATRR No. 236, 1/18/66); and another containing only a conditional divestiture requirement (U.S. v. Aluminium, Ltd., p. A-4, ATRR No. 274, 10/11/66). All but the Alcoa and General Dynamics judgments are consent decrees.

Time Limits

Almost all future-merger clauses are effective for a specified number of years -- usually ten years. Only three of the eighteen future-merger clauses written by the FTC in the last two years (all in either consent orders or settlements of court review proceedings) deviate from the ten-year norm. Two prohibit mergers for only five years (Reynolds Metals Co., Docket 7009, p. A-13, ATRR No. 256, 6/7/66; Broadway-Hale, Inc., Docket C-1057, p. A-2, ATRR No. 250, 4/26/66), and the third forbids Foremost Dairies, Inc. (Docket C-1161, p. A-4, ATRR No. 291, 2/7/67) to make any future acquisitions of pharmaceutical manufacturers, without limitation as to time. In a joint-venture case (Phillips Petroleum Co., Docket C-1088, p. A-19, ATRR No. 265, 8/9/66), the Commission's consent order adds a fifteen-year prohibition of joint ventures. The consent order allowing Procter & Gamble Co. to retain J. A. Folger Co., a coffee processor (Docket C-1169, p. A-15, ATRR No. 293, 2/21/67), added a seven-year ban on acquisition of "any household product company" to its ten-year prohibition for coffee manufacturers or sellers.

Ten years is the most common time limit in the future-merger bans negotiated by the Antitrust Division, too. Of the seventeen future-merger clauses obtained by the Division in the last two years, only four set other time periods. In U.S. v. Hat Corp. (p. A-6, ATRR No. 300, 4/11/67) and for one defendant in U.S. v. Valley National Bank of Arizona (p. A-24, ATRR No. 275, 10/18/66), the term is fifteen years. For two other defendants in Valley National Bank and in U.S. v. National Cleaning Contractors, Inc. (p. A-8, ATRR No. 259, 6/28/66), U.S. v. Pittsburgh Brewing Co. (p. A-15, ATRR No. 251, 5/3/66), and U.S. v. Von's Grocery Co. (pp. A-1, X-1, ATRR No. 291, 2/7/67), the sentence is cut to five years. In U.S. v. American Smelting & Refining Co. (p. A-20, ATRR No. 292, 2/14/67), the ban is to be effective only so long as the defendant continues to hold stock in the company it was charged with acquiring unlawfully. All of the deviations, except that of the Von's case, appear in consent decrees.

Future-merger bans are always limited to the particular industry involved, but only in exceptional circumstances are they limited to specified geographical areas. None of the FTC's future-merger orders set geographical limits. But area boundaries have been written into the decrees ending nine Justice Department suits. U.S. v. Peabody Coal Co. (p. A-2, ATRR No. 324, 9/26/67); U.S. v. First National Bank of Lexington (p. A-15, ATRR No. 317, 8/8/67); U.S. v. Gulf & Western Industries, Inc. (p. A-8, ATRR No. 316, 8/1/67); U.S. v. Chicago Title and Trust Co. (A-18, ATRR No. 250, 2/26/66); U.S. v. Schlitz Brewing Co., 253 F.Supp. 129 (p. A-8, ATRR No. 247, 4/5/66); U.S. v. Valley National Bank; U.S. v. National Cleaning Contractors; U.S. v. Pittsburgh Brewing Co.; and U.S. v. Von's Grocery Co. In the two bank-merger cases the defendant banks lacked authority to do business anywhere except in the areas covered by the future-merger restrictions.

Approval Requirement

All of the FTC antimerger orders entered in 1966 and 1967 require that advance Commission approval be obtained for any merger consummated during the time period set by the order. The same uniformity does not prevail in the court decrees obtained by the Antitrust Division. In the Pittsburgh Brewing Case, the decree requires nothing more than advance notice of any merger to be consummated during the next five years. Defendants in four cases (U.S. v. Herff Jones Corp., p. A-2, ATRR No. 305, 5/16/67; U.S. v. Monsanto Co., p. A-27, ATRR No. 292, 2/14/67; U.S. v. Kimberly-Clark Corp., p. A-8, ATRR No. 306, 5/23/67; U.S. v. Schlitz Brewing Co.) are required to get advance consent from the Justice Department and, if denied it, are specifically accorded a right to seek relief from the court. Peabody Coal and Von's Grocery also need the Attorney General's consent before proceeding with a merger, but no provision is made for court review of a denial of consent. Five of the Antitrust Division's decrees (U.S. v. National Steel Corp., p. A-10, ATRR No. 293, 2/21/67; U.S. v. Newmont Mining Corp., p. A-16, ATRR No. 243, 3/8/66; U.S. v. First National Bank of Lexington; U.S. v. American Smelting; and U.S. v. Gulf & Western) say nothing about consent from anyone; they simply prohibit acquisitions for the designated period of time. The Hat Corp., Valley National Bank, National Cleaning, and Chicago Title decrees impose what appear to be absolute prohibitions for some defendants or for a portion of the time period covered, but only consent requirements for other defendants or time periods.

Eight of the FTC orders (of which six are consent orders) and four of the court's consent decrees rely entirely upon future-merger prohibitions to effect a remedy for the alleged antitrust violation and fail to require divestiture of the companies said to have been unlawfully acquired. The Commission's power to restrict future mergers in a Section 7 Clayton Act case without ordering divestiture was challenged by Commissioner Elman, dissenting in National Tea Co., Docket 7453 (pp. A-1, X-1, ATRR No. 245, 3/22/66). He insisted (1) that the Commission must find a violation before it can issue any order at all and (2) that, if it finds a violation, it must order divestiture. The Commission's majority did find Section 7 violations by National Tea but concluded that "dynamic features of the industry" will dissipate their effects if no further acquisitions are permitted.

Neither Chairman Dixon's majority opinion nor Commissioner Elman's dissent nor Commissioner Jones' answering concurrence mention the similar order of the Federal District Court for Eastern Pennsylvania in U.S. v. Jerrold Electronics, Inc., 187 F.Supp. 545 (E.D. Pa. 1960). The Section 7 portions of that decree, though, were based on quite different findings. The district judge found that none of the acquisitions that had occurred so far raised a sufficient anticompetitive threat to violate Section 7. But he imposed a three-year ban on future mergers because the defendant's acquisitions "are approaching, if not beyond, the point where it can be said that it is a reasonable probability that they will have the prohibited effect."

The Jerrold Electronics order was the first of the Antitrust Division's litigated judgments to restrict future mergers. But the inclusion of future-merger provisions in consent decrees began as early as U.S. v. National Food Products Corp., March 4, 1926 (S.D.N.Y.). Except for the Times Mirror opinion of the Federal District Court for Central California, there do not seem to be any precedents specifically exploring the power of a federal district court to enjoin a class of future mergers. There are decisions, though, that a federal court has all its traditional equity powers in an antitrust injunction suit and that it can prohibit otherwise lawful conduct when such a prohibition is necessary to remedy an antitrust violation. U.S. v. Ward Baking Co., 376 U.S. 327 (pp. A-5, X-12, ATRR No. 139, 3/10/64); U.S. v. Loew's, Inc., 371 U.S. 38 (1962); U.S. v. Bausch & Lomb Optical Co., 321 U.S. 707 (1944).

FTC Jurisdiction

Administrative future-merger bans have a shorter historical base than court decrees of that nature, for it was not until 1957 that an FTC order first prohibited a class of future mergers. International Paper Co., 53 FTC 1192. A year earlier, in Farm Journal, Inc., 53 FTC 26 (1956), an initial decision that became the Commission's decision without formal review deplored the Commission's lack of "general equity power." Without it, the examiner reasoned, the Commission cannot do anything in a Section 7 Clayton Act case except order divestiture. Apparently the examiner was influenced by the declaration of the Supreme Court in Arrow-Hart that "the Commission is an administrative body possessing only such powers as are granted by statute. It * * * has not the additional power of a court of equity to grant other and further relief." Yet in Ekco Products Co., Docket 7770 (p. A-10, ATRR No. 157, 7/14/64), the Commission imposed a twenty-year prohibition on future mergers that the Court of Appeals for the Seventh Circuit found "rather harsh" but "within the broad scope allowed the Commission in such cases." Ekco Products Co. v. FTC, 347 F.2d 745 (p. A-1, ATRR No. 207, 6/29/65).

In a dissenting opinion in Foremost Dairies, Inc., 60 FTC 944, 1093 (1962), Commissioner Elman explored the question somewhat more fully and arrived at the conclusion that the Commission can issue a Section 7 order against a class of future acquisitions. But two of the three cases he relied on were Section 5 FTC Act cases (Jacob Siegel Co. v. FTC, 327 U.S. 608 (1946); FTC v. National Lead Co., 352 U.S. 419 (1957)), and the third was a Section 2 Clayton Act case (FTC v. Ruberoid Co., 343 U.S. 470 (1952).

The Siegel opinion recognized the Commission's "wide discretion in its choice of remedy" under Section 5. Earlier, FTC v. Eastman Kodak Co., 274 U.S. 619 (1927), had denied that the Commission, even under Section 5, has been "delegated the authority of a court of equity," but that reasoning seems to have been abandoned in view of the present court's statement in Pan American World Airways v. U.S., 371 U.S. 296, 312, n. 17 (1963), that "authority to mold administrative decrees is indeed like the authority of courts to frame injunctive decrees." That footnote cited FTC v. Mandel Bros., 359 U.S. 385 (1959), which allowed the Commission "wide discretion" in choosing a remedy under the Fur Products Labeling Act. Section 8 (a)(2) of the Fur Products Act says the Commission shall have "the same jurisdiction, powers and duties as though all applicable terms and powers of the Federal Trade Commission Act were * * * made a part of this Act."

Conclusions

In FTC v. Ruberoid Co., the Supreme Court, rejecting objections to a general prohibition of future price discrimination, reasoned that a Clayton Act order prohibiting future transactions must be read as prohibiting only those that are actually violations of the Act. The meeting-competition and cost-justification defenses must be read into a Section 2 order. The same inherent limit was attributed to Section 5 FTC Act orders in FTC v. National Lead. If that reasoning is applicable to Section 7 of the Clayton Act, which is tied to the same enforcement language as Section 2, a future-merger ban adds nothing substantive to the statutory prohibition. If only illegal future mergers are prohibited by such a decree, moreover, there was no need for the court in the Times Mirror case to "prejudge" the future of the newspaper market with "certainty." The Times Mirror could defend any subsequent merger covered by the decree on the same grounds as it could use in the absence of a decree.

In any event, the eventual outcome of the dispute over the authority of the courts and the Commission to prohibit a designated category of future acquisitions may well be of less than vital importance to antitrust enforcement. As the statistics show, a substantial majority of future-merger prohibitions come into existence by consent, not as a result of litigation. Presumably, administrative or judicial power to enjoin future mergers is not relevant to consent orders. The consenting party seems estopped to deny that the court had power to enter the judgment he consented to. Swift & Co. v. U.S., 276 U.S. 311, 327 (1928).

The preponderance of consents is likely to continue, many antitrust experts feel, because there are so many merger cases in which the defendants are delighted to give up something they may never want -- or may never get a chance to buy -- in order to keep some of what they now have and know they want. And there are many situations in which the enforcement agencies can well afford to drop divestiture demands in return for consent to orders barring future acquisitions. Those situations are not limited to cases in which the government's evidence is weak. As Commissioner Elman's dissent in the Foremost case suggests, prohibitions against future mergers in an industry can be powerful devices for preserving competition and halting a trend toward concentration. Solid blocks of these decrees in some industries might prove more significant than piecemeal divestiture.

Power in the courts or the FTC to forbid future acquisitions may be most significant for situations in which the enforcement agency wants to add such a prohibition to full divestiture. If it were to become established that blanket prohibitions against future mergers are outside the powers of a court or the FTC, then the government would no longer be in a strong position to negotiate decrees containing such prohibitions when it is now willing to give up its goal of divestiture.

Litigation of more cases might well put an end to much of the uniformity that appears in the future-merger clauses described above, since litigation adds another variable factor: a court. But one provision likely to stay is that requiring the defendant or respondent to seek government clearance before making another acquisition. In fact, there would seem to be no reason why the privilege of seeking the government's consent to a merger would not be available even to a company whose decree simply forbids it to make further acquisitions. Consequently, the Antitrust Division's amended motion in the Times Mirror case may not have been much of a retreat for the government.

An interesting and unanswered question regarding future merger clauses is raised by the Supreme Court's most recent opinion in the El Paso case -- California v. El Paso Natural Gas Co., 386 U.S. 129 (pp. A-18, X-1, ATRR No. 294, 2/28/67). Can members of an industry intervene to demand relief from future acquisitions when the government does not demand it? (See analysis, "Intervention in Government Antitrust Suits," p. B-1, ATRR No. 301, 4/18/67).

- 0 -

PART III — PRICE DISCRIMINATION

Subject: The "Commerce" Requirement   (Published 10/17/67)

Question

Is it essential to proof of a Section 2(a) Clayton Act violation that at least one of the two sales at discriminatory prices be shown to have crossed a state line?

References

Willard Dairy Corp. v. National Dairy Products Corp., 309 F.2d 943 (6th Cir. 1962), review denied, 373 U.S. 934

Borden Co. v. FTC, 339 F.2d 953 (7th Cir.) (pp. A-4, X-1, ATRR No. 182, 1/5/65)

Foremost Dairies, Inc. v. FTC, 348 F.2d 674 (5th Cir.) (p. A-10, ATRR No. 210, 7/20/65), review denied, 382 U.S. 959

Shreveport Macaroni Mfg. Co., Inc. v. FTC, 321 F.2d 404 (5th Cir. 1963), review denied, 375 U.S. 971

Rangen, Inc. v. Sterling Nelson & Sons, 351 F.2d 851 (9th Cir.)(pp. A-2, X-3, ATRR No. 225, 11/2/65)

Background

Section 2(a) of the Clayton Act, as amended by the Robinson-Patman Act, makes it "unlawful for any person engaged in commerce, in the course of such commerce *** to discriminate in price between different purchasers of commodities of like grade and quality, where either or any of the purchases involved in such discrimination are in commerce," provided the discrimination has certain anticompetitive potentiality.

As originally passed by the House of Representatives, the bill that evolved into the Robinson-Patman Act contained additional language: "It shall also be unlawful for any person, whether in commerce or not, *** to discriminate in price between different purchasers of commodities of like grade and quality where in any section or community and in any line of commerce such discrimination may substantially lessen competition in commerce among either sellers or buyers or their competitors." According to the conference committee report on the bill finally enacted, this additional language was omitted because "the preceding language already covers all discriminations, both interstate and intrastate, that lie within the limits of federal authority." H.R. Rep. No. 2951, 74th Cong., 2d Sess. 6 (1936).

In the last three or four years there has been litigation over the significance of the requirement that "either or any of the purchases involved" be "in commerce." It has been suggested that this language is the only one of the three jurisdictional "commerce" requirements in Section 2(a) that has any real importance. If one of the two sales alleged to have been made at discriminatory prices was "in commerce" -- i.e., actually crossed a state line -- it would appear that the seller is necessarily "engaged in commerce" and the discrimination occurred "in the course of such commerce." Rowe, Price Discrimination Under the Robinson-Patman Act, 78 (Little, Brown & Co., 1962). In the Willard case, the Court of Appeals for the Sixth Circuit upheld dismissal of a treble-damage suit brought by a local competitor complaining about discrimination in the prices charged by the local plant of a large multi-state dairy company. In requiring evidence that the local plant also made interstate shipments, the Sixth Circuit declared immaterial the fact that the multi-state dairy made interstate shipments from plants other than the one involved in this particular litigation.

When the Supreme Court refused to review the Sixth Circuit's decision, Mr. Justice Black dissented. He regarded the Sixth Circuit's decision as irreconcilable with Moore v. Mead's Fine Bread Co., 348 U.S. 115 (1954). In that case, the Court sustained a Section 2(a) treble-damage suit against a New Mexico bakery for a discriminatory reduction of its wholesale bread prices in a single New Mexico town where it had competition from the treble-damage claimant. The defendant bakery had not reduced its prices elsewhere, including a Texas community it served with a bread truck operating out of New Mexico. Because the price cut complained of was supported by an interstate "treasury," the Supreme Court reinstated a treble-damage judgment the Court of Appeals for the Tenth Circuit (208 F.2d 777) had set aside. The Tenth Circuit had reasoned that the territorial price cut had caused injury to only a purely local competitor whose business was in no way related to interstate commerce. While the Moore opinion did refer to interstate sales at prices higher than those charged in the complaining competitor's territory, Mr. Justice Black insisted that it had condemned "the monopolistic practice under which profits made in nondiscriminatory interstate transactions are used to offset losses arising from discriminatory price cutting at the local level."

Although the Federal Trade Commission has primary responsibility for interpreting and applying Section 2(a), it has never really made clear its position on the need for proof that at least one sale crossed state lines. First, in Foremost Dairies, Inc., FTC Docket 7475 (p. A-2, ATRR No. 100, 6/11/63), Commissioner Elman wrote an opinion to the effect that a large multi-state dairy did violate Section 2(a) when it charged different prices on sales in New Mexico of milk processed at a New Mexico dairy. Commissioner Elman relied on evidence that much of the milk processed in the New Mexico plant originated on out-of-state farms, and he rejected a suggestion that the brief processing at the New Mexico plant "negatives the interstate character of these transactions." But he also stressed the fact that "Foremost is a large interstate corporation with major offices in Florida and California."

Then, in Borden Co. FTC Docket 7474 (p. A-14, ATRR No. 138, 3/3/64), Chairman Dixon declared that local sales by a multi-state dairy corporation are sales "in commerce" and therefore subject to Section 2(a). But only three Commissioners participated in the decision; one of them concurred only in the result; and Commissioner Elman dissented, taking the position that the rule Chairman Dixon wanted to use applies only to territorial price discrimination threatening injury to the discriminating seller's competitors, and not to price discriminations said to injure competition among the seller's customers.

When the issue came up again in National Dairy Products Corp., Docket 7018 (pp. A-10, X-1, ATRR No. 266, 8/16/66), the Commission dropped a Section 2(a) count based on local sales by a multi-state dairy, even though its hearing examiner had found illegal price discrimination. Chairman Dixon's majority opinion reversed the examiner for lack of detailed evidence of the Dairy's internal operations to show the relationship and interdependence of the dairy's various branches, zones, and divisions.

In the Borden case, the Commission was reversed by the Court of Appeals for the Seventh Circuit, which followed the lead of the Sixth Circuit's decision in the Willard Dairy case and also pointed out that in Standard Oil Co. v. FTC, 340 U.S. 231 (1951), the Supreme Court said that, in order for sales to come under the Robinson-Patman Act, "they must have been made in interstate commerce." In the Foremost case, on the other hand, the Commission's order was upheld by the Fifth Circuit. That court did not rely, though, on the theory that the seller's general involvement in interstate commerce can eliminate the need for proof that one of the two sales at discriminatory prices was made across state lines. Rather it agreed with the Commission's reasoning that milk obtained from out-of-state farms and processed in a local dairy for local sale remained in commerce until the final retail sale was made and therefore that the discrimination did directly involve sales made in commerce.

Previously, though, the Fifth Circuit had played down the importance of interstate sales in the Shreveport Macaroni case listed in the references. In applying Section 2(d)'s ban on discriminatory promotional allowances, the Fifth Circuit recognized the existence of text authorities supporting the need for proof that one of the two sales evidencing discrimination crossed a state boundary. But it refused to read the statute "so narrowly." Although the court did have evidence of the involvement of interstate sales, it went on to say it was enough that the manufacturer paying the discriminatory allowances and the two favored customers all did an interstate business in the products on which the discriminatory allowances were paid, and that the allowances were made or used in interstate commerce. Section 2(d) makes it unlawful "for any person engaged in commerce" to pay discriminatory allowances "in the course of said commerce," but it does not contain the language, "where either or any of the purchases involved in such discrimination are in commerce."

The issue has also come up in the application of the "brokerage" ban in Section 2(c) of the Clayton Act. Like Section 2(d), the brokerage provision does not contain the language, "where either or any of the purchases involved in such discrimination are in commerce." In fact, it does not speak at all in terms of discrimination in two or more separate sales or in dealings with two or more separate customers. In Rangen, Inc. v. Sterling Nelson & Sons, 351 F.2d 851 (9th Cir.)(pp. A-2, X-3, ATRR No. 225, 11/2/65), the Court of Appeals for the Ninth Circuit applied Section 2(c) to what it recognized as being a purely intrastate sale. As the court read the Borden and Willard Dairy cases, they "tend to support the view that transactions of the character involved in our case are not 'in the course' of interstate commerce." However, it was decided that the rationale of Moore v. Mead's Fine Bread was controlling. "In Moore, defendant was able to reduce local prices because of the financial resources provided by its interstate business. In our case, Rangen was better able to compete in his interstate business because he was receiving an unfair preference in his local Idaho business. *** The concept to which we refer is something more than the broader test of 'affecting interstate commerce,' which is applied under the Sherman Act. Critical here is the fact that Rangen's payments *** gave it a definite advantage in its own interstate dealings -- the 'beneficiary' was its interstate business -- and therefore the payments must be regarded as having been made in the course of its own interstate commerce."

Conclusions

At first glance, the statement in the conference committee report on the Robinson-Patman Act that the intent of Section 2(a) was to cover "all discriminations, both interstate and intra-state, that lie within the limits of federal authority" might seem to support an argument that it is not necessary to show a sale actually crossing a state line. In 1936 when the Act was passed, however, the requirement of a sale "in commerce" meant a sale crossing state boundaries. Of course, "the limits of federal authority" over commerce have greatly expanded since 1936, and it may be contended that Congress intended to make full use of any subsequent extension of those limits. In applying other statutes -- e.g., the Fair Labor Standards Act and the Sherman Act -- the courts have tended to allow the statutorily covered area to expand with changes of constitutional interpretation. And under those statutes jurisdiction has been asserted over intra-state activities that have a direct, substantial, and intended impact on interstate commerce. Yet the precedents outlined above clearly require that, in a Section 2(a) case, one of the sales at discriminatory prices must have crossed state lines. Despite some wavering at the FTC, most of its decisions have made a point of finding that one or more of the sales involved did cross a state line. And no matter what language the Supreme Court used in its opinion in Moore v. Mead's Fine Bread, that case, too, involved a seller who sold across state lines at unreduced prices. Mr. Justice Black's dissent in the Willard case is an indication of some sentiment on the Supreme Court for a broader application of Section 2(a), but the Supreme Court does not take as many Robinson-Patman Act cases as Sherman Act and Section 7 Clayton Act cases.

At the same time, it seems incongruous to apply a different rule under Subsections (c) and (d), as was done in the Shreveport Macaroni and Rangen cases. Despite the variations in jurisdictional language concerning "commerce," the courts have tended to look at these subsec-tions as means of preventing circumvention of Section 2(a)'s ban on discriminatory pricing and to adjust their scope to that of Section 2(a). FTC v. Henry Broch & Co., 363 U.S. 166 (1960); Thomasville Chair Co. v. FTC, 306 F.2d 541 (5th Cir. 1962). Compare FTC v. Simplicity Pattern Co., 360 U.S. 55 (1959).

Possibly, the Rangen and Shreveport Macaroni decisions reflect a thrust similar to that of Commissioner Elman's dissent in Borden and of the interstate commerce cases under other statutes. Where price discrimination by a multistate business injures one of its interstate com-petitors, as in Rangen, or when the discrimination is among buyers operating interstate, as in Shreveport, it can be contended that the discrimination had a direct, substantial and intended effect on interstate commerce and is thus within the expanded interstate commerce power. Where, however, the only alleged impact of an intrastate transaction is on intrastate commerce, the Robinson-Patman Act and the commerce power simply do not cover the situation.

One point the decisions do make clear is that, once there is a sale across state lines, it is unlawful to discriminate in favor of or against the purchaser even if the entire anti-competitive effect is felt by purely local commerce.

- 0 -

Subject: Competitive Injury in Geographical-Pricing Cases   (Published 8/1/67)

Question

How does the Utah Pie decision affect pricing practices of national sellers?

References

Utah Pie Co. v. Continental Baking Co., 386 U.S. 685, 35 LW 4373 (pp. A-16, X-17,
ATRR No. 302, 4/25/67)
Analysis, "Geographical Pricing," p. B-1, ATRR No. 24, 3/29/66, reprinted at p. 203,
Antitrust & Trade Regulation Today: 1967

Background

As originally conceived, the purpose of the Clayton Antitrust Act's curb on discrimination in price was to forbid "great and powerful combinations * * * to lower prices of their
commodities, oftentimes below the cost of production in certain communities and sections
where they had competition, with the intent to destroy and make unprofitable the business of
their competitors, and with the ultimate purpose in view of thereby acquiring a monopoly in the
particular locality or section in which the discriminating price is made." H. Rept. 627, 63rd
Cong., 2d Sess., pp. 8 and 9 (1914). Section 2 of the 1914 Clayton Act declared unlawful any
price discrimination whose effect "may be to substantially lessen competition or tend to
create a monopoly in any line of commerce." As amended in 1936 by the Robinson-Patman
Act, Section 2(a) now bans price discrimination "where the effect of such discrimination may
be substantially to lessen competition or tend to create a monopoly in any line of commerce,
or to injure, destroy, or prevent competition with any person who either grants or knowingly
receives the benefit of such discrimination or with customers of either of them."

In its Utah Pie decision, which two dissenting Justices read "as protecting competitors,
instead of competition," the Supreme Court found sufficient proof of competitive injury to
sustain a jury determination that three frozen-pie makers selling nationwide had violated the
Robinson-Patman Act when they cut prices in only the Sale Lake City market.

When Utah Pie Co. entered the frozen-pie market, its location in Salt Lake City gave it
natural advantages, and it entered the market at a price below the then going prices for pies
sold by the three defendant companies, Pet Milk Co., Continental Baking Co., and Carnation
Co. During most of the period involved, 1958-1961, in the suit, Utah's prices were the lowest in the Salt Lake City market. It began selling at a price of $4.15 per dozen, and at the time
the suit was filed its price was $2.75 per dozen. Pet, which was offering pies at $4.92 per
dozen at the beginning of the period, was offering pies at $3.56 per dozen in March and April
of 1961. Carnation's price in early 1958 was $4.82 per dozen, but it was selling at $3.56 per
dozen at the conclusion of the period, meanwhile its price was as low as $3.30 per dozen.
The price range experienced by Continental during the period covered by the suit ran from a
1958 high of more than $5 per dozen to a 1961 low of $2.85 per dozen.

Pet, which shipped to Salt Lake City from its California plant, sold, during seven of the
44 months involved in the suit, at prices lower than it charged in the California market, even
though selling at Salt Lake City involved a $.30-.35 freight cost per dozen pies. In addition,
Pet admitted it had sent an industrial spy into Utah Pie's plant to seek information of use
to Pet in convincing a grocery chain not to buy from Utah. Continental made two two-week
offers in Salt Lake City at a price less than its direct cost plus an allocation for overhead.
A large supermarket chain responded to one offer by purchasing a five-week supply of
frozen pies. At the same time, Continental sold the pies at a higher price outside Salt
Lake City. Carnation, in order to get new business, reduced its prices in Salt Lake City
to a price below its cost level.

During 1958, the year before the price cuts, Utah Pie had 66.5 percent of the Salt Lake City sales, Carnation had 10.3, Continental 1.3, and Pet 16.4. In 1959, Utah's market share dropped to 34.3, Carnation had 8.6, Continental's share was 2.9, and Pet had 35.5. Utah Pie increased its market share in 1960 to 45.5 percent, Carnation had 12.1, Continental had 1.8 and Pet dropped to 27.9. In 1961 the market share of Utah Pie was 45.3 percent, Carnation's was 8.8, Continental's was 8.3, and Pet had 29.4 percent.

Impressed by evidence of predatory intent and below-cost sales, the Supreme Court rejected suggestions that a competitive-injury finding is foreclosed by the complaining competitor's increasing sales volume, continued profits, and ability to make responsive price cuts. Mr. Justice White, who wrote the majority opinion, found unconvincing the notion that "there is no reasonably possible injury to competition as long as the volume of sales in a particular market is expanding and at least some of the competitors in the market continue to operate at a profit. Nor do we think that the Act only comes into play to regulate the conduct of price discriminators when their discriminatory prices consistently undercut other competitors."

He recognized that many of the "primary-line cases" -- Robinson-Patman Act cases attacking price discrimination said to injure competition among sellers, rather than among buyers -- that have been litigated in the courts involved "blatant predatory price discriminations employed with the hope of immediate destruction of a particular competitor." In such a case, Mr. Justice White went on, it is easy to find injury to competition. But "we believe that the Act reaches price discrimination that erodes competition as much as it does price discrimination that is intended to have immediate destructive impact. In this case, the evidence shows a drastically declining price structure which the jury could rationally attribute to continued or sporadic price discrimination."

One of the factors relied upon by the Court of Appeals for the Tenth Circuit (349 F.2d 122, p. A-6, ATRR No. 206, 6/22/65) in setting aside the jury's award of damages was evidence that Utah Pie had responded to a competitor's price cut by reducing its own price to 10 cents below the competitor's. In Mr. Justice White's view, the jury could "reasonably conclude that a competitor who is forced to reduce his price to a new all-time low in a market of declining prices will in time feel the financial pinch and will be a less effective competitive force." He also insisted that consideration be given to the consequences of this price cutting on other producers who might want to enter the market.

The Court distinguished "fierce competitive instincts" from illegal anticompetitive behavior. "Actual intent to injure another competitor does not, however, fall into [the fierce-competitive-instincts] category, and neither, when viewed in the context of the Robinson-Patman Act, do persistent sales below cost and radical price cuts themselves discriminatory. Nor does the fact that a local competitor has a major share of the market make him fair game for the discriminatory price cutting free of Robinson-Patman Act proscriptions."

The three defendant pie companies argued that prior court and FTC decisions in which no primary-line injury to competition was found established a standard that compelled affirmance of the court of appeals' holding. However, the Supreme Court majority disagreed. In Anheuser-Busch, Inc., v. FTC, 289 F.2d 835 (7th Cir. 1961), there was no general decline in price structure attributable to the defendant's price discrimination. Nor was there any evidence that price discriminations were "a single lethal weapon aimed at a victim for predatory purposes." In Borden Co. v. FTC, 339 F.2d 953 (7th Cir. 1965), the court reversed the Commission's decision on price discrimination in one market for want of sufficient interstate connection, and the Commission's charge regarding another market failed to show any lasting impact upon prices caused by the single, isolated incident of price discrimination proved.

Conclusions

First of all, the Utah Pie decision deals only with the question of injury to competition; it does not involve the question of impact of an antitrust violation upon Utah Pie itself. See Analysis, "Proof of the Fact of Injury and Causation in a Damage Suit," p. B-1, ATRR No. 305, 5/16/67 (page 133, infra). The question whether Utah Pie itself was injured as a result of the antitrust violations is not yet settled. The Tenth Circuit has not yet dealt with that and other questions raised on appeal, although it stated that none of the defendants "had taken or would take in the future any appreciable amount of frozen pie business from Utah Pie." Of course, Utah Pie did not need to show that it actually operated in the red. Its damage verdict will stand if the jury has evidence that Utah Pie would have made more money but for the price discrimination. See, Analysis, "Measure and Proof of Damages in Private Suits," p. B-1, ATRR No. 293, 2/21/67, reprinted at p. 308, Antitrust & Trade Regulation Today: 1967.

The Utah Pie decision is further evidence of the Supreme Court's belief that jury trials are the best method for handling antitrust disputes. There is little doubt of the esteem in which the Supreme Court holds treble-damage suits as an antitrust enforcement tool or of its dislike of summary judgments. See Radiant Burners Co., Inc., v. Peoples Gas, Light, & Coke Co., 364 U.S. 656 (1961); Continental Ore v. Union Carbide and Carbon Corp., 370 U.S. 690 (pp. A-24, X-13, ATRR No. 50, 6/26/62); and Poller v. CBS, 368 U.S. 464 (pp. A-5, X-1, ATRR No. 32, 2/20/62).

The dissenters' assertion that the majority is "protecting competitors, instead of competition" seems to turn the spotlight once again on what some critics consider to be a dichotomy between the Sherman and Robinson-Patman Acts. Assuming the discrimination "had any effect," Mr. Justice Stewart stated, "that effect must have been beneficial. * * * Lower prices are the hallmark of intensified competition."

Both the legislative history and the language of the Robinson-Patman Act -- "injure, destroy, or prevent competition with any person" -- demonstrate that it is aimed at the protection of smaller competitors. On the other hand, the Sherman Act, as it is interpreted today, is consumer-oriented. Its policy is to protect competition by channeling business into the hands of the most efficient, and thereby to give consumers the best possible product at the lowest possible price. Those who view "deteriorating" or "drastically declining" price structures as a good thing for consumers are clearly thinking in Sherman Act terms. Yet, it can be argued that Utah Pie, by having its plant in Salt Lake City, is more efficient than the three defendants whose plants are distant from the Salt Lake City market.

According to the critics, the dichotomy between the Sherman Act and the Robinson-Patman Act is a fact of life. The two statutory policies cannot be completely reconciled, and therefore the Utah Pie decision is significant. A national company is confronted with a very real problem when it wants to enter a new market. If the entry is tried by temporarily setting a lower price than the company is charging elsewhere, then local competitors may well complain, particularly if that lower price is below cost. And all three defendants in the Utah Pie case sold below cost. The Court's opinion stressed "persistent sales below cost and radical price cuts themselves discriminatory."

- 0 -

Question

To what extent has the Robinson-Patman Act's impact on private-brand discounts been eased by the Fifth Circuit's decision that such discounts do not injure competition if they merely reflect consumer preference?

References

Borden Co. v. FTC, 381 F.2d 175 (5th Cir.) (pp. A-4, X-1, ATRR No. 314, 7/18/67). Analysis, Private-Label Price Differentials (p. B-1, ATRR No. 252, 5/10/66), reprinted at p. 207, Antitrust & Trade Regulation Today: 1967.

Background

Manufacturers willing to produce and pack their products under the private brands of their customers often sell the private-brand items at lower prices than those charged for products bearing the manufacturer's brand. For private-brand products, the manufacturer does not spend money on brand advertising. If the private-brand product is made to the buyer's unique specifications, the manufacturer is probably not obligated to maintain any price relationship between that product and those he makes and markets under his own brand. The Robinson-Patman Act inhibits price discrimination only when it occurs on sales of products of "like grade and quality." (And see Quaker Oats Co., FTC Docket 8112 (pp. A-3, X-10, ATRR No. 177, 12/1/64).) But the Federal Trade Commission has applied the Act to private-brand price differentials when the only difference between the products as they leave the factory is in their labels.

In FTC v. Borden Co., 383 U.S. 637, 34 LW 4288 (pp. A-1, X-6, ATRR No. 246, 3/29/66), the Supreme Court, reversing the Court of Appeals for the Fifth Circuit (339 F.2d 113, pp. A-1, X-1, ATRR No. 178, 12/8/64), sustained the FTC's rule that consumer preference for a premium label is not, standing alone, a difference in "grade or quality" for Robinson-Patman Act pricing purposes. Since the Supreme Court endorsed the view of the Attorney General's National Committee to Study the Antitrust Laws that consumer preference "should receive due legal recognition in the more flexible 'injury' and 'cost justification' provisions of the statute," that element of price determination was not eliminated from price-discrimination cases. Nevertheless, ATRR analyzed the Borden holding as "loaded with problems for the business community." Little hope for saving private-brand differentials was seen in recognizing the cost differences of promoting a premium brand, because "proof of cost justification is always difficult." It was pointed out that, in entering the Robinson-Patman Act order (Docket 7129, pp. A-17, X-1, ATRR No. 74, 12/11/62) being reviewed in the Borden case, the FTC had refused to let Borden prove cost justification by comparing average distribution costs for Borden-brand evaporated milk with the average for private-brand evaporated milk. Apparently the Commission wanted a comparison of costs for separate classifications of Borden-brand customers with costs for individual private-label customers. In carrying out the Supreme Court's mandate that it conduct "further proceedings consistent with this opinion," however, the Court of Appeals for the Fifth Circuit did not have to deal with the cost-justification issue. Before it reached that problem, the Fifth Circuit discovered a lack of evidence to support either the FTC's finding that Borden's lower price for evaporated milk packed under private labels caused injury to competition between Borden and other milk processors or its finding that the price difference injured competition among Borden's customers.

The Commission's finding of injury to primary-line competition -- between Borden and other milk processors -- was based on the testimony of officials of several of Borden's competitors that they were unsuccessful in competing for business with Borden -- that Borden was able to sell private-label milk for a lower price than they could.

But the court of appeals pointed out that this testimony relates to the price difference between Borden's private-label milk and its competitor's private-label milk; it does not relate to the price difference between the brands of milk marketed by Borden, which is the precise price discrimination alleged in the complaint. "Therefore, injury proved in the primary line, if any, is not the effect of the price difference in issue."

In rejecting FTC findings that secondary-line competiton -- among Borden's customers -- was hurt, the Fifth Circuit reasoned that, if a private-brand price differential "reflects no more than a consumer preference for the premium brand, the price difference creates no competitive advantage to the recipient of the cheaper private brand product on which injury could be predicated. '[R]ather it represents merely a rough equivalent of the benefit by way of the seller's national advertising and promotion which the purchaser of the more expensive branded product enjoys.' (Report on the Antitrust Laws, 159.) The record discloses no evidence tending to show that Borden's price differential exceeds the recognized consumer appeal of the Borden label. Nor has it been suggested that the prices are unreasonably high for Borden-brand milk on the one hand, or unrealistically low for the private-label milk on the other. * * * No customer has been favored over another."

Although the Fifth Circuit once again set aside the Commission's cease-and-desist order, this time the Commission could not persuade the Solicitor General to seek Supreme Court review.

Conclusions

Any assessment of the Fifth Circuit's ruling necessarily begins with recognition that the court has granted Robinson-Patman Act clearance to any bona fide private-brand price differential -- that is, one that truly reflects a difference in market value attributable to a difference in consumer brand preference. True, the court's "no competitive advantage" rationale eliminates only the possibility of injury to secondary-line competition and is not relevant in determining whether a private-brand differential has hurt the manufacturer-seller's own competition. (After all, it makes no difference to the competing manufacturers being undersold that they are losing the market to a rival who is favoring "no customer * * * over another.") But the no-causation reasoning with respect to proof of injury to primary-line competition would seem to make that route as well a difficult one for the Commission to follow. The Commission's evidence of injury to primary-line competition in Robinson-Patman Act cases has generally consisted of sales losses and customer alienations attributable to the difference between the injured competitors' prices and the lower price the respondent seller charged on some sales. The Fifth Circuit now says it is "immaterial" that the respondent seller's prices on other sales were higher. Apparently the Commission can no longer leave to inference the proposition that the customer-diverting price cuts were possible only because the seller was able to charge more elsewhere. At least one other federal court has seen a need for separate proof in a primary-line case that the lower prices were financed by higher prices on other sales. Shore Oil & Gas Co., Inc., v. Humble Oil & Refining Co., 224 F.Supp. 922 (D.N.J.) (pp. A-1, X-1, ATRR No. 129, 12/31/63).

There are a few considerations, though, that may limit the impact of the Fifth Circuit's decision on private-brand pricing. First of all, while the court assigns the FTC the burden of proving that a private-brand differential exceeds the name brand's consumer appeal, the issue arises only when there is a "recognized" consumer preference for this brand over the customer's private label. If that is true, the retail chain that promotes its "private" brand into national prominence loses its right to negotiate for a private-brand discount.

Second, some antitrust lawyers think the Fifth Circuit's reasoning on secondary-line competition is likely to gain acceptance only for those situations in which the manufacturer makes private-brand manufacture and pricing available to all his customers. But uniform availability may wipe out actionable discrimination in any case based on injury to secondary-line competition. When the first Borden appeal was argued, the FTC indicated it would settle for uniform availability in a secondary-line situation.

Such a requirement, however, would give most manufacturers problems and would foreclose private-brand pricing to many. Manufacture under private labels at reduced prices is economically feasible for many manufacturers only if the number of brands to be handled is relatively few and the volume of production under each brand is relatively large. Otherwise, the administrative and management detail become sufficiently burdensome to wipe out the cost savings attributable to the absence of a need for advertising. In the food industry, the National Commission on Food Marketing found private brands to be available in a wide range of products. While the greater volume of private-label business is in the hands of the big grocery chains, the Commission discovered that all categories of retailers sell private-brand foods. Yet the concept of "uniform availability" may not even exist in the processing of natural products such as fruits, vegetables, and fish. In those product lines, a packer first appropriates the quality and quantity he wants for his own advertised brand and then offers only the excess for private-brand sale.

Third, there is reason to doubt that the FTC will let the matter rest as it now stands. The Commission did ask the Solicitor General to petition for Supreme Court review of the Fifth Circuit's ruling, indicating that it has not given up the fight.

General acceptance of the Fifth Circuit's principles would apparently magnify the Commission's task in private-label cases based on injury to secondary-line competition. Proving that the price differential exceeds recognized consumer preference will be greatly complicated by such factors as price changes, special prices, cents-off labels, local and temporary price cuts, and even price-marking errors.

Moreover, the Commission is not likely to acquiesce very readily in the Fifth Circuit's ruling that the difference between the price of Borden-brand milk and the price of private-brand milk was "immaterial" to a finding of injury to primary-line competition. The principle embodied in that ruling is broad enough to take in all the Commission's primary-line Robinson-Patman Act cases. There is no reason for supposing that a geographical price difference, for example, is more "material" than a private-brand differential to the issue whether injury to competition for the trade of customers offered the lower price was caused by the price differential.

While the Commission has no pending private-brand cases in which complaints have been filed, it can be expected to keep an eye open for another appropriate fact situation that might give it a new path to the Supreme Court. A conflicting decision from another court of appeals would probably induce the Solicitor General to seek review.

The end result is that at least some of the Antitrust Bar expects the FTC to go on attempting to apply Robinson-Patman to private-brand pricing but to exercise restraint in its choice of cases. Some lawyers are prepared to advise their clients to go ahead with deals for private-brand discounts but to make sure they are kept well within limits reasonably related to consumer brand preference. Unfortunately, that advice may have no meaning for the client. There are people in the food industry who insist that the Fifth Circuit's key phrase, "recognized consumer brand preference" is meaningless to them because housewives shop for prices in the grocery store; brand preference is ordinarily manifested only when there is no price differential. It must not be overlooked though, that the court was talking about a price differential charged wholesalers and retail chains, not a retail price differential. The admitted fact that brand is considered by the housewife when prices are equal establishes that value, and therefore a price differential can be attributed to a name brand.

- 0 -

Subject: Pricing "Systems" and the Meeting-Competition Defense   (Published 4/8/69)

Question

When, if ever, can a discriminatory pricing or advertising-allowance "system", plan, or formula be defended as meeting a competitor's price or allowance?

References

Surprise Brassiere Co., Inc. v. FTC, 406 F.2d 711, 1969 Trade Cases Para. 72,692 (5th Cir.) (p. A-15, ATRR No. 397, 2/18/69)
Analyses, "Meeting-Competition Defense," p. B-1, ATRR No. 96, 5/14/63; p. B-1, ATRR No. 170, 10/13/64; p. B-1, ATRR No. 275, 10/18/66; reprinted, pp. 189-202, Antitrust and Trade Regulation Today: 1967

Background

Section 2(b) of the Clayton Act, as amended by the Robinson-Patman Act, provides that "nothing contained herein shall prevent a seller rebutting the prima facie case thus made by showing that his lower price or the furnishing of services or facilities *** was made in good faith to meet an equally low price of a competitor, or the services or facilities furnished by a competitor." When a seller receives word from salesmen or customers that he is about to lose trade because a competitor is offering a lower price, he may sometimes be able to obtain details of the competitive offer and then meet that offer to a particular customer. In other situations, he may decide to make temporary adjustments in his pricing schedule or formula to accommodate an entire class of customers likely to be receptive to the competitor's offer. Sometimes the competitor's new price is part of a pricing system or formula designed to attract a whole class of buyers rather than a simple offer to one prospective buyer. There has been a good deal of litigation over the extent to which the involvement of general pricing "systems" or formulae, as opposed to specific offers to individual buyers, affects the "good faith" of a seller who makes defensive but discriminatory price adjustments.

The distinction between "pricing systems" and "individual competitive situations" derives from the Supreme Court's opinion in FTC v. A.E. Staley Mfg. Co., 324 U.S. 746 (1945), where the Court stated that the meeting competition defense puts "emphasis on individual competitive situations rather than upon a general system of competition." Section 2(b)'s proviso, the Court reasoned, "presupposes that the person charged with violating the Act would, by his normal, nondiscriminatory pricing methods, have reached a price so high that he could reduce it in order to meet the competitor's equally low price. *** Respondents have never attempted to establish their own nondiscriminatory price system, and then reduced their price when necessary to meet competition. Instead they have slavishly followed in the first instance a pricing policy which, in their case, resulted in systematic discriminations. *** Moreover, there is no showing that if respondents had charged nondiscriminatory prices, they would be higher in all cases than those now prevailing under their basing point system. Hence it cannot be said that respondents' price discriminations have resulted in 'lower' prices to meet equally low prices of a competitor." 324 U.S. at 754-5. Under those circumstances, the Court concluded that the proferred meeting-competition defense rested "upon the assumption that the statute permits a seller to maintain an otherwise unlawful system of discriminatory prices, merely because he has adopted it in its entirety, as a means of securing the benefits of a like unlawful system maintained by his competitors" -- which the Supreme Court rejected as a "startling conclusion."

Neither the Supreme Court nor the FTC has ever attempted to define the word "system" as used in stating the rule that use of a pricing system negates "good faith." Under the "basing point" system involved in the Staley case, each customer's price was computed by adding to the Chicago price the freight rate from Chicago to the place of delivery, even though the seller's plant was not in Chicago and therefore some sales involved no freight charge or a lower charge than that added to the Chicago price.

In Standard Oil Co. v. FTC, 233 F.2d 649, 653 (7th Cir. 1956), the Court of Appeals for the Seventh Circuit interpreted the "Staley and kindred cases" as relating only to inherently illegal pricing systems that are used "to stabilize or increase but never to lower price" or that eliminate "all price competition." That limitation of the Staley doctrine was not endorsed by the 5-4 Supreme Court majority that affirmed the Seventh Circuit. FTC v. Standard Oil Co., 355 U.S. 396 (1958). Rather, the Court found that the FTC had not proved the discriminatory price reductions under attack to have been made "pursuant to a pricing system."

Standard Oil had been using a "dual price system" under which retail service stations paid a "tank-wagon" price one and a half cents per gallon higher than the "tank-car" price paid by "jobbers," who sold at both wholesale and retail. In its petition to the Supreme Court the FTC insisted that this "dual price system" was industry-wide, but the Court found this claim not to be alleged in the Commission's complaint or supported by its findings. Looking solely at Standard's pricing practices, the Court found the "jobber" discount to have been granted in a context of "a prolonged period of haggling" and "numerous attempts" by competitors to lure the jobbers away with cut-rate prices lower than Standard's. These factors convinced the Court that Standard's prices to the jobbers "were reduced as a response to individual competitive situations."

On the basis of the Staley opinion, the FTC, in Forster Mfg. Co., Docket 7207 (p. A-5, ATRR No. 80, 1/22/63), refused to apply the meeting-competition defense to price cuts offered to all customers in a designated area. The Commission decided that discriminatory price cuts can be defended under Section 2(b) only when they are made on a customer-by-customer basis, with knowledge of the competitor's identity and the amount of his price. In Callaway Mills Co., FTC Docket 7634 (pp. A-10, X-1, ATRR No. 139, 3/10/64) the Commission required a seller asserting the meeting-competition defense "to identify with particularity both his goods and the competing goods whose price was met" and rejected a defense based on proof of "a formal pricing system of universal application." The companies involved in Callaway Mills were textile manufacturers that, upon entering the carpet industry, found their no-volume discount policies to be seriously impeding their development and felt compelled to adopt the cumulative volume discount system prevailing among the old-line carpet manufacturers.

Courts of Appeals

The Commission's orders in both the Forster and the Callaway Mills cases were set aside by courts of appeals. In the Forster case, the First Circuit (335 F.2d 47, pp. A-1, X-1, ATRR No. 160, 8/4/64) called attention to statements by the Supreme Court in the Staley opinion that the defense "does not require the seller to justify price discriminations by showing that in fact they met a competitive price." Rather, Staley held, "the statute at least requires the seller, who has knowingly discriminated in price, to show the existence of facts which would lead a reasonable and prudent person to believe that the granting of a lower price would in fact meet the equally low price of a competitor."

Applying this "reasonable and prudent person" rule, the First Circuit decided the Commission was expecting too much of a seller when it required proof that the seller knew in advance the amount of his competitors' offers and the identity of each competitor who made them. Later (p. A-2, ATRR No. 213, 8/10/65) the Commission made new findings of fact -- based largely on "below-cost" sales and again rejected Forster's meeting-competition defense for failure to meet the "reasonable and prudent person" test. Forster's second review petition to the First Circuit was dismissed (361 F.2d 340, p. A-10, ATRR No. 255, 5/31/66).

In Callaway Mills, the Fifth Circuit likewise stressed the Staley opinion's "reasonable and prudent person" language and sustained a meeting-competition defense for a "discount system, thoughtfully tailored by both petitioners to meet their individual problems in the market, * * * a mature and reasoned approach to a very real and difficult competitive program." After checking the Supreme Court's Staley opinion, the court of appeals found "nothing wrong per se in adopting a 'pricing system' used by competitors." There were a number of factors in the case that the court of appeals seems to have regarded as making it unreasonable to expect "individual competitive" responses: (1) each carpet manufacturer markets such a wide variety of types and styles at different prices that it would be "practically unfeasible" for a manufacturer to get the competitive information it would need for an "individual competitive" response; (2) the cumulative volume discount was uniformly established throughout the industry (indeed, was protected by an antitrust consent decree, U.S. v. Institute of Carpet Manufacturers, 1 F.R.D. 636 (S.D.N.Y. 1941); and (3) no workable alternative pricing response was available.

Advertising Allowances

In Rabiner & Jontow, Inc., Docket 8629 (p. A-4, ATRR No. 273, 10/4/66), the Commission refused to ease its standards of specificity in proof of meeting competition when that defense is offered to justify discriminatory promotional allowances in an industry where the practice of granting such allowances is widespread. (For a discussion of Section 2(b)'s applicability to advertising allowances, see the first of the analyses cited in the references.) The Commission stuck to its rule that the defense is available only when "the particular discrimination is made in a genuine defensive response to another seller's offer in a specific transaction." On appeal, the seller challenged only the propriety of enforcing an order against it while its competitors remain free to follow the same illegal practices. The Second Circuit upheld the Commission's order (386 F.2d 667, p. A-21, ATRR No. 335, 12/12/67), pointing out that the meeting-competition defense is "implicit in every order issued under" the Robinson-Patman Act. A suggestion that the order should leave the seller free "to meet competition generally without showing that any particular payment was made to meet a specific competitor's offer" was rejected.

Discrimination in advertising allowances was the context of another FTC definition of its Section 2(b) proof requirements in Surprise Brassiere Co., Inc., Docket 8584 (p. A-18, ATRR No. 313, 7/11/67). "Respondent must prove that its discriminatory allowances were responsive to offers by other sellers in specific competitive situations and that it had reason to believe it was meeting such offers." As he has in this entire series of Section 2(b) opinions, Commissioner Elman dissented, objecting to "rigid standards imposing unrealistic and impossible duties of inquiry and predictions on businessmen."

Relying on the Callaway Mills decision, Surprise Brassiere asked the Fifth Circuit to hold that it can meet competition generally through meeting a plan or system of its competitors. In the opinion cited in the references, however, the Fifth Circuit took the position that Surprise Brassiere's argument has no factual support in the record of the FTC proceeding. Unlike Callaway Mills, the court of appeals explained, "Surprise was not confronted with the problem of trying to match its prices with the prices of competitors that varied according to the cumulative annual purchases of each customer. It was faced with specific competitive situations but its proof did not show that it limited its variances to specific competitive situations." In the Fifth Circuit's view, the FTC "required no more than is taught in Staley. The Court there did not think it an impossible burden to require '*** a showing of diligence on the part of respondents to verify the reports which they received, or to learn of the existence of facts which would lead a reasonable and prudent person to believe that the granting of a lower price would in fact be meeting the equally low price of a competitor.' 324 U.S. at p. 759."

More applicable to Surprise's pricing practices, the Fifth Circuit said, are the Rabiner & Jontow case and Exquisite Form Brassiere Inc., v. FTC, 360 F.2d 492 (D.C. Cir.)(pp. A-8, X-1, ATRR No. 208, 7/6/65), where "the courts upheld the view that a seller cannot deviate from promotional advertising programs in order to meet competition generally as opposed to meeting competition in individual competitive situations." In Exquisite Form, the D.C. Circuit explicitly held that the Staley rule against adoption of a discriminatory system to meet a discriminatory system is as applicable to advertising allowances as it is to prices and discounts therefrom.

Conclusions

The Fifth Circuit's opinions in Callaway Mills and Surprise Brassiere are not inconsistent, since Surprise Brassiere's meeting-competition evidence established that it had made a general response to "specific competitive situations." Unlike Callaway, the Fifth Circuit explained, "Surprise was not confronted with the problem of trying to match its prices with the prices of competitors that varied according to the cumulative annual purchases of each customer."

In making this distinction, the Fifth Circuit seems to have given exalted status to a practice the Staley case is often cited as outlawing -- the adoption of a discriminatory pricing system to meet a competitor's discriminatory pricing system. In fact, however, the basing-point pricing system used by Staley was not a defensive response to price reductions made by a competitor. Rather, Staley had, without attempting to develop a nondiscriminatory price schedule of its own, adopted a system that, for some customers, permitted the maintenance of higher prices than would otherwise be charged. Some Robinson-Patman Act practitioners believe, therefore, that a general, discriminatory pricing response can be made to a competitor's discriminatory pricing "system" whenever the response is made in "good faith" as to the seller's knowledge (or related diligence) of the competitive offer and whenever the response is no broader in scope than the demands of the competitive situation and is reasonable in the light of the available alternatives. The distinction often made is between a discriminatory system, like Callaway Mills', adopted in a genuinely defensive response to competition, and one, like Staley's, adopted as the seller's own pricing plan. If that is true, the lack of an authoritative definition of what constitutes a pricing "system" may not be significant.

Other lawyers, however, feel just as strongly that the FTC's "individual competitive response" requirement will still prevail in such a situation if the seller proceeded against is not a newcomer to an industry in which no reasonable alternative course of action is available. They regard the Callaway Mills decision as a special exception for the new entrant like the limited clearance given tying arrangements in U. S. v. Jerrold Electronics Corp., 187 F. Supp. 545 (E.D. Pa. 1960).

- 0 -

Subject: Advertising Allowances in Dual-Distribution Systems   (Published 5/14/68)

Question

What effect is the Supreme Court's decision in the Fred Meyer case likely to have on dual-distribution marketing techniques?

Reference

FTC v. Fred Meyer, Inc., 390 U.S. 341, 36 LW 4233 (pp. A-13, X-10, ATRR No. 349, 3/19/68) (See ANALYSIS, "Advertising Allowances in Dual-Distribution Systems," p. B-1, ATRR No. 101, 6/18/63, reprinted, p. 225, Antitrust and Trade Regulation Today: 1967).

Background

The practice in consumer-product industries of marketing partly through independent wholesalers or jobbers and partly through direct-buying retail chains causes problems of interpretation and enforcement under the Robinson-Patman Act. Section 2(a) of the Clayton Act, as amended by Robinson-Patman, does not prohibit manufacturers or other sellers from choosing wholesalers, retailers, and even consumers as their customers and charging all of them the same price. There is no price "discrimination" in identical prices. The fact that direct-buying retailers paying the same price as wholesalers may thereby obtain an advantage over their retail competitors who buy from wholesalers at higher prices has been the subject of congressional committee hearings, but no legislative action has been taken to modify the existing prohibition of "discrimination."

Sometimes direct-buying retailers enjoy further advantages over wholesaler-supplied competitors by obtaining from a manufacturer price concessions or advertising assistance not made available to wholesalers or to the wholesalers' retailer customers. Moreover a manufacturer frequently gives special discounts or promotional assistance to direct-buying retailers as a means of extending his sales into new geographic markets. Unless justified by cost differences or as good-faith attempts to meet competition, the straight price concessions may violate Section 2(a) of the Clayton Act, as amended by the Robinson-Patman Act. Section 2(a) makes it "unlawful for any person * * * to discriminate in price between different purchasers * * * when the effect of such discrimination may be * * * to injure, destroy, or prevent competition with any person who either grants or knowingly receives the benefit of such discrimination, or with customers of either of them."

Determination of the legality of advertising assistance given in the form of cash allowances involves quite different considerations, however, for Section 2(d) of the Act makes discriminatory advertising allowances unlawful only when paid "to or for the benefit of a customer" and requires that any such allowance be made "available on proportionally equal terms to all other customers competing in the distribution of such products or commodities." Until its 1963 decision in the Fred Meyer case (Docket 7492, p. X-1, ATRR No. 92, 4/16/63), the FTC had interpreted these references to "customers" and "competing customers" as meaning that allowances can properly be offered to direct-buying retailers alone, since wholesalers do not compete with such retailers in resale of the products and since retailers purchasing from wholesalers are not "customers" of the manufacturer. Ligget & Myers Tobacco Co., 56 FTC 221, 250-252 (1959). Yet in Elizabeth Arden, 39 FTC 288, 305 (1944), the Commission had ordered the furnishing of advertising services "to competing retailers on proportionally equal terms" even though some of the retailers traded with wholesalers rather than with the manufacturer supplying the services. Section 2(e) of the Act prohibits discrimination among "purchasers" in the furnishing of "services or facilities."

The New Jersey Federal District Court held, in Krug v. International Telephone and Telegraph Corp., 142 F.Supp. 230, 236 (1956), that a wholesaler can maintain a treble-damage suit against his manufacturer-supplier for granting advertising allowances only to direct-buying retailers. That decision was cited with approval by the Commission in the Fred Meyer case, which was not a proceeding against a manufacturer but one against a direct-buying retailer. The Commission's order prohibits Fred Meyer from inducing or receiving promotional allowances when Meyer knows or should know that such allowances are not made available by its supplier on proportionally equal terms to wholesalers who resell to retailers competing with Meyer.

The Commission's order was set aside by the Court of Appeals for the Ninth Circuit (359 F.2d 351, p. A-14, ATRR No. 246, 3/29/66) for lack of evidence (1) that Meyer's manufacturer-suppliers had in some way dealt directly with retailers competing with Meyer and (2) that products sold by the manufacturer-suppliers could be traced through wholesalers to the shelves of the competing retailers. These two requirements were imposed by the Ninth Circuit as elements of the "indirect customer" doctrine, under which the Commission and the courts have required nondiscriminatory promotional payments to indirect-buying retailers if the manufacturer exercises control over the selection of wholesaler's customers. American News Co. v. FTC, 300 F.2d 104 (2d Cir 1962); K. S. Corp. v. Chemstrand Corp., 198 F.Supp. 310 (S.D.N.Y. 1961); Kay Windsor Frocks, Inc., 51 FTC 89 (1954).

The Supreme Court parted company with both the FTC and the Ninth Circuit and held that the indirect-buying retailers competing with Meyer, and not their wholesaler-suppliers, are the disfavored buyers entitled to receive the manufacturers' promotional allowances on proportionally equal terms with Meyer. In reaching that result, the Supreme Court did not question the validity of the "indirect customer" doctrine. The key element leading the Supreme Court to conclude that the Commission did not need to resort to the "indirect customer" doctrine was the FTC finding -- unchallenged by the court of appeals -- that Meyer competed in the resale of these manufacturers' products with retailers who purchased through wholesaler customers of the manufacturers. "Whether suppliers deal directly with disfavored competitors or not, they can, and here did, afford a direct buyer the kind of competitive advantage which Section 2(d) was intended to eliminate."

As for Meyer's contention that the indirect-buying retailers were not "customers" of the discriminating manufacturers within the meaning of Section 2(d), "it rests on a narrow definition of 'customer' which becomes wholly untenable when viewed in light of the central purpose of Section 2(d) and the economic realities with which its framers were concerned." That purpose is "to curb and prohibit all devices by which large buyers gained preferences over smaller ones by virtue of their greater purchasing power." FTC v. Henry Broch and Co., 363 U.S. 166, 168 (1960)."

To an FTC suggestion that it will often not be feasible for suppliers to bypass their wholesalers and grant promotional allowances directly to their many retail outlets, the Supreme Court replied that "our decision does not necessitate such bypassing. * * * Nothing we have said bars a supplier, consistently with other provisions of the antitrust laws, from utilizing his wholesalers to distribute payments or administer a promotional program, so long as the supplier takes responsibility, under rules and guides promulgated by the Commission for the regulation of such practices, for seeing that the allowances are made available to all who compete in the resale of his product."

Conclusions

As it did in other opinions such as FTC v. Sun Oil Co., 371 U.S. 505 (1963), and FTC v. Henry Broch & Co., 363 U.S. 166 (1960), the Supreme Court has again seen in the Robinson-Patman Act a general "requirement of proportional equality" in the treatment of competitors. And Commissioner Elman seemed to have had a similar thought in mind when, dissenting from the FTC order against Fred Meyer, he insisted that Section 2(d) should be applied in the same manner as Section 2(e) -- that is, to prohibit discrimination among competing retailers even if some buy through wholesalers. But proportional equality may be difficult to achieve as long as a manufacturer is free to sell to both wholesalers and retailers at the same price.

The extent to which the Meyer decision will in fact assist wholesaler-supplied retailers depends on how manufacturers and independent wholesalers react to the problems the decision is likely to create for them. The number, scope, and severity of the manufacturer's problems in maintaining equality in advertising assistance to retailers depends on the perishability, unit

value, service requirements, and other features of the product he markets, the number of retailers involved, the geographical scope of his market, retailer and wholesaler inventory-
turnover rates, and other characteristics of his market such as relative importance of advertising as opposed to price competition. Some dual-distributing manufacturers may find the administration of an advertising program that complies with the "proportional equality" standard
so burdensome that they will terminate all such programs. A few may even simply stop selling
to wholesalers, confident that direct-buying retail chains offer ample markets for many lines
of products. That solution may have limited value, though, for a manufacturer willing to sell
directly to anyone may have to market his product through wholesalers because some retailers
need the wholesalers' full-line service.

Actually, the typical manufacturer weighing the continuation or initiation of retailer-
advertising assistance has no way of knowing what he must do to avoid Robinson-Patman Act
litigation, for the ruling in the Meyer case raises more questions than it answers. How does
a manufacturer find out which direct-buying retailers have competitors who obtain the manufacturer's product through wholesalers and therefore must be given notice of any available advertising assistance? If he finds a direct-buying retailer who has no such competition, how
can he be sure that competition will not develop, after the advertising program starts, by
reason of a delayed sale from a wholesaler's inventory? How can he give indirect-buying
retailers adequate notice without prohibitive expense? One producer thinks he has solved
that one by printing the notice prominently on his shipping carton. What formula for computing
the advertising allowance will assure "proportional equality" among retailers of greatly dis-
parate sizes and purchase volumes? A percentage of purchase volume won't do; the manufacturer wouldn't have a uniform or accurate price base for evaluating the purchases of wholesaler-
supplied retailers.

Perhaps anticipating these problems for manufacturers, the Supreme Court made it
clear that it was not barring a supplier "from utilizing his wholesalers to distribute payments
or administer a promotional program." But how much supervision of the wholesaler then becomes necessary? Could a manufacturer's careful supervision of his wholesaler to assure
equality reach a point of refinement that it might be considered a vertical conspiracy in restraint of trade and hence a Section 1 Sherman Act violation? And could the policing of the
wholesaler's activity reach the point where the wholesaler's customers would become the
manufacturer's "indirect customers" entitled to buy at the same price as direct-buying retailers? Can a manufacturer who gives wholesalers a functional discount require them to use
part of the discount? More significantly, perhaps, is the wholesaler going to get something
for his greater effort? Even if manufacturers decide generally to continue using wholesalers,
it may be difficult for wholesalers to survive in a distribution system depending on manufacturer-
retailer cooperation in advertising. Some manufacturers consider their independent wholesalers much too apathetic about retailer-advertising assistance to be counted on for a vital
role in administration of a cooperative-advertising program. The Fred Meyer opinion made
it clear that the manufacturer who so uses independent wholesalers nevertheless retains "responsibility, under rules and guides promulgated by the Commission," for the proportional
equality of the program. Under its guides or advisory-opinion program, the Commission
might supply answers to some of the questions listed above. If the current law-enforcement
trend at the Commission continues, it seems unlikely that the agency will supply many of the
answers in litigation. It has filed only three Robinson-Patman Act complaints -- and has entered consent orders in only six other new Robinson-Patman cases -- in the last twelve months.
Therefore, it may be that the most substantial immediate hazard for manufacturers who stray
from the narrow path of "proportional equality" is treble-damage liability in private civil
actions. In this connection, manufacturers must keep in mind the threat of retailer class
actions under new Rule 23 of the Federal Rules of Civil Procedure (see ANALYSIS, "Class
Actions," p. 143).

- 0 -

PART IV – FRANCHISING

Subject: Customer Restrictions   (Published 7/25/67)

Question

Under what conditions and by what sort of contractual arrangements can a manufacturer lawfully restrict choice of customers by independent merchants in a franchised marketing program?

References

U. S. v. Arnold, Schwinn & Co., 388 U. S. 365, 35 LW 4563 (pp. A-1, X-1, ATRR No. 309, 6/13/67)

Analysis, "Territorial Dealer and Distributor Franchises" (p. B-1, ATRR No. 90, 4/2/63; p. B-1, ATRR No. 122, 11/12/63), reprinted at p. 55, Antitrust Trade Regulation Today: 1967

Analysis, "Territorial and Customer Restrictions on Franchised Dealers" (p. B-1, ATRR No. 189, 3/23/65), reprinted at p. 60, Antitrust and Trade Regulation Today: 1967

Background

Webster's Third New International Dictionary defines a franchise as "the right granted to an individual or group to market a company's goods or services in a particular territory" or "the territory involved in such a right." Much of the business community, though, has come to think of a "franchise" more in terms of a right to use or exploit a trademark or trade name than to market a product. They do not tie it so closely to the concept of a "territory." And for years the FTC and the Antitrust Division have been taking a position that would divorce "territory" entirely from "franchise." The agencies have taken the position that under Section 1 of the Sherman Act a franchised merchant may be neither guaranteed an exclusive territory nor forbidden to sell outside it. The legality of a ban on out-of-territory sales and other restrictions on choice of customers was litigated in an Antitrust Division injunction suit against Arnold, Schwinn & Co., which was finally resolved by the Supreme Court on the last day of its 1966-1967 term.

Schwinn was charged with conspiring with its wholesale distributors, jobbers, and retailers to fix the retail prices of Schwinn bicycles, allocate exclusive territories to wholesalers and jobbers, and confine Schwinn merchandise to "franchised" retail dealers. The charges were based on a marketing program initiated by Schwinn in 1952 after a year in which it had accounted for the largest single share of the United States bicycle market -- 22.5 percent. During the first 10 years of the program's operation, Schwinn increased substantially its dollar and unit sales, but its share of the market fell to 12.8 percent. In the same period, Murray Ohio Mfg. Co., a producer for Sears Roebuck and other mass merchandisers, became the leading bicycle manufacturer in the country. Murray increased its market share from 11.6 percent in 1951 to 22.8 percent in 1961. Most bicycles are sold under private label, including 40 percent distributed by national manufacturers and distributors that operate their own stores and "franchise" others and another 20 percent by giant chains and mass merchandisers such as Sears and Montgomery Ward. Schwinn, on the other hand, sells only under the Schwinn label and markets its products primarily to or through 22 wholesale distributors. Most sales to the public are made by bicycle specialty shops that also provide servicing. Schwinn sold its bicycles in three principal ways: (1) to bicycle distributors, to B. F. Goodrich Co. for resale in Goodrich "franchised" stores, and to hardware jobbers; (2) to retailers by means of consignment or agency arrangements with the distributors; and (3) to retailers under the so-called Schwinn Plan, which involves direct shipment by Schwinn to the retailer, invoices to the purchasing retailer, extension of credit, and payment of a commission to the distributor taking the order. Each distributor was assigned a specific territory and agreed to sell only to "franchised" Schwinn retailers located in that territory. Retail dealers were "franchised" only as to

designated locations; each was allowed to purchase only from or through a distributor authorized to serve his area; and each was authorized to sell only to consumers, not to
other retailers.

In the district court (237 F.Supp. 323 (N.D. Ill.), pp. A-6, X-3, ATRR No. 182,
1/5/65), the government failed to prove the price-fixing count in its complaint; the court found
that in non-fair-trade states, Schwinn dealers have at all times been free to establish their own
retail prices. In addition, the limitation of the distributors' choice of customers to "franchised"
retailers was upheld as a reasonable means of competing with giant bicycle merchants, as was
Schwinn's rule that "franchised" retailers may not sell to anyone but consumers. The territorial restriction on distributors was sustained for Schwinn Plan transactions on the theory that
the distributors were true agents in that situation. But it was outlawed for any transaction in
which the distributor makes delivery from his own warehouse and sets price, regardless of
whether Schwinn keeps title under some "agency" or "consignment" arrangement.

Only the government appealed, and it did not challenge the dismissal of the price-fixing
charge. Mr. Justice Fortas wrote the Supreme Court's opinion. He began by pointing out that
the restrictions imposed by Schwinn would clearly be illegal per se if they were either imposed
at the urging of the distributors themselves -- in which case they would represent a horizontal
combination rather than the "truly vertical arrangement" involved here -- or were part of a
scheme involving unlawful price fixing. "At the other extreme," Mr. Justice Fortas noted, is
proper use of the Colgate Doctrine, 250 U.S. 300 (1919) -- "franchising" that amounts to nothing more than the manufacturer's selection of the customers with whom he will deal. "If nothing more is involved than vertical 'confinement' of the manufacturer's own sales of the merchandise to select dealers, and if competitive products are readily available to others, the restriction on these facts alone, would not violate the Sherman Act." As Mr. Justice Fortas
viewed them, Schwinn's marketing practices fall somewhere between those two extremes.

Schwinn's restrictions were found to fall partly on one side of the line of illegality and
partly on the other, and the dividing line chosen is "the ancient rule against restraints on
alienation." "Proper application of Section 1 of the Sherman Act to this problem requires dif-
ferentiation between the situation where the manufacturer parts with title, dominion, or risk
with respect to the article, and where he completely retains ownership and risk of loss." To
permit a manufacturer to reserve control over his product's destiny after sale "would sanction
franchising and confinement of distribution as the ordinary instead of the unusual method which
may be permissible in an appropriate and impelling competitive setting, since most merchandise is distributed by means of purchase and sale." On the other hand, as indicated in White
Motor [372 U.S. 253, pp. A-1, X-1, ATRR No. 86, 3/5/63], we are not prepared to introduce
the inflexibility which a per se rule might bring if it were applied to prohibit all vertical restrictions of territory and all franchising, in the sense of designating specified distributors
and retailers as the chosen instruments through which the manufacturer, retaining ownership
of the goods, will distribute them to the public. Such a rule might severely hamper smaller
enterprises resorting to reasonable methods of meeting the competition of giants and of merchandising through independent dealers, and it might sharply accelerate the trend towards
vertical integration of the distribution process."

Applying that passage-of-title test, the Court declared that Schwinn's restrictions on resale of purchased bicycles are illegal per se -- that no distinction can be made between territorial and customer restrictions. (Actually, the government had not asked the Court for a rule
of per se illegality; see the report of the argument at p. A-7, ATRR No. 302, 4/25/67.) Applying the rule of reason to the agency, consignment, and Schwinn Plan deals, the Supreme
Court rejected the government's contention that the impact of Schwinn's customer restrictions
for those transactions is unreasonably restrictive of competition. First, Schwinn's "scheme
of confining distribution outlets" is "unencumbered by culpable price fixing." Second, they are
"truly vertical" restrictions. Third, they were adopted "in a competitive situation dominated
by mass merchandisers which command access to large-scale advertising and promotion,
choise of retail outlets, both owned and franchised, and adequate sources of supply." In
short, "there is nothing in the record -- after elimination of the price-fixing issue -- to

lead us to conclude that Schwinn's program exceeded the limits reasonably necessary to meet the competitive problems posed by its more powerful competitors. In these circumstances, the rule of reason is satisfied."

Not always, Mr. Justice Fortas was careful to say, will the necessity of meeting competition from mass merchandisers justify the unilateral adoption by even a single manufacturer of an agency or consignment pattern to confine distribution outlets. But there are two other critical factors present: (1) the availability to bicycle distributors and retailers of competing brands that are apparently reasonably interchangeable with Schwinn's products and (2) the freedom and willingness of Schwinn distributors and retailers to handle other brands of bicycles.

In an earlier portion of his opinion, Mr. Justice Fortas mentioned two other possible factors as relevant to a showing that a vertical restraint is sheltered by the rule of reason because not anticompetitive -- evidence that the manufacturer is either a newcomer seeking to break into or stay in the business or is a "failing company." While Schwinn falls within neither of those categories, it did argue that it had adopted its restrictive distribution program for the purpose of enabling it and the small independent merchants in its distribution chain to compete more effectively in the market place -- that it was seeking a better method of distribution that would promote sales, increase stability of its distributors and dealers, and augment profits.

But Mr. Justice Fortas points out that every restrictive practice is designed to augment profit and competitive position. "The antitrust outcome does not turn merely on the presence of sound business reason or motive. * * * Our inquiry is whether, assuming nonpredatory motives and business purposes and the incentive or profit and volume considerations, the effect upon competition in the marketplace is substantially adverse."

Mr. Justice Stewart and Mr. Justice Harlan dissented from that part of the opinion that found Schwinn's restrictions illegal per se when they are applied to bicycles Schwinn has sold. They feel the majority reached out "to adopt a potent per se rule" justified by "no previous antitrust decision of this Court." In fact, the majority's per se rule "completely repudiates the only case in point, White Motor." The ancient doctrine that a manufacturer has no legitimate interest in what happens to his products once he has sold them "no longer holds true in a day of sophisticated marketing policies, mass advertising, and vertically integrated manufacturer-distributors. Restrictions like those involved in a franchising program should accordingly be able to claim justification under the ancillary restraints doctrine."

Conclusions

Since most distributors and retail dealers buy and resell rather than merely serve as agents or consignees of their suppliers, the majority's per se rule does appear to take the "territory" out of many "franchises." Yet the true scope of its holding may depend on what it means when it says something is illegal "per se." Both Webster and Black define "per se" in a way that indicates something is illegal per se when it is illegal "by, of, or in itself," "inherently," or "unconnected with other matters." Yet at one point the majority opinion seems to suggest that a vertical territorial restriction on distributors who buy and resell might not be illegal when imposed by a manufacturer who is a "newcomer" or a "failing company." Similarly, in U.S. v. Sealy, Inc., 388 U.S. 350, 35 LW 4511 (pp. A-3, X-9, ATRR No. 309, 6/13/67), the Court in a footnote characterized horizontal market splitting among competitors as illegal per se and then in the body of its opinion suggested that small grocers might be permitted to justify an allocation of territories.

When the Court leaves open the possibility that there are circumstances under which conduct is illegal per se and others under which it is not illegal per se, it is not using the term in accordance with its dictionary definition, for the conduct is not being tested "by, of, or in itself." What the Court is really saying, then, is that most -- or perhaps almost all -- business enterprises are foreclosed from justifying restraints classified as per se Sherman Act violations but that some who find themselves in a few limited types of competitive emergencies are entitled to special consideration. Certainly this is not the type of "per se" rule that has been applied in price-fixing or boycott cases. But it is similar to the type of hedging the Supreme Court engaged in when it announced that tying arrangements "are unreasonable in and of themselves whenever a party has sufficient economic power with respect to the tying product to appreciably restrain free competition in the market for the tied product and a 'not insubstantial' amount of commerce is affected." Northern Pacific R. Co. v. U.S., 356 U.S. 1 (1958). For many restraints, the "per se" rule does not appear to be as harsh as it is cracked up to be.

In any event, it would appear that the government did not give up anything when it decided to argue for the per se rule against vertical territory and customer restrictions. The tenor of the Court's opinion makes it clear that the Court would not have applied a per se rule to customer choice restrictions for consignment, agency, or Schwinn Plan transactions even if it had been asked to. Regardless of what limitations the Court is putting on the per se rule, the result reached in the Schwinn case demonstrates the importance of the rule in antitrust enforcement. As applied here, the "rule of reason" lets Schwinn go on with all the wholesale-level territorial and customer restrictions attacked in the government's suit. All it needs to do is to revise its contractual arrangements with its distributors in terms that do away with all sales for resale and transfer all bicycle marketing to consignment or agency arrangements or to the Schwinn Plan.

While the Court in this particular case lets a very substantial competitor in a market restrict its distribution outlets in this fashion -- as long as no coercive-price-maintenance or "horizontal" element intrudes -- the Court says its concern is for "smaller enterprises resorting to reasonable methods of meeting the competition of giants" and against "the trend towards vertical integration of the distribution process." If franchising and confinement of distribution is to remain "the unusual method" of merchandising, as the Court seems to desire, territorial and customer restrictions enforced through agency, consignment, or similar arrangements will be permitted only when there is ample interbrand competition and when exceptional "competitive problems" are "posed by more powerful competitors."

In summary, then, the Court has announced two general rules for franchised marketing programs: (1) a manufacturer or distributor may impose no restrictions on the territories in which the customers to whom his customer resells an item of merchandise to which title has been transferred and (2) a manufacturer or distributor can impose such restrictions if he retains title and dominion over the merchandise through an agency or consignment arrangement and if the impact of the restrictions is not "unreasonably" restrictive of competition.

But there are actually new principles set out in the opinion that go far beyond franchising. Apparently the rule against restraints on alienation is now absolute in the marketing of consumer products; this seems to be the first time the Court has applied the principle outside a context of resale price maintenance. On the other side of the scales, the opinion seems to read new life into the consignment method of controlling distribution, provided the control does not take the form of coercive price fixing in a "vast distribution system." Simpson v. Union Oil Co., 377 U.S. 13 (pp. A-8, X-1, ATRR No. 145, 4/21/64). Even when the vertical restriction relates to price, some antitrust experts think it will fail to pass Sherman Act muster only when the consignment form of transaction is tied to what is really an outright sale by a dominant seller. But there are also antitrust experts who think the Court would never apply such a line of reasoning to the top three or four companies in the major consumer-product industries such as automobiles, appliances, and gasoline. And, since consignment selling is not practicable in drug stores and supermarkets, they think the revival of consignments will have little impact in the business community.

Wholesaler trade associations are in an uproar over the Schwinn opinion, viewing it as a spur to vertical integration that will wipe out still more independent distributors. The per se rule applied to resale restrictions will cause a manufacturer to think in terms of forward integration into the distribution function whenever he wants to confine the retailing of his product to outlets of his choice. Since he can't lawfully induce retailers to agree not to resell to "unfranchised retailers, he can retain tight control over the choice of retail outlets only by putting the retailer on an agency or consignment basis. At that point, the question arises whether it is administratively or legally possible to designate both the distributor and the retailer as agents or consignees of the manufacturer.

For control at the wholesale level only, however, there are still ways left open -- in addition to consignment and agency -- for marketing through independent distributors. If a manufacturer has confidence in his distributors' willingness to adhere voluntarily to otherwise unenforceable rules, he can operate what amounts to a "franchised" marketing program in the dictionary sense through use of the Colgate Doctrine referred to in the Court's opinion -- that is, by simply dropping distributors who ignore territorial restrictions. Since the purpose is to protect distributors from competition with each other, a manufacturer can unilaterally adopt a policy of selling only to one distributor in any particular geographical market area. An agreement with such a merchant not to set up additional sales locations or not to establish any shop outside a specified radius without the manufacturer's consent would seem to be lawful if Boro Hall Corp. v. General Motors, 124 F.2d 822, 130 F.2d 196 (2d Cir. 1942) is good law. And Mr. Justice Fortas said nothing that would invalidate the district judge's statement that a manufacturer "has a right to assign primary responsibility to a distributor in an area or territory."

- 0 -

Subject: "Inherent Coercion"   (Published 3/4/69)

Question

Can franchisors safely accept "commissions" on sales made to their franchisees by independent suppliers?

Reference

FTC v. Texaco, Inc., 393 U.S. 223, 37 LW 4059 (pp. A-1, X-1, ATRR No. 388, 12/17/68)

Background

As look-alike hamburger, fried chicken, and ice cream stands; "chain" restaurants and motels; dancing schools; rug-cleaning and car-repair shops; greeting-card stores; and the like spread across the country, lawyers representing the franchising promoters of these establishments are keeping a wary eye on an emerging concept of antitrust law. In a series of recent opinions, the Supreme Court has manifested an increasing concern for the economic independence of small distributors or retailers in their dealings with large suppliers. U.S. v. Arnold, Schwinn & Co., 388 U.S. 365 (pp. A-1, X-1, ATRR No. 309, 6/13/67); FTC v. Brown Shoe Co., 384 U.S. 316 (pp. A-7, X-4, ATRR No. 256, 6/7/66); Simpson v. Union Oil Co., 377 U.S. 13 (pp. A-8, X-1, ATRR No. 145, 4/21/64); Kiefer-Stewart Co. v. Seagram & Sons, 340 U.S. 211 (1951).

The economics of many franchised marketing systems pivot around a single set of business decisions: choosing the franchisee's suppliers. Franchisees often contract to buy from their franchisor or suppliers designated by the franchisor all products that are to be resold or used in connection with the main product or service marketed under the franchise. While the term encompasses a broad range of marketing systems, much of the business community has come to think of a "franchise" as primarily a device for exploiting an established trademark or trade name. And one of the obligations imposed upon a trademark owner, at the risk of losing his trademark rights, is to insure that any licensee maintains the quality-control standards associated with the product or service. Dawn Donut Co. v. Hart's Food stores, 267 F.2d 358 (2d Cir. 1959). When reasonably ancillary to the protection of a trademark or trade name, exclusive-dealing and supplier-selection licensing restrictions, which might otherwise be unlawful, have been upheld. Carvel Corp., FTC Docket 8574 (pp. A-14, X-1, ATRR No. 212, 8/3/65); Susser v. Carvel Corp., 332 F.2d 504 (2d Cir.) (p. A-11, ATRR No. 149, 5/19/64); Purity Cheese Co. v. Ryser, 153 F.2d 88 (7th Cir. 1946). Cf. Arthur Murray, Inc. v. Reserve Plan, Inc., 1969 Trade Cases Para 72,700 (8th Cir.) (p. A-3, ATRR No. 397, 2/18/69).

In addition to profits from the manufacture and/or distribution of products bearing their brands, franchisors have various ways of obtaining compensation for the use of their trademarks and the know-how they pass along to franchisees. Some collect a lump-sum franchise fee when the contract is signed; others collect royalties based on sales. In addition, almost all franchised retail and service operations sell or use supplementary, non-trademarked lines of products, accessories, or equipment. And it is often to the franchisor's advantage to take on the task of supplying his franchisees with these requirements. Cf. Griff's of America, Inc., et al., FTC Dockets C-1253-7, 3 Trade Reg. Rep. Para 18,071 (p. A-9, ATRR No. 326, 10/10/67). Other franchisors, while not attracted into the business of selling these items to their franchisees, do accept a commission from suppliers of these items on all sales to franchisees.

Such a three-party "commission" arrangement was the subject of the Supreme Court's most recent expression of concern for a small retailer's freedom to conduct his business as he sees fit. FTC v. Texaco, cited as the reference, rejected a court of appeals' suggestion that proof of overt coercion was essential to the result reached in Atlantic Refining Co. v. FTC, 381 U.S. 357 (pp. A-11, X-5, ATRR No. 203, 6/1/65; analyzed, p. B-1, ATRR No. 207, 6/29/65, reprinted at p. 76, Antitrust and Trade Regulation Today: 1967). The Atlantic opinion upheld an FTC order outlawing, as an unfair method of competition violating Section 5 of the FTC Act, an arrangement by a major oil company to receive a commission from a tire manufacturer on all sales of the tire company's tires, batteries, and accessories (TBA) by service stations retailing the refiner's gasoline. Atlantic and Texaco were each ordered to cease making or continuing in effect any contract with a TBA supplier under which the oil company would receive anything of value in connection with the sale of TBA to its dealers.

In reaching the same result in Texaco despite the lack of evidence of overt coercion, the Court found "dominant economic power" of an oil company over its retail dealers to be "inherent in the structure and economics of the petroleum distribution system." The crucial elements in "the structure and economics" of the industry are (1) one-year service-station leases terminable on 10 days' notice; (2) the oil company's right to terminate without advance notice if "housekeeping" provisions in the lease are not fulfilled; and (3) one-year gasoline-supply contracts terminable on 30 days' notice. In such a market, the opinion goes on, "the sales commission system for marketing TBA is inherently coercive. A service station dealer whose very livelihood depends upon the continuing good favor of a major oil company is constantly aware of the oil company's desire that he stock and sell the recommended brand of TBA."

Actually, the Court of Appeals for the Fifth Circuit had already held, in Shell Oil Co. v. FTC, 360 F.2d 470 (p. A-5, ATRR No. 250, 4/26/66), the other of the Commission's trilogy of TBA cases, that proof of overt coercion is not essential. The Fifth Circuit had rejected, though, a suggestion that in the Atlantic opinion the Supreme Court had adopted a rule of per se illegality for the TBA commission arrangements. While the Texaco opinion does not discuss the issue in terms of per se illegality, Mr. Justice Marshall, a member of the Texaco majority, has since described the opinion as adding the TBA commission arrangements to the list of per se antitrust violations, U. S. v. Container Corp. of America, 393 U.S. 333, 37 LW 4077 (pp. A-19, X-21, ATRR No. 392, 1/14/69).

A "per se rule of 'inherent' coercion" was also detected in Texaco by Mr. Justice Stewart, who dissented. He was not joined in dissent this time by Mr. Justice Harlan, who explained his change of views since the Atlantic decision, when he did join Mr. Justice Stewart in dissent: "Candor compels me to say that further reflection has convinced me that the portions of the Commission's order which the Court today sustains were within the authority granted to the Commission under Section 5 of the Federal Trade Commission Act."

The rationale of the Texaco opinion has brought expressions of dismay from the franchising industry and its lawyers. It is conceivable that many or most companies marketing products or services through franchised outlets and accepting "commissions" from independent suppliers could be found to display all the same indicia as the oil industry of "dominant" economic power" over their franchisees and to be supervising a marketing system that "is inherently coercive." Almost any franchisee operating under a one-year contract would appear to be as conscious as a Texaco dealer that his livelihood "depends upon the continuing good favor" of his franchisor. Under the typical franchise contract (unlike gasoline dealers' contracts), a terminated franchisee must look for an entirely new occupation or line of business, for he has signed a "covenant not to compete." Franchise systems for marketing services or food are likely to impose stricter "housekeeping" requirements than the oil industry. In some systems, franchise operating manuals impose such detailed standards as frequency of haircuts for countermen or clerks.

Conclusions

The Texaco case warrants close examination because the small retailer-large supplier relationship is so common in our economic system. And it is clear, from the Supreme Court's repeated expressions of concern for small retailers' freedom in business, that the "inherent coercion" doctrine evolved in the Texaco case is one that is likely to be applied in any typical franchised marketing system -- that is, any in which the franchisor is economically dominant.

For many franchisors, the Texaco opinion may mean that they can comply with the law only by avoiding any involvement with their franchisees' purchases from third-party suppliers of products that are not used in close enough association with the franchised mark to make restrictions on their source reasonably ancillary to protection of the mark. Disparity of size and economic strength between a franchisor and his franchisees makes the softest type of sales effort suspect. Indeed, absence of any sales effort at all may not save a "commission" arrangement, for "it is difficult to escape the conclusion that there would be little point in paying substantial commissions to oil companies were it not for their ability to exert power over their wholesalers and dealers." Atlantic Refining Co. v. FTC, 381 U.S. at 376.

The FTC orders upheld by the Supreme Court outlaw only the "sales commission plans" the oil companies have with TBA suppliers. The orders do not reach arrangements by which the oil companies might buy tires, batteries, and accessories and resell them at profits equal to the commissions they received from the tire companies. It is clear that the oil companies could not lawfully enter into exclusive-dealing arrangements with their retailers (Standard Oil Co. of California v. U.S., 337 U.S. 293 (1949)) or otherwise coerce the retailers into buying exclusively or primarily from them. But some antitrust lawyers feel that a purchase-and-sale marketing technique by the oil companies would free them to engage in more sales effort than the "inherent coercion" doctrine permits them to exercise on behalf of third-party suppliers.

Other lawyers point out, however, that the Supreme Court's tough talk about freedom of choice for retailers lends itself to extension well beyond third-party arrangements like the TBA commission plan. According to this school of thought, the scope and impact of the Texaco case on franchising in general depends on what use the Federal Trade Commission makes of the "inherent coercion" doctrine, for the Court stressed again that the Commission has "the task of defining 'unfair methods of competition.'" For example, it may be found unlawful for a large supplier to announce "suggested resale prices" if its retailer customers are small, operate under short-term contracts subject to termination on short notice, operate under strict "housekeeping" rules, and are subject to other restrictions typical of franchised market systems. But that is merely a possible extension of the "inherent coercion" theory; the Texaco opinion does not go that far.

Many of the characteristics of the petroleum distribution system that led to the finding of inherent coercion -- short-term leases, easy termination, housekeeping rules, etc. -- are of the sort cited by Congress as justification for the Automobile Dealers Act, 15 U.S. Code 1221-5. That Act requires "good faith" of car manufacturers "in performing or complying with *** the franchise or in terminating, canceling, or not renewing the franchise." "Good faith" is defined as the duty to act "so as to guarantee the one party freedom from coercion, intimidation, or threats of coercion or intimidation from the other party." Automobile dealers have had little success in suits brought under that Act (see analysis, "Automobile Dealers' Suits Against Manufacturers," p. B-1, ATRR No. 44, 5/15/62; reprinted at p. 47, Antitrust and Trade Regulation Today: 1967). None of the reported cases discloses any attempt to invoke an "inherent coercion" rationale.

- 0 -

Subject: Government Contractors   (Published 5/21/68)

Question

What antitrust pitfalls are present when a businessman sells to the government?

References

Armed Services Procurement Regulations, Paras. 1-311, 1-330, 4-118.
Department of Defense Directive 3200.9, July 1, 1965
U. S. v. General Dynamics Corp., 258 F.Supp. 36 (S.D. N.Y. 1966) (pp. A-1, X-1,
    ATRR No. 269, 9/6/66).
U. S. v. Johns-Manville Corp., 259 F.Supp. 440 (E.D. Pa. 1966) (p. A-12, ATRR No.
    274, 10/11/66)
U. S. v. Concentrated Phosphate Export Assn., 273 F.Supp. 263 (S.D. N. Y. 1967)
    (p. A-7, ATRR No. 323, 9/19/67), reversed and remanded, 393 U.S. 199 (pp.
    A-1, X-17, ATRR No. 385, 11/26/68)

Background

For most years since Pearl Harbor the federal government has contracted for goods and services on a vast scale. For example, for the government's fiscal year ending June 30, 1967, the Department of Defense alone awarded new contracts with a value exceeding $43 billion. Of this almost $23 billions were made without any form of competition as follow-on contracts or other single-source procurements. "Military Prime Contract Awards - July 1966-June 1967" published by the Office of the Secretary of Defense.

A practice of noncompetitive procurement has coincided with placing much of government procurement in a handful of business concerns. For the year ending June 30, 1967, the Department of Defense awarded some $25.6 billion in new contracts to 100 companies and their subsidiaries, and this was about 65 percent of the total amount of new contracts made that year by the Department. Indeed, 20 corporations took over 40 percent and the first ten about 30 percent of this $25.6 billion (BNA's Federal Contracts Report (FCR) No. 98, 12/4/67, Sec. D).

Government antitrust enforcement in the context of government procurement is commonplace as to collusive bidding. E.g., U.S. v. Carnation Co. of Washington, E.D. Wash., Justice Department Antitrust Case No. 1654, March 16, 1962 (p. A-21, ATRR No. 36, 3/20/62); U.S. v. Ward Baking Co., S.D. Fla., Justice Department Antitrust Case No. 1593, March 6, 1961. Indeed, the government procuring agencies are under a statutory duty to refer to the Attorney General any bid that evidences violation of the antitrust laws (see 10 U.S.C. 2305(d); 41 U.S.C. 252(d)). And Section 4A of the Clayton Act, 15 U.S.C. 15a, explicitly authorizes the recovery by the United States of any actual damages "in its business or property by reason of anything forbidden in the antitrust laws" -- a provision the government has sometimes invoked with success, most spectacularly in the early 1960's against manufacturers of heavy electrical equipment. But the impact of antitrust on government procurement is less clearly defined with respect to possibly anticompetitive conduct other than the bid-rigging and procurement-splitting agreements that traditionally have been the subject of federal antitrust litigation against government contractors. The government contractor operates in a market quite different from that of the ordinary businessman in that the contractor's market is created, defined and controlled by the government's procurement policies and practices. Consequently, some of the market factors that have competitive significance in other segments of the economy may become inoperative in government procurement.

This analysis examines briefly some antitrust problems government contractors may encounter in the contexts of (1) team-bidding arrangements for major weapons systems, (2) the sole-source supplier, and (3) bidding below cost, known as "buying in."

Team Bidding

A major development in defense procurement since World War II, given formal recognition and impetus by Secretary McNamara, is known as "weapons systems contracting." DoD Directive 3200.9 (July 1, 1965). An extension of it is called "total-package procurement." See ASPR 1-330. (See also "Problem Areas in the Weapon Systems Procurement Process," FCR No. 103, 2-7-66, Sec. K). Weapon systems procurement, as it has evolved, differs from ordinary government contracting in that the prime contractor is given full responsibility for the design and development of a total weapons system, such as a ship, aircraft or missile, the components of which usually transcend company and even industry product lines. Under "total-package procurement" the contractor's responsibilities also include the production and support of the weapons system. By contrast, under conventional government procurement, weapons were formerly built by contractors to detailed government specifications and major equipment components, usually the products of other industries (e.g., engines for aircraft, propulsion machinery for ships, weapons and communications equipment for ships and aircraft) were obtained by the government by means of competitive procurement and furnished by the government to the contractor for installation.

The scope and complexity of weapons-systems contracting and total-package procurement in transcending the resources and skills of individual companies and industries have made it necessary for companies to form teams, known as "contractor team arrangements," in order to compete for and perform weapons-systems and total-package contracts. Typically, the teams are formed in anticipation of the government's request for proposals for a particular weapons system.

When a number of manufacturers so pool their resources for a government contract, a specific but limited statutory antitrust exemption may be available. Section 708 of the Defense Production Act, 50 U.S.C. App. 2158, authorizes presidential approval "of voluntary agreements and programs to further the objectives of this Act." And Section 708(b), 50 U.S.C. App. 2156(b), provides that no action taken under an approved agreement relating solely to the exchange of "technical or other information" concerning military equipment "shall be construed to be within the prohibitions of the antitrust laws." In addition, Section 11 of the Small Business Act, 15 U.S.C. 640, exempts defense-production and research-and-development pools formed by small businesses with the approval of the Small Business Administration. But these exemptions are relatively narrow, and few approved pools have been in operation since World War II when the statutory exemption from antitrust was much broader (50 U.S.C.App. 1111).

Paragraph 4-118 of the Armed Services Procurement Regulation provides for Department of Defense recognition of "the integrity and validity of contractor team arrangements" that are fully disclosed, and further states that the Department "normally will not require or encourage dissolution of contractor team arrangements." However, that Department policy does "not authorize arrangements in violation of the antitrust laws." ASPR 4-118(a) defines a "contractor team arrangement" to be "one whereby two or more companies form a partnership or joint venture to act as a potential prime contractor or whereby a potential prime contractor agrees with one or more companies to act as his subcontractor(s) under a specified government procurement or program."

Joint Ventures

Lacking exemption, a typical weapons-system team arrangement may raise a number of antitrust problems quite unaffected by the contracting agency's recognition of the arrangement. Nor are these problems eliminated by the likelihood that the team-bidding arrangement can be considered a joint venture, for anticompetitive restrictions imposed by, or inherent in, joint ventures remain subject to the antitrust laws. Timken Roller Bearing Co. v. U.S., 341 U.S. 593 (1951); U.S. v. Minnesota Mining and Mfg. Co., 92 F.Supp. 947 (D. Mass. 1950); U.S. v. Imperial Chemical Industries, 100 F.Supp. 504 (S.D. N.Y. 1951). Indeed, if an attempt is made to give the joint venture strength and continuity through the incorporation of a separate team-bidding entity or through one prime venturer's purchase of substantial or controlling

ownership interest in the other participants, the combination becomes subject to the relatively broad antimerger provisions in Section 7 of the Clayton Act. U.S. v. Penn-Olin
Chemical Co., 378 U.S. 158 (pp. A-9, X-11, ATRR No. 154, 6/23/64).

However, if the members of the team remain independently owned joint venturers, their
entry into a joint venture is not necessarily an antitrust violation. After all, if they must combine forces to have the know-how and facilities to prepare a bid or perform the contract, their
combination increases competition for the procurement. A joint venture violates the antitrust
laws only if the purpose or effect of its formation, or the purpose or effect of terms in the joint-
venture agreement is to restrain trade or to monopolize. U.S. v. Imperial Chemical Industries,
100 F.Supp. at 557. In fact, one of the FTC's most recent advisory opinions (No. 245, p. A-9,
ATRR No. 357, 5/14/68) condemns as a "combination to fix prices" a proposed joint venture by
five producers -- actual or potential competitors of each other -- to bid on and perform a contract that is beyond the capacity of any one of them to perform alone. The Commission's staff
will not say whether a government procurement is involved.

There are several terms or conditions that, if found in otherwise lawful team arrangements, would raise antitrust questions. A commitment by each team member that he will not
quote prices to competing teams is clearly an agreement in restraint of trade even if its only
purpose is to prevent disclosure of technical know-how. An agreement by each member that he
will fill particular needs for the contract exclusively by purchase from team members is challengeable under both Section 1 of the Sherman Act and Section 3 of the Clayton Act, unless the
scope of the team's functions is limited and there is ample competition from other bidders of
comparable strength. With or without any specific restrictions on team members, an understanding that the team will stick together for subsequent procurements might give the venture
the stature of a conspiracy to monopolize in violation of Section 2 of the Sherman Act if the scope
of the team's activities is broad and competing bidders scarce or weak. Even in the absence of
that understanding, the members' "intimate association * * * in day-to-day manufacturing operations, their exchange of patent licenses and industrial know-how, and their common experience in marketing and fixing prices may inevitably reduce their zeal for competition inter
sese in the [private or future-government-procurement] market." U.S. v. Minnesota Mining
and Mfg. Co., 92 F.Supp. at 963.

Other conditions under which team members deal with each other may also create
anticompetitive influences for the private, nongovernmental market for the same or related
products. If team members or nonmember subcontractors and suppliers are selected for their
loyalty as customers of team members, the team may be engaging in the type of "reciprocity"
declared violative of Section 1 of the Sherman Act -- when it affects a "not insubstantial" amount
of commerce -- in U.S. v. General Dynamics Corp., 258 F.Supp. 36, 48-49 (S.D. N.Y. 1966)
(pp. A-1, X-1, ATRR No. 269, 9/6/66). Still, joint ventures have been recognized as legitimate devices of doing business and even as important means of financing research and development and of creating new competition in markets that need it. U.S. v. Pan American World
Airways, Inc., 193 F.Supp. 18 (S.D. N.Y. 1961), reversed on other grounds, 371 U.S. 296
(1963). The necessity for some ancillary restraints on the competitive activities of the joint
venturers themselves has also been acknowledged. U.S. v. Bausch and Lomb Optical Co., 45
F.Supp. 387 (S.D. N.Y. 1942), affirmed, 321 U.S. 707 (1944). The lawfulness of the ancillary
restraints depends on their reasonableness. Some of the "rule of reason" cases, such as U.S.
v. Morgan, 118 F.Supp. 621 (S.D. N.Y. 1953), and Appalachian Coals, Inc., v. U.S., 288
U.S. 344 (1933), involved joint ventures with some features closely paralleling those of
weapons-systems teams. A key element in both the investment bankers (Morgan) and the
Appalachian Coals ventures was combination pricing, and the factor that saved each was the
absence of power to control the market's price. In each instance, there was plenty of outside
competition to influence the price set by the joint venture. In the original landmark "rule of
reason" case -- Chicago Board of Trade v. U.S., 246 U.S. 231 (1918), control of market price
would have been possible, but the combination imposed only a temporary freeze of prices that
was effective when the Board of Trade was closed. The temporary freeze substantially increased the market's efficiency.

In most weapons-system procurement situations, there is competition at least between
two teams that may suffice to prevent a single weapons-system team from controlling the

procurement. In addition, the government itself could become a fearsome potential competitor quite capable of producing the item itself if the winning team's price were too high or its terms of doing business otherwise appeared to stifle long-term competition. The government is also protected by price negotiations based on the certification as to the accuracy, completeness and currency of detailed cost data of the winning team. Moreover, reasonableness can be written into team arrangements in the form of a specific limit on the life of the team or a provision removing all restrictions on team members once some other team or prime contractor is awarded the contract. If, as often happens, habit of association causes the team members to come back together each time proposals for a new weapons system procurement are requested, team-agreement language terminating the arrangement after each procurement may get little weight in an assessment of the reasonableness of any anticompetitive restrictions.

Yet it should be recognized that the weapons-system method of procurement for the large projects that transcend industry product lines makes the team arrangements necessary if these contracts are not to be made on a sole-source basis. This inducement and encouragement of team arrangements, particularly by the Department of Defense in order to create a competitive environment, may in itself lead to antitrust violations by the team members in their efforts to come together and bid on these projects. Thus it would appear that a result of this method of procurement by the Department of Defense has been to increase the risks of antitrust violation for contractors who engage in weapons systems procurement.

Sole-Source Suppliers

It would be a mistake to assume there is no competition for government contracts that are awarded on the basis of negotiation rather than competitive bidding. Indeed, the thrust of 10 U.S.C. 2304(g) is to require the solicitation of competition and the conduct of discussions among competing firms, to the maximum practicable extent, for negotiated procurements that exceed $2,500 and set a delivery time permitting such discussions. Competitive negotiation under this statutory mandate accounted for some $11 billion of new contracts awarded by the Department of Defense in the year ending June 30, 1967.

Nevertheless, some $22.7 billion in new contracts amounting to 52.5% of all Defense Department contract awards were also negotiated by the Department during the 1967 fiscal year without any form of competition. Hence in defense procurement at least the predominant position of the sole-source supplier may invite antitrust scrutiny.

In the sole-source situation, the possible antitrust violation lies in the monopoly the sole-supplier has apparently obtained in the market. Even if the government is his only possible customer, this monopolist gets no antitrust immunity under the procurement statutes such as 10 U.S.C. 2304. The statutes regulating federal procurement practices seem to have no bearing on the behavior of the industry into which the government goes to negotiate a contract and in which there may or may not be competition. Implied exemptions from the antitrust laws are strongly disfavored, even in federally regulated areas of business activity. U.S. v. Phila. Nat'l. Bank, 374 U.S. 321 (1963). Since the primary emphasis of 10 U.S.C. 2304(a) and (g) is on procurement by formal advertising or by competitive negotiation, it seems doubtful that Congress intended to confer antitrust immunity by virtue of the statutory authorization of a sole-source procurement.

The legality of the monopoly held by the government's sole-source supplier depends on the manner of its acquisition. If the contractor is a sole-source supplier because it is the only enterprise technologically capable of producing a project that will meet the government's needs, the only one with an essential patent, or simply a sole survivor "as a consequence of a superior product, business acumen, or historic accident" (U.S. v. Grinnell Corp., 384 U.S. 563, 571 (pp. A-2, X-14, ATRR No. 257, 6/14/66)), presumably its monopoly is lawful. But there are other ways of becoming a sole-source government supplier that may bring a contractor into collision with the antitrust laws. For example, creation of exclusive technological capability in a single source through formation of an unnecessarily broad team would produce an illegal monopoly.

If, moreover, the only manufacturer of a particular product has been marketing that product through distributors, he cannot, by halting deliveries to them, prevent those distributors from competing with him for government procurements. U.S. v. Klearflax Linen Looms, 63 F.Supp. 32 (D. Minn. 1945). Similarly, a sole producer of an item essential to performance of the particular type of government contract probably cannot refuse to supply competing bidders with that item. Fred Johnson Cement Block Co. v. Waylite Co., 182 F.Supp. 914 (D. Minn. 1960); Curtiss-Wright Corp., FTC Complaint, Docket 8703 (p. A-3, ATRR No. 267, 8/23/66).

"Lobbying"

Another way of becoming a sole source is to persuade the procuring agency to issue product specifications so narrowly drawn as to eliminate the products of competitors. Whether influence that obtains narrow specifications eliminating otherwise acceptable products is applied unilaterally by a single business enterprise or jointly by several manufacturers, difficult questions arise as to the antitrust status of the conduct. In U.S. v. Johns-Manville Corp., 259 F.Supp. 440, 452 (E.D. Pa. 1966), it was held that activities engaged in to influence the decisions of public procurement officials on product specifications "are constitutionally protected and cannot be the basis of a finding of violation of the antitrust laws * * * regardless of the intent with which they were undertaken." The decision was based on Eastern Railroad Presidents' Conference v. Noerr Motor Freight, Inc., 365 U.S. 127 (1961), and United Mine Workers v. Pennington, 381 U.S. 657 (pp. A-1, X-1, ATRR No. 204, 6/8/65).

In the Noerr case, the Supreme Court declared that "no violation of the [Sherman] Act can be predicated upon mere attempts to influence the passage or enforcement of laws. * * * We think it equally clear that the Sherman Act does not prohibit two or more persons from associating together in an attempt to persuade the legislature or executive to take particular action with respect to a law that would produce a restraint or monopoly." 365 U.S. at 135-6. The Pennington opinion described the Noerr decision as shielding "from the Sherman Act a concerted effort to influence public officials regardless of intent or purpose. * * * Joint efforts to influence public officials do not violate the antitrust laws even though intended to eliminate competition." As applied in the Johns-Manville case, the antitrust exemption accorded efforts to influence government actions is broader than the exemption as expressed and applied in the Noerr case. In both language and result, the Noerr opinion involved only attempts to influence "the passage or enforcement of laws." While Pennington spoke broadly of "attempts to influence public officials," there, too, the Court was dealing with efforts to influence the enforcement of laws. Under attack in Pennington were efforts of the United Mine Workers and some coal-mine operators to persuade the Secretary of Labor to set higher minimum wage rates under the Walsh-Healey Public Contracts Act, 41 U.S.C. §35 et seq., and to induce the Tennessee Valley Authority to curtail its "spot market" purchases of coal, many of which are exempt from the Walsh-Healey Act. Similarly, in Schenley Industries, Inc., v. N.J. Wine & Spirit Wholesalers, 272 F.Supp. 872 (D. N.J. 1967)(p. A-1, ATRR No. 319, 8/22/67), Noerr was read as exempting any "private effort to influence government action" even if the effort takes the form of actions that violate state law. But the opinion dealt with what it called "lobbying" without giving any further description of the acts involved.

In Johns-Manville, on the other hand, the district court gave antitrust exemption to combinations to influence the government's actions when it is functioning, not in a legislative or sovereign capacity, but when it is acting in the capacity of a buyer in the marketplace. Since the Justice Department elected not to take an appeal from dismissal of the Johns-Manville complaint, the district court's decision remains as precedent. But there are antitrust lawyers who believe that opinion gave unwarranted scope to the Noerr doctrine and predict that on further reflection the courts will extend full Sherman Act protection to the federal government when it is buying or selling in a commercial market.

Unfortunately, there is no clear line of distinction between actions taken by the Government as sovereign and those it takes as a buyer. The government often uses its massive buying power to advance policy -- to discourage racial discrimination in employment, for example. In fact, in the Pennington case, a TVA election to use Walsh-Healey Act procurement rather than spot-market purchases could be motivated either by a desire to give full effect to the statute or by a business purpose related to advantages of doing business with larger, more dependable suppliers of coal.

At any rate, antitrust exemption has been denied to influence that took the form of bribery. Rangen, Inc. v. Sterling Nelson & Sons, 351 F.2d 851 (9th Cir. 1965). And in Harman v. Valley Nat'l Bank, 339 F.2d 564 (9th Cir. 1964), the Ninth Circuit refused to apply the Noerr doctrine to a conspiracy in which the relevant government official is "a participating conspirator," although it did accord exemption to the acts of informing the official of "irregularities" in a competitor's conduct and persuading him to take enforcement action. One commentator has suggested that a distinction must be made between influencing government officials' policy or political decisions and influencing their business or "proprietary" decisions. Noerr granted full antitrust exemption to conduct designed to affect policy making. But if proprietary decisions are involved, applicability of antitrust law depends upon another distinction -- between appeals to a government official based on "considerations legitimate in the formulation of government policy" and appeals to a government official who "is himself interested in, or at least aware of, the improper approach to him." Note, Application of the Sherman Act to Attempts To Influence Government Action, 81 Harv. L. Rev. 847 (1968).

Mergers

A third way to become a sole-source supplier or at least reduce the competition is by acquisition of one's competitors. The manufacture and sale of products for which only the federal government has use apparently can represent a relevant market, national in geographical scope, for purposes of applying the antimerger provisions in Section 7 of the Clayton Act. U.S. v. Ling-Temco Electronics, Inc., 1961 Trade Cases 70,160 (N.D. Tex. 1961). Presumably, an anticompetitive merger in such a market might also constitute a combination in restraint of trade under the doctrine of U.S. v. First Nat'l. Bank & Trust Co. of Lexington, 376 U.S. 665 (pp. A-1, X-1, ATRR No. 143, 4/7/64).

Combinations that stop short of merger have also been attacked when they eliminate competition for government procurements. In U.S. v. Concentrated Phosphate Export Association, 273 F.Supp. 263 (S.D. N.Y. 1967) (p. A-7, ATRR No. 323, 9/19/67), a government Section 1 Sherman Act injunction complaint attacked the use of a common selling agency by five fertilizer producers to sell fertilizer to the Republic of Korea under the United States Foreign Aid Program. The complaint was dismissed on the theory that the common sales agency is entitled to antitrust exemption under the Webb-Pomerene Export Trade Association Act, 15 U.S.C. 61-65. The government has persuaded the Supreme Court to review that order (p. A-4, ATRR No. 351, 4/2/68) with a jurisdictional statement declaring that "however sweeping an agency's regulatory powers over procurement might be, they cannot supplant the antitrust laws as the basic safeguard of the competitive process." Moreover, the Comptroller General has recently ruled that, even though the Webb-Pomerene Act may exempt combinations in restraint of trade from the application of the antitrust laws, such exemption does not authorize procuring agencies to engage in procurements of coal for export that restrict available competition. Comp. Gen. Dec. B-159868. (Nov. 7, 1967, April 18, 1968, p. A-16, FCR No. 219, 4/29/68).

Buying In

There is no government procurement policy providing for the rejection of "buy-in" bids or proposals -- that is, offers that knowingly quote prices below anticipated costs -- and the absence of such a policy has provoked congressional criticism. Indeed, as a result of investigating an Army helicopter procurement said to have involved such "buying in," the House Armed Services Subcommittee for Special Investigation has recommended that the Department of Defense revise its policies "to provide contracting officials with sufficient direction and authority to dispose of, by rejection or otherwise, any attempted 'buy-ins' in accordance with DoD's stated policy on the subject." (See FCR No. 193, 10/30/67, Sec. K.)

The Defense Department response to this recommendation has been to restate its policy on buying in so as to stress the use of procurement methods such as multi-year procurement and priced options for additional quantities that will avoid or minimize the opportunities for buying in. The revised Department policy, set forth in ASPR 1-311, does not, however, specifically provide for the rejection of buy-in bids and proposals (p. A-17, FCR No. 219, 4/29/68).

In the absence of such a policy the Comptroller General has in at least three cases refused to approve the rejection of bids or proposals alleged to buy in. Comp. Gen. Decs.

B-156888 (July 2, 1965), B-158326 (May 5, 1966), and B-160065 (Nov. 17, 1966). For a discussion of the decisions and the ASPR policy on buying-in, see FCR No. 193, 10/30/67, Sec. K).

The Comptroller General's rulings are consistent with his historical reluctance to allow exceptions to the lowest-bidder test for making awards. After all, a price floor is usually the death of meaningful competition. But see Appalachian Coals, Inc. v. U.S., 288 U.S. 344 (1933). At the same time, there are market situations in which drastic price cutting can be the ultimate weapon in the destruction of competition. Predatory pricing is a common element of proven violations of the monopolization ban in Section 2 of the Sherman Act. U.S. v. Grinnell Corp., 236 F.Supp. 244 (D.R.I. 1964)(pp. A-1, X-1, ATRR No. 177, 12/1/64), reversed in part on other grounds, 384 U.S. 563 (pp. A-2, X-14, ATRR No. 257, 6/14/66). The legality of a buy-in under Section 2 of the Sherman Act depends upon a number of market and competitor characteristics. By definition, the successful bid is below the bidder's costs; if it is high enough to cover his costs, then he is not spending anything to "buy in." But even pricing below costs is not forbidden by Section 2 when the bidder is trying merely to stay alive in a market dominated by larger competitors, to get started in a market that is new to it, or to maintain certain skills or a particular staff organization needed for later profitable contracts. Nor does below-cost price cutting violate Section 2 when it is a defensive response to competitors' pricing practices. Union Leader Corp. v. Newspapers of New England, Inc., 180 F.Supp. 125 (D.Mass. 1959), modified and affirmed, 284 F.2d 582 (1960). Each of these circumstances negatives the existence of either actual monopoly or "exclusionary intent."

Size of Market

Another relevant factor is the scope of the market involved. If the government procurement involves an ordinary consumer product or one widely used in private industry, success merely in getting the government part of the business will often not involve either monopolization or impairment of the competitive strength of the other producers in the industry. The problem is a different one, though, if the procurement involves a product used only by the government. In that situation, the low bidder obtains at least a temporary monopoly in the market. True, someone will win such a monopoly every time the government satisfies its needs in a single contract. But even in a market where only one competitor can survive, the successful bidder must avoid "unfair weapons" and must rely on "superior skill, foresight, and industry." And below-cost pricing is an "unfair weapon" whose use shows the existence of an illegal exclusionary intent, unless the price reduction was defensive. Union Leader Corp. v. Newspapers of New England, 180 F.Supp. at 139, 284 F.2d at 586-7.

When the government procurement involves a product or service sold or used extensively by nongovernment buyers, another statute is relevant -- the Robinson-Patman Act, 15 U.S.C. 13-13c. That statute contains not only expanded price-discrimination restrictions first enacted as Section 2 of the Clayton Act, but also a prohibition against "unreasonably low prices." On the theory that a statute will not be construed as a restriction on government activities unless it is expressly made applicable to the government, the Attorney General has declared the Act inapplicable to sales to the government. 38 Ops. Atty. Gen. 539 (1936). See also General Shale Products Corp. v. Struck Const. Co., 37 F.Supp. 598, 602-03 (W.D. Ky. 1941); Rowe, "Price Discrimination Under the Robinson-Patman Act" 84 (1962). But the fact that a "buy-in" on a government procurement was accomplished by a bid lower than the price charged other buyers of the same or a similar product can be evidence of illegal monopolization, or of an attempt to monopolize, in violation of Section 2 of the Sherman Act. Union Leader Corp. v. Newspapers of New England, Inc., 180 F.Supp. at 139-147.

It would appear that buying-in is more likely to be treated as an antitrust problem by the Justice Department when it involves a product sold also to nongovernment buyers than when the government is the only buyer. As a sole buyer, the government has means of protecting itself that are not available to industry or consumers when they must buy from a seller who, by predatory procurement of a big government contract, has gained control of the market and thereafter increased his price. When the government is the product's only user and buyer, the "buying-in" problem under the current ASPR policy, the Comptroller General has observed, can be resolved by insuring that the contractor does not cut corners in performance and "that any amounts possibly excluded in the original contract price are not recovered in the pricing of change orders or of follow-on procurements." Comp. Gen. Dec. B-156888 (July 2, 1965). Some experts are skeptical about the effectiveness of that policy. In any event, a government supplier always faces potential competition, since the government has sufficient resources to develop its own production facilities or establish other sources if necessary.

Conclusions

While the markets involved are sometimes strikingly different from those that normally give rise to antitrust litigation, government contractors and government contracts remain generally subject to antitrust curbs even when the government is the only buyer. But the Justice Department's Antitrust Division and the Federal Trade Commission are likely to continue their policy of taking action against only hard-core violations like price fixing and government-contracting practices that can be shown to impair competition in non-government markets. Otherwise, the enforcement agencies are prone to view federal contractors as akin to members of a regulated industry and to leave control of their activities -- at least in the first instance -- to the procuring agencies and the General Accounting Office. Wise government procurement procedures can nullify even the dangers of frozen team membership in complex weapons-system procurements.

While both the Antitrust Division and the FTC have business review or advisory procedures that permit the solicitation of antitrust advice in advance of undertaking a proposed course of conduct, those procedures are too time-consuming to be of value to government contractors in most situations. By the time a contractor prepares his bid or proposal in response to a government request, there is not enough time left to clear it with the Antitrust Division or the FTC before it must be submitted.

Moreover, an Antitrust Division clearance letter or an FTC advisory opinion would at best give assurance only that the government will not sue the contractor seeking advice. It would give no protection against an antitrust suit by an unsuccessful bidder for three times the profits he would have realized if the contract had not been taken from him by anticompetitive practices. Private treble-damage recoveries are the most severe sanction imposed upon antitrust violators. Presumably, a government contractor who gets his contract by violating antitrust laws will be liable for treble damages to only one of the unsuccessful bidders -- the one who would have gotten the contract had there been no antitrust violation -- and perhaps that bidder's suppliers and subcontractors. The other unsuccessful bidders and their suppliers probably could not causally relate their losses to the antitrust violation.

When the contract has been negotiated without competitive bidding, it will sometimes be difficult for any unsuccessful bidder to establish that he lost the contract by reason of the successful bidder's antitrust violation. More often than not an award of a negotiated contract is based on factors beyond price, specifications, and bidder dependability -- including the predilections and prejudices of the contracting officer, who is a likely witness for the defense.

Nevertheless, the bigness of government procurement in relation to the total economy has increased the risks to government contractors of antitrust violation and liability. The risks are enhanced by the weapon-systems contracting method of procurement, which necessitates team arrangements that unavoidably may limit or inhibit competition. The vast extent of sole-source government procurement coupled with the concentration of government contracts among a relatively few large corporations tends to further reduce meaningful competition for a large share of defense procurement.

The Department of Defense in fashioning its procurement policies and in its procurement practices has a major responsibility for these increased risks of antitrust violation faced by government contractors and subcontractors. It is unlikely that Congress would afford any relief from these added risks, concerned as it is by the extent of noncompetitive procurement. The result appears to be that for many government contractors the antitrust implications of their dealings must be continuously and carefully appraised in connection with obtaining and performing government contracts, particularly those entered into without effective competition.

- 0 -

Subject: Bank Merger Act — The "Convenience and Needs" Defense   (Published 4/9/68)

Question

> What burden of proof is assumed by merging banks when they defend their merger
> on the ground that its anticompetitive effects are "clearly outweighed" by its
> effect "in meeting the convenience and needs of the community"?

References

> Analysis, "Bank Merger Act of 1966," p. 242, Antitrust and Trade Regulation Today:
>   1967
> Analysis, "Early decisions under the 1966 Bank Merger Act," p. 247, Antitrust and
>   Trade Regulation Today: 1967
> U.S. v. Third National Bank in Nashville, 391 U.S. 171 (pp. A-3, X-8, ATRR No. 347,
>   3/5/68)
> U.S. v. First City National Bank of Houston, 386 U.S. 361 (pp. A-8, X-33, ATRR No.
>   298, 3/28/67)
> U.S. v. Provident National Bank, 280 F.Supp. 1 (E.D. Pa.) (pp. A-1, X-1, ATRR No.
>   345, 2/20/68)
> U.S. v. Crocker-Anglo National Bank, 277 F.Supp. 133 (N.D. Calif.) (pp. A-10, X-1,
>   ATRR No. 330, 11/7/67)

Background

Under Section 18(c)(5) of the Federal Deposit Insurance Act, as amended by the 1966
Bank Merger Act (p. X-1, ATRR No. 248, 4/12/66), none of the three bank regulatory agencies
may approve any bank merger that may substantially lessen competition, tend to create a monopoly, or be in restraint of trade unless it "finds that the anticompetitive effects of the transaction are clearly outweighed in the public interest by the probable effect of the transaction in
meeting the convenience and needs of the community to be served." The "public interest" factors are then listed as "the financial and managerial resources and future prospects of the existing and proposed institutions, and the convenience and needs of the community to be served."

In the Houston Bank case cited above, the Supreme Court rejected the conclusion of a
number of district courts that the government has the burden of proving the absence of "public
interest" elements justifying an anticompetitive bank merger. Rather, the Court saw in the
legislative history of the 1966 Act an intent to make antitrust standards "the norm and anticompetitive bank mergers, the exception." The Justices therefore applied the "general rule"
that the burden of proof falls on one who "claims the benefits of an exception to the prohibition
of a statute."

Despite that holding and despite a ruling in the same opinion that a court reviewing a
merger approved by an agency should make an "independent determination of the issues," the
government continued to lose bank-merger cases in the district courts. In U.S. v. Third National Bank in Nashville, 260 F.Supp. 869 (M.D. Tenn.)(pp. A-1, X-1, ATRR No. 281, 11/29/66),
and the Crocker-Anglo case listed in the references, the district courts found the government's
evidence insufficient to show a substantially adverse effect on competition. Both also went on to
determine that, in any event, any competitive injury that may result from the mergers is clearly outweighed by enhancement of the merged banks' ability to compete more vigorously and to
provide new or expanded services to their communities.

They parted company, however, in finding changes made by the 1966 Bank Merger Act
in the rules for testing the competitive effect of bank mergers. The Middle Tennessee Federal
District Court saw in the Act an intent to return to the more permissive merger criteria of
U.S. v. Columbia Steel Co., 334 U.S. 495 (1948), whereas the Northern California Federal
District Court recognized the continuing importance for bank mergers of the market-concentra-
tion test of cases like U.S. v. Von's Grocery, 384 U.S. 270 (pp. A-11, X-1, ATRR No. 255,
5/31/66), and U.S. v. Pabst Brewing Co., 384 U.S. 546 (pp. A-4, X-23, ATRR No. 257, 6/14/66).
The Northern California judges viewed the Act's omission of the Clayton Act's Section 7 phrase

"in any line of commerce" as expanding the relevant market for testing competitive effect from commercial banking alone to "the wider and more realistic field of all institutions which compete either for the savings or investment dollar or for the extension of credit." The Tennessee judge, on the other hand, stuck to the "commercial banking" market, doubting that "such an important change in established antitrust law would be made by mere omission" of the phrase "line of commerce." The Nashville Bank decision has been reversed by the Supreme Court, but the Justice Department has decided not to take an appeal from the Crocker-Anglo judgment.

One federal district judge has enjoined a bank merger approved by the Comptroller of the Currency and attacked by the Antitrust Division, but he did so "reluctantly." In the Provident National Bank case cited in the references, the Philadelphia Federal District Court read the Supreme Court's Houston opinion and the Act's legislative history as indicating "that the convenience and needs test must be read restrictively. *** It merely allows bank mergers in those cases where the needs and convenience of the community are so compelling that competition will be enhanced rather than decreased by the merger. This will occur in only a very few instances." Describing the banks' burden of proof under the Act as "indeed a heavy one," the district judge assessed the competitive-effects and public-interest evidence before him as producing "at best *** a tie. However, in a tie situation, the banks necessarily lose."

Supreme Court

The latest word on the scope and impact of the "convenience and needs" or "public interest" test comes from the Supreme Court in its reversal of the district-court judgment in the Nashville Bank case. Speaking for a 5-2 majority, Mr. Justice White recognized that "securing better banking service for the community is a proper element for consideration in weighing convenience and need against the loss of competition." And he had no doubt the merger before the Court "would very probably end the managerial problems" that led the district judge to characterize the bank to be acquired as "not disposed to compete." According to Mr. Justice White, however, the district court's analysis overlooks a vital element: the possibility that "convenience and need" requirements could be satisfied without resort to merger. Although the district judge had discussed the Nashville bank's efforts to recruit new management and had concluded that management procurement is difficult for banks in general and an "almost insoluble" problem for the Nashville Bank, Mr. Justice White said the lower court should have made it clear "just how insoluble" the problem is. The district judge was instructed on remand to ascertain whether the bank's ownership had made "concrete efforts to recruit new management" and to assess the possibility of a sale of the bank to other owners who might be willing to face up to the management difficulties over a more extended period.

In assessing the competitive effect of the Nashville Bank merger, the Supreme Court rejected the district judge's suggestion that the 1966 Bank Merger Act revived the Columbia Steel doctrine. The Supreme Court agreed with the Justice Department's position that Congress had "no intention to adopt a different 'antitrust standard' for bank cases than that used generally in the law." To that statement, the Supreme Court also added a footnote disposing of the relevant-market issue that had divided the district courts. The footnote accepts the Middle Tennessee Federal District Court's determination that commercial banking in Davidson County, Tennessee, is the relevant market for appraising the competitive effects of the merger. The Justices found in the 1966 Bank Merger Act "no intention to alter the traditional methods of defining relevant markets."

Conclusions

The Supreme Court's decisions on the "convenience and needs" defense seem to support the Philadelphia Federal District Court's observation that the burden of proof assumed by merging banks relying on that defense is "indeed a heavy one." The Nashville Bank opinion clearly adds a criterion not explicit in the statute -- that the banks must show they do not have less anticompetitive means of procuring the community benefits that outweigh the anticompetitive effects of the merger. Yet the Supreme Court was careful to say it was adopting a test that "does not demand the impossible or the unreasonable." All that is required is "a showing * * * that the gain expected from the merger cannot reasonably be expected through other means."

Necessarily a premise for the Court's line of reasoning is acceptance of the concept that an anticompetitive bank merger can be justified even if only in extreme circumstances. Therefore, the Philadelphia Federal District Court seems clearly to have gone too far when it said "the needs and convenience of the community" must be "so compelling that competition will be enhanced rather than decreased by the merger." In fact, to require enhanced competition would be to impose a stricter antimerger rule than existed prior to enactment of the 1966 Act. Subsequent portions of the district judge's own opinion indicate a willingness to look for merger-justifying factors other than enhancement of competition. He carefully evaluated -- and found wanting -- evidence offered in support of the banks' claims that their merger would create an enterprise offering a broader range of services than are now available to the community and attracting job-creating enterprises to help solve the community's lagging employment growth.

Without saying so, the Supreme Court may also have interred a contention the Justice Department made in the Crocker-Anglo case -- that the "convenience and needs" defense is merely a restatement of the "failing company" doctrine. The Supreme Court's direction to the Nashville Federal District Court to check alternative ways of solving the acquired bank's managerial problems implies that, if no alternatives are available, the merger could be justified as a method of solving these problems, even though they fall short of putting the acquired bank in a "failing" condition.

In fact, even as far back as U.S. v. Philadelphia National Bank, 374 U.S. 321, 372, n. 46 (pp. A-9, X-7, ATRR No. 101, 6/18/63), the Supreme Court acknowledged that "arguably, the so-called failing company defense *** might have somewhat larger contours as applied to bank mergers because of the greater public impact of a bank failure." It would seem similarly "arguable" that what the Nashville Federal District Court called the "stagnant and floundering" condition of a merging bank will be given full weight both in assessing the merger's anticompetitive effect and in balancing such effect against public-interest gains.

Actually, there are two reasons why a true "failing bank" case is not likely to be litigated in court. First, the banking agencies would be derelict in their duties if they were to permit a bank to reach "failing company" conditions as that term is defined in International Shoe Co. v. FTC, 280 U.S. 291 (1930). Second, if a bank were found in such dire straits, the merger would probably be handled -- pursuant to paragraph (6) of the 1966 Act -- on an emergency basis, without the waiting periods provided for in the 1966 Act. Once consummated, paragraph (7)(C) provides that a bank merger is not challengeable under the antitrust laws unless it amounts to a violation of Section 2 of the Sherman Act.

- 0 -

Subject: The Webb-Pomerene Act   (Published 1/21/69)

Question

What future has the antitrust exemption of export trade associations?

References

U.S. v. Concentrated Phosphate Export Assn., 393 U.S. 199, 37 LW 4045 (pp. A-1, X-17, ATRR No. 385, 11/26/68)
"Webb-Pomerene Associations: A 50-Year Review," FTC Economic Report (p. A-11, ATRR No. 367, 7/23/68)

Background

Armed with a 1916 Federal Trade Commission report deploring the disadvantages faced by small U.S. businessmen in competing for foreign markets with foreign cartels and citing the threat of Sherman Act prosecution as a deterrent to potential exporters, a coalition of national business organizations persuaded Congress in 1918 to pass the Webb-Pomerene Export Trade Act, 15 U.S.C. 61. Section 2 of that Act exempts from the Sherman Act any association established "for the sole purpose of engaging in export trade." Exemption is granted the association's agreements and activities provided it does not act in a way (1) that is "in restraint of trade within the United States," (2) that is "in restraint of the export trade of any domestic competitor of such association," or (3) that "enhances or depresses prices within the United States." Under Section 5 of the Act, every association seeking to qualify for exemption must submit to the FTC a statement of its organization, membership, business, and practices. The Commission is authorized to investigate if it believes the law may have been violated and to recommend readjustment of the conduct of association business.

The debates that led to enactment of the statute revealed a controversy between those citing the advantages of cooperative arrangements to small U.S. exporters and those warning of anticompetitive effects upon domestic trade. Congress saw a clear need to encourage U.S. companies to look abroad for sales. The Act was expected to help American exporters in four ways: (1) by reducing the cost of exporting; (2) by making increased financial resources available to smaller American producers seeking to enter foreign markets to compete with powerful combination; (3) by obtaining higher prices and improved sales terms for American exporters; and (4) by obtaining lower shipping rates and other export service charges through concerted bargaining efforts.

In 1946, a study prepared partly by a Senate subcommittee, partly by the FTC, and partly by the Justice Department indicated that Webb-Pomerene associations were accounting for only 7% of annual U.S. exports, that few association members were small firms, and that even those associations made up of small firms were not able to compete more effectively in world markets by reason of any cost advantages derived from cooperation made possible by the Webb-Pomerene Act.

The Justice Department's portion of the report described the statute as "demonstrably capable of serious abuse" and observed that "where the association appears successful, the industry is likely to be one in which monopoly symptoms, such as market sharing, delivered price systems, patent control and the like, have been found." Small Business and the Webb-Pomerene Act, Senate Subcommittee Print No. 11, 79th Cong., 2d Sess. (August 21, 1946).

About the same time, FTC reports on the Copper Industry (1947), International Equipment Cartels (1948), International Phosphate Cartels (1946), International Steel Cartels (1948), the Sulphur Industry and International Cartels (1947), and the Fertilizer Industry (1950) found domestic anticompetitive results from association participation in international cartels. In addition, the Commission has struck down a Webb-Pomerene association contract requiring members to sell all their products exclusively through the association (Pacific Forest Industries and Export Trade Assn., 40 FTC 843, n. 1 (1940)), restrained activities aimed at buying out foreign competitors to seal off American "home markets" (Export Screw Assn., 43 FTC 980-1074 (1947)), and prohibited combination with other than association members even when the association's activities were apparently sanctioned by the Webb-Pomerene Act (Carbon Black Import, Inc., 46 FTC 1425 (1949)).

Court Decisions

In U.S. v. United States Alkali Export Assn., 86 F.Supp. 59 (S.D.N.Y. 1949), the first court decision under Webb-Pomerene, the Sherman Act was held violated by agreements of association members with foreign associations and companies dividing markets, assigning international quotas, and fixing prices in certain territories. "Congress did not intend * * * to abandon the rule of competition as applied to our export trade," the district court declared. In addition, the Alkali opinion outlawed the use of an export trade association to stabilize domestic prices by removing surplus products from the domestic market.

U.S. v. Minnesota Mining & Mfg. Co., 92 F.Supp. 947 (D. Mass. 1950), on the other hand, marked out areas of allowable conduct under the statute: "Now it may very well be that every successful export company does inevitably affect adversely the foreign commerce of those not in the joint enterprise and does * * * affect adversely the members' competition in domestic commerce. * * * But if there are only those inevitable consequences, an export association is not an unlawful restraint. The Webb-Pomerene Act is an expression of congressional will that such a restraint shall be permitted."

The dispute that characterized the debates leading to enactment of the Webb-Pomerene Act reappeared in the 1955 report of the Attorney General's National Committee to Study the Antitrust Laws. After reviewing the Alkali and Minnesota Mining cases, a majority of the Committee supported a view that the Act may help small business to deal with combinations authorized under foreign law. In any event, "the practical significance of the Webb-Pomerene exemption may easily be exaggerated," since only 44 export associations were registered in 1954 and 104 such associations had been dissolved. A dissent was noted by "several members" who viewed the Act as representing "a philosophy antithetic to that of the Sherman Act," one that "has occasionally been abused," and one that "has certainly not significantly helped small American exporters."

In mid-1967, the then Assistant Attorney General in charge of the Antitrust Division flatly recommended repeal of the Act. He noted that the number of active Webb-Pomerene associations had dropped to about 27 and that they accounted for only about 4 percent of total American exports. In his view, the Webb-Pomerene exemption no longer serves any useful purpose. It promotes misallocation of resources at home and "provides an unfortunate precedent for foreign nations." Donald F. Turner, "U.S. Antitrust Policy and American Foreign Commerce," International and Comparative Law Center, Dallas (p. X-1, ATRR No. 311, 6/26/67).

Congressional Hearings

Mr. Turner repeated his recommendation at hearings before the Senate Antitrust Subcommittee in June 1967 (p. A-19, ATRR No. 312, 7/4/67). In his prepared statement to the Subcommittee, Mr. Turner expressed the view that foreign buying cartels pose no threat to U.S. exporters and are not likely to develop into a problem in view of developing antitrust legislation abroad, especially in England and the Common Market. Furthermore, "the existence of an antitrust exemption for export associations inevitably affects competition at home (and thereby affects the American consumer). Every export agreement that affects the amount of a product sold abroad must inevitably affect the amount sold at home. And to the extent that the agreement allows exporters artificially to control prices abroad, it is likely to misallocate resources at home."

An earlier witness -- Professor Robert L. Curry, Jr., Sacramento State College -- had testified (p. A-17, ATRR No. 311, 6/27/67) that the activities of export trade associations sometimes inhibit foreign trade. He claimed that price-fixing agreements had been made for markets where the U.S. exporters had no effective competition and that the resulting price support tended to depress sales there. His solution was not repeal but reform -- an amendment giving the FTC power (1) to investigate the need for a proposed export trade association before it is allowed to begin operations and (2) to order the disbanding of any existing association for which it finds no need.

At those same hearings, though, the Commerce and Treasury Departments supported retention of the Webb-Pomerene exemption as contributing to expansion of exports and improvement of our balance of payments.

In July 1968 the FTC released a 50-year report on Webb-Pomerene associations. In general, the report confirms the statistics on the extent to which the statute is being used and the size of the companies able to take advantage of its provisions. It finds that associations that remained active for any length of time usually consisted of members producing a homogeneous product. "Efforts to market differentiated or branded products under the aegis of a Webb-Pomerene association have had little success." According to the Commission, three product categories have accounted for most of the active associations: food products, chemicals, and wood and paper products. It concludes that the Act's standards for antitrust exemption should be modified to make exemption available only to firms that can demonstrate need and that the standards for judging domestic anticompetitive effects be based on probable future effects rather than actual effects.

Cases arising under the Webb-Pomerene Act have reached the Supreme Court only twice. In United States Alkali Export Assn. v. U.S., 325 U.S. 196 (1945), the Supreme Court sustained the Justice Department's authority to file a Sherman Act suit against a Webb-Pomerene association without prior FTC investigation or recommendation. Last November, in the decision cited in the references, the Court held that a sale of goods procured under the U.S. foreign aid program is not "export trade" within the meaning of the Act and that, therefore, an agreement fixing prices for such sales is not exempt from the Sherman Act. The Court saw no intent on the part of Congress "to insulate transactions initiated, controlled, and financed by the American government, just because a foreign government is the nominal 'purchaser.' * * * The major impact of allowing the combination appellees desires would not be to encourage American exports; it would be to place the burden of noncompetitive pricing on the shoulders of the American taxpayer."

Concern for the American taxpayer has been expressed by the Comptroller General of the United States in a decision involving Webb-Pomerene protected activities. In 47 Comp. Gen. 223 (1967), the Comptroller General held that the disclosure of prices and allocations among competitors involved in protected Webb-Pomerene activities inevitably restricts competition in violation of the Armed Services Procurement Regulation requiring "maximum competition."

Conclusions

Whatever their merits, the persistent criticisms of the Webb-Pomerene Act have created a climate that causes some lawyers to advise businessmen not to rely on the statute as written. The Act's antitrust exemption is an effective shield for only those associations that stick closely to the statute's original justifications: collaboration of small firms for promotion of physical exports by joint sales efforts that include a minimum of concerted pricing and production planning and leave members free to deal outside the organization.

If it were not clear from the Supreme Court's general attitude on antitrust matters, the Concentrated Phosphate decision confirms that the Court takes a restrictive view of the Act. And the Justice Department's hostility to Webb-Pomerene associations is sufficiently well known to have been cited by a number of antitrust lawyers as one of the reasons why the Act and its antitrust exemption have not become a major factor in the development of export trade.

Moreover, some experts feel that Webb-Pomerene associations and their members should be alert to the possibility of enforcement action against them under new foreign antitrust laws such as the Common Market's rules on competition. Europe now has antitrust laws that reach import cartels and could be the basis for penalties against Webb-Pomerene associations.

The dispute running throughout the history of the Webb-Pomerene Act is a reflection of a conflict between two basic public policies: (1) the public interest in promoting export trade, especially in view of our current balance-of-payments problem, and (2) the public interest in promoting efficient allocation of our resources through competition. The statute's antitrust exemption has been getting the worst of that conflict for a number of reasons. First, critics like Prof. Curry have been able to point to instances when the pricing practices of Webb-Pomerene associations have suppressed exports. Second, the failure of Webb-Pomerene associations to attract small companies has convinced others that the exemption is used only when it is unnecessary for its intended purpose. Third, the efficacy of the statute's exemption in promoting exports is measured against all our export trade and, when so measured, appears slight, whereas its side effects on domestic competition and prices are viewed in the context of the few industries involved and therefore are seen as significant.

If there is a public interest in promoting export trade, some experts see no reason for turning down any trade stimulated through use of Webb-Pomerene associations, even if it represents a small percentage of our export commerce. In 1966 the deficit in our balance of payments amounted to less than 5% of our exports of merchandise. This view, however, does not face up to the real issue -- whether promotion of this relatively small amount of export trade is of such overriding importance as to justify an exception to a fundamental national policy.

It is also the view of some experts that elimination of official hostility to Webb-Pomerene associations would result in greater use of such associations to boost exports and perhaps make the exemption worthwhile. But there is no guarantee that the increased use will not bring with it the historical ratios of big business that don't need antitrust exemption and of artificial price increases that suppress export trade.

Nevertheless, resolution of the conflict is not likely to be worked out in favor of pure antitrust theory -- that is, of promotion of maximum competition to insure efficient allocation of resources. Too many other policies and influences are operative in foreign trade. Even if its use were stimulated by easing of Sherman Act enforcement, the Webb-Pomerene exemption would still represent an insignificant leak in the efficient-allocation-of-resources dike when compared with the anticompetitive results of the protections domestic businesses have obtained against imports. Both diversions from the route to maximum competition need to be related to a broad public interest involving considerations in addition to antitrust policy: national defense and foreign aid, as well as balance of payments.

- 0 -

Subject: Foreign Acquisitions   (Published 12/10/68)

Question

To what extent do the antitrust laws apply to foreign acquisitions by U.S. corporations?

References

U.S. v. Gillette Co., Civil Action No. 68-141-W, U.S. District Court, Massachusetts,
   filed February 14, 1968 (p. A-9, ATRR No. 345, 2/20/68)
"Inflation's Role in the World Economy," by William H. Chartener, Assistant Secretary
   of Commerce, September 25, 1968, Stanford Research Institute, San Francisco

Background

A book published in France in the Fall of 1967 predicted that "the third industrial
power in the world, following the United States and the Soviet Union could well be in fifteen
years not Europe but the American industry in Europe. Already today, in the ninth year of
the Common Market, the organization is essentially American." Jean-Jacques Servan-Schreiber,
"The American Challenge" (1967).

On the first day of 1968, the President of the United States announced foreign-investment
restrictions, including severe limits on new capital investments in foreign subsididaries, but
President-elect Nixon has said he will remove the restrictions. In any event, the curbs imposed
by President Johnson were backed up by a campaign by the Foreign Direct Investment Program
to encourage U.S. firms to borrow funds abroad to finance their overseas investments. As a
result, during the first two quarters of this year U.S. businessmen borrowed $1.1 billion on
bonds alone from foreign sources to finance foreign investments. William H. Chartener,
Assistant Secretary of Commerce for Economic Affairs, "Inflation's Role in the World Economy," Address, September 25, 1968, Stanford Research Institute, San Francisco.

In the meantime, a merger trend within Western Europe's own business organizations
may be making it difficult for U.S. firms to establish or enlarge beachheads there. In a recent
report on the causes and possible results of this trend, Business Week warns U.S. companies
operating in Europe that they will hereafter (1) be "dealing with tougher competitors who no
longer think exclusively of national markets" and (2) find fewer European enterprises to acquire
or join in joint ventures "as mergers gobble up hundreds of small companies." "Europe's
Merger Boom Thunders a Lot Louder," Business Week, November 23, 1968.

Enforcement Policy

Until recent years, foreign acquisitions had been attacked by the U. S. government only
incidentally in litigation aimed at broad conspiratorial or monopolistic patterns of conduct of
which the acquisitions constituted only parts. U.S. v. National Lead Co., 63 F.Supp. 513
(S.D. N.Y. 1945), Aff'd 332 U.S. 319 (1947); U.S. v. Imperial Chemical Industries, 105 F.Supp.
209 (S.D. N. Y. 1952). A foreign acquisition, standing alone, was first attacked in U.S. v.
Jos. Schlitz Brewing Co., 253 F.Supp. 129 (N.D. Calif. 1966), but the government's real object
was to prevent Schlitz control of a California brewery operated by a subsidiary of the acquired
foreign company.

On February 14 of this year the Justice Department filed an injunction suit under Section 7 of the Clayton Act attacking the stock acquisition by The Gillette Co. of a German manufacturer of electric shavers. However, the purpose of the suit was not to protect or promote
the export trade of the United States but to preserve a potential competitor for the domestic
shaving-instrument market.

One of the Federal Trade Commission's recent enforcement proceedings -- W. R.
Grace & Co., Docket C-1182 (p. A-3, ATRR No. 297, 3/21/67) -- attacked the acquisition of the third largest domestic producer of chocolate by a company that had no other
chocolate production facilities in the United States but whose South American factories
made it one of the world's six largest producers. The Commission's Section 7 complaint

attacked the tendency "to create a monopoly throughout the United States, or in portions thereof." Grace was described as "a leading exporter to the United States."

The legislative history of the antimerger provisions in Section 7 of the Clayton Act gives no clue to the intent of Congress regarding foreign acquisitions. Nor does the 1955 Report of the Attorney General's National Committee to Study the Antitrust Laws say anything about international mergers. "Antitrust Developments 1955-1968," the ABA Antitrust Section's supplement to that Report, devotes only a single paragraph to "Joint Activities and Mergers Abroad" (p. 59). Yet acquisition of a foreign competitor is a transaction to which the antitrust laws have been applied. U.S. v. Jos. Schlitz Brewing Co., 253 F.Supp. 129 (N.D. Calif. 1966); Dresser Industries, Inc., FTC Docket 7095 (p. A-7, ATRR No. 108, 8/6/63). The "commerce" protected by the antitrust laws is defined as including "trade or commerce * * * with foreign nations."

The Schlitz decision is the only reported court opinion exploring the impact of the antitrust laws specifically on a foreign acquisition unrelated to other anticompetitive conduct. But there no longer seems to be any doubt about the power of U.S. courts to apply the antitrust laws to foreign mergers. Contracts made and transactions consummated outside the boundaries of the United States and lawful where made or consummated have been held subject to the antitrust laws if they have an impact on the foreign or domestic commerce of the United States. U.S. v. American Tobacco Co., 221 U.S. 106 (1911); U.S. v. Aluminum Co. of America, 148 F.2d 416, 444 (2d Cir. 1945). And the federal courts ordered termination of joint foreign interests in the National Lead and Imperial Chemical Industries cases cited above.

The antitrust curb most frequently applied against mergers is Section 7 of the Clayton Act. In addition, an agreement by one corporation to acquire another or the actual acquisition itself is a "contract, combination * * * or conspiracy" that can be "in restraint of trade" and hence a violation of Section 1 of the Sherman Act. U.S. v. First National Bank & Trust Co. of Lexington, 376 U.S. 665 (1964). And in recent years the Federal Trade Commission has made gradually intensified efforts to subject consolidations, mergers, and acquisitions of businesses to the "unfair methods of competition" ban in Section 5 of the FTC Act. See, e.g., Beatrice Foods Co., FTC Docket 6653, (pp. A-11, X-1, ATRR No. 201, 5/18/65).

Clayton Act

These three statutes differ significantly in the jurisdictional language that determines their applicability to foreign acquisitions. Section 7 of the Clayton Act applies only to the acquisition by one corporation "engaged in commerce" of "another corporation engaged also in commerce," if the acquisition may substantially lessen competition "in any line of commerce in any section of the country." Section 1 of the Clayton Act defines "commerce" as including "trade or commerce with foreign nations." Acquisition of a foreign company falls within Section 7, therefore, only if the acquired firm is actually "engaged" in the foreign commerce of the United States and if its acquisition may lessen competition "in any line of commerce in any section of the country."

A foreign company has been treated as "engaged in commerce" for Clayton Act purposes because it produces and sells a product that flows continuously into the United States. U.S. v. Jos. Schlitz Brewing Co., 253 F.Supp. 129 (N.D. Calif. 1966). By analogy, a foreign business would seem to be "engaged in commerce" if it buys products flowing continuously from the United States, for "commerce" has been held to include the whole sequence of purchase, transportation, and sale. U.S. v. Sanders, 99 F.Supp. 113 (W.D. Okla.), aff'd 196 F.2d 895 (10th Circ. 1952). But there do not seem to be any decisions on the issue whether acquisition of such a foreign buyer could ever be regarded as affecting competition "in any section of the country" -- that is, whether competition among U.S. exporters occurs in this country or in their foreign markets.

Sherman Act

Section 1 of the Sherman Act, on the other hand, prohibits "every contract, combination * * * or conspiracy" in restraint of "commerce among the several states, or with foreign nations," and adds no requirement that the conspirators be themselves "engaged in commerce." A U.S. corporation might be found in violation of the Sherman Act -- though not of the Clayton Act -- if, in order to increase its power over a foreign market, it should acquire a foreign competitor that never produces for the U.S. market or buys U.S. exports. The Sherman Act's phrase "commerce *** with foreign nations" has been given broad scope. In Pacific Seafarers, Inc. v. Pacific Far East Line, Inc., 404 F.2d 804 (D.C. Cir.) (p. A-1, ATRR No. 378, 10/8/68), it was read as including U.S.-flagship-transport service between foreign ports.

Such an acquisition of a foreign company that has no direct connection with U.S. commerce may be subject to Sherman Act challenge for the acquisition's impact on U.S. export trade. One federal court has specifically based a Sherman Act order requiring dissolution of foreign joint ventures upon a finding that American-owned foreign factories precluded "American competitors from receiving business they might otherwise have received from the markets served by these jointly owned foreign factories. *** Nor is it any excuse that the use of foreign factories has increased the movement of raw materials from American to foreign shores. We may disregard the point that the books are not in balance when raw materials actually transported are set off against finished products potentially transported. It is more significant that Congress has not said you may choke commerce here if you nourish it there." U.S. v. Minnesota Mining & Mfg. Co., 92 F.Supp. 947, 961-2 (D. Mass. 1950).

The Sherman Act's impact is not limited to corporations; acquisitions of or by partnerships or associations are also subject to its ban on combinations in restraint of trade.

FTC Act

Section 5 of the FTC Act could be used as a powerful supplement to Section 7 of the Clayton Act; the FTC Act does not require that both the merging companies be "engaged in commerce." Like the Clayton Act, the FTC Act defines "commerce" as including "commerce *** with foreign nations." Furthermore, its substantive and enforcement provisions are explicitly made applicable, in Section 4 of the Webb-Pomerene Act, 15 U.S.C. 64, to "unfair methods of competition used in export trade against competitors engaged in export trade, even though the acts *** are done without the territorial jurisdiction of the United States." Unlike the Sherman Act, the FTC Act can apparently be used against acquisitions that merely threaten to harm competition or to eliminate potential competition. The Supreme Court has given the Commission broad discretion in implementing the language of Section 5. Atlantic Refining Co. v. FTC, 381 U.S. 357 (1965); FTC v. Colgate-Palmolive Co., 380 U.S. 374 (1965). Like the Sherman Act, though, the FTC Act is not limited to corporations.

As a practical matter, government civil proceedings to enforce any one of these statutes may be subject to no time limit. Under Section 7, the legality of a merger is tested by its anticompetitive potentiality at the time of litigation, regardless of how much time has passed and how much the market has changed since the merger was consummated. U.S. v. duPont, 353 U.S. 586 (1957). But see "The Backward Sweep Theory and the Oligopoly Problem," 32 ABA Antitrust Law Journal 306 (1966). And a corporate merger that constitutes a restraint of trade or an unfair method of competition is likely to remain so and thus remain subject to attack under the Sherman or FTC Act.

All the foregoing principles are equally applicable to the second major device by which U.S. companies enter foreign markets -- the joint venture. Any doubt that Section 7 of the Clayton Act applies to the transaction whereby a joint venturer obtains his stock ownership in the joint venture was eliminated by the Supreme Court's 1964 decision in U.S. v. Penn-Olin Chemical Co., 378 U.S. 158 (pp. A-9, X-11, ATRR No. 154, 6/23/64). In U.S. v. Monsanto Co., 1967 Trade Cases Para. 72,001 (W.D. Pa.) (p. A-27, ATRR No. 292, 2/14/67), the government obtained a consent order forcing a domestic corporation to drop out of a joint venture with a foreign competitor. The complaint was based on both Section 1 of the Sherman Act and Section 7 of the Clayton Act.

Conclusions

While theoretically there is much that could be done under the antitrust laws to stop foreign acquisitions, they have apparently not yet been selected by enforcement officials as an appropriate area for pioneering on a large scale. Despite the favorable ruling the Justice Department got in the Schlitz case, foreign acquisitions as such have been attacked by the government only incidentally in litigation aimed primarily at consolidations affecting domestic commerce. In the government's view, the Gillette case involves a foreign acquisition that would eliminate a strong future competitor for the domestic shaving-equipment industry and one that, assuming it to be a product-extension or conglomerate merger, clearly falls within either paragraph 18(a)(i) or paragraph 18(a)(iv) of its Merger Guidelines (p. X-1, ATRR No. 360, 6/4/68; analyzed, p. B-1, ATRR No. 367, 7/23/68).

Moreover, any extensive antitrust enforcement program in foreign commerce would probably be coordinated, through action of higher executive authority, with the many other government programs affecting foreign trade, including those related to the balance of payments, the national defense, foreign aid, and tariffs. In the present climate of antitrust enforcement, it seems probable that the threat of antitrust enforcement action hangs over the acquisition of a foreign company only if that acquisition is part of a larger anti-competitive scheme or if the acquired company is a competitor of the buyer that does business in the United States or is a likely potential competitor in the United States market.

Use of the antitrust laws to eliminate American ownership and support of foreign competition reducing the export trade of the United States would not be easy. Application of the Clayton Act's relatively broad antimerger provisions would raise serious jurisdictional problems. See Interview with Donald Turner, 37 ABA Antitrust Law Journal 290, 304 (Spring Meeting, April 4, 1968). And efforts to coordinate strong antitrust enforcement with such other unrelated policies as balance of payments might result in distortions of antitrust law. As now written, the antitrust laws are designed to "yield the best allocation of our economic resources." Northern Pacific R. Co. v. U.S., 356 U.S. 1, 4 (1958). Protection of one area of the business community from competitive encroachments by another -- e.g., U.S. exporters from U.S.-owned foreign factories -- has always been regarded as inconsistent with that purpose.

The recent increase in private antitrust litigation is also unlikely to raise any threat to foreign acquisitions by United States business enterprises. Antitrust litigation tends to be extremely lengthy, costly, and uncertain in outcome. When the suit complains of conduct affecting foreign enterprises and foreign commerce, the complexities and costs -- and hence the length and uncertainty -- of the litigation increase. Discovery programs, already burdensome, will often become unmanageable when access to foreign document files becomes necessary. Problems of market definition and proof of anticompetitive impact take on new dimensions. It is not surprising, therefore, that private antitrust litigation, to an even greater extent than government enforcement efforts, has concentrated on domestic commerce.

- 0 -

PART VII – RELIEF IN GOVERNMENT CASES

Subject: Anti-Monopolization Decrees   (Published 7/30/68)

Question

What special powers and duties, if any, does a federal court have in writing an injunction occasioned by a Section 2 Sherman Act violation?

References

U.S. v. United Shoe Machinery Corp., 391 U.S. 244, 36 LW 4412 (pp. A-7, X-34,
    ATRR No. 358, 5/21/68)
U.S. v. Grinnell Corp., 384 U.S. 563 (pp. A-2, X-14, ATRR No. 257, 6/14/66)

Background

"The kind of remedies courts apply in monopolization cases are as important an element of the present law on size as the standards of liability on which they make judgments." Kaysen and Turner, "Antitrust Policy" (1959), p. 109.

By its terms, the Sherman Act adds nothing to the traditional relief powers of a court of equity; it merely extends them to Sherman Act violations. Section 4 simply says "The several district courts of the United States are invested with jurisdiction to prevent and restrain violations of this Act; and it shall be the duty of the several United States Attorneys, in their respective districts, under the direction of the Attorney General to institute proceedings in equity to prevent and restrain such violations."

"The problem of the district court does not end with enjoining continuance of the unlawful restraints nor with dissolving the combination which launched the conspiracy. Its function includes undoing what the conspiracy achieved." U.S. v. Paramount Pictures, Inc., 334 U.S. 131, 171 (1948). In monopolization cases, the decree must "neutralize the extension and continually operating force which the possession of the power unlawfully obtained has brought and will continue to bring about." Standard Oil Co. v. U.S., 221 U.S. 1, 78 (1911).

The Supreme Court has repeatedly indicated that dissolution or divestiture is the remedy it expects the federal district court to try first as a means of undoing what an illegal monopoly has achieved. U.S. v. Paramount Pictures, Inc.; Schine Chain Theatres, Inc., v. U.S., 334 U.S. 110, 127-8 (1948); U.S. v. Crescent Amusement Co., 323 U.S. 173, 189 (1944). In "Antitrust Policy," Kaysen and Turner called "for a widespread application of dissolution remedies, on the ground that an increase in numbers and reduction of concentration is the surest and most durable way of reducing market power" (pp. 113-4). ("'Dissolution' is generally used to refer to a situation where the dissolving of an allegedly illegal combination or association is involved; it may include the use of divestiture and divorcement as methods of achieving that end. 'Divestiture' refers to situations where the defendants are required to divest themselves of property, securities or other assets." Oppenheim & Weston, Federal Antitrust Laws, 3d Ed., p. 858.)

Since World War II there have been at least five Sherman Act cases in which the government has asked for a decree of dissolution or divestiture against tight oligopolies or dominant single firms. U.S. v. Alcoa, 148 F.2d 416 (2d Cir. 1945); U.S. v. National Lead Co., 332 U.S. 319 (1948); U.S. v. Paramount Pictures; U.S. v. Grinnell Corp.; and U.S. v. United Shoe Machinery Corp. So far, the government has succeeded in obtaining a divestiture decree in only two of those cases -- Paramount Pictures and Grinnell.

Divestiture was granted against Paramount Pictures on appeal after such relief had been denied by the district court. The government sought to separate motion-picture film production from distribution. The district court, however, merely enjoined the producers from expanding their theater holdings in any manner and directed that all their films be marketed through competitive bidding. Because it considered the district court's findings on monopoliza-tion inadequate and the competitive-bidding procedure unworkable, the Supreme Court set aside both decree provisions and ordered the district court "to make an entirely fresh start on the whole of the problem." On remand, the district court granted the requested divestiture relief. 85 F.Supp. 881 (S.D. N.Y. 1949).

The Alcoa case was litigated during World War II and was decided on appeal before it was possible "to say what will be Alcoa's position in the industry after the war," (148 F. 2d at 446), since much of Alcoa's business was being conducted in plants leased from the government. Under the Surplus Property Act of 1944, 50 U.S.C. App. 1622, those leased plants were to be disposed of after the war in a manner designed "to discourage monopolistic practices and to strengthen and preserve the competitive position of small business concerns." Eventually, 91 F.Supp. 333 (S.D. N.Y. 1950), domestic divestiture was denied, although the district court saw danger in common control of Alcoa and Aluminium, Inc., a Canadian affiliate, and ordered their common stockholders to sell their shares in one or the other. The decree also struck down grant-back clauses in Alcoa's patent-licensing contracts. The district judge not only found the two domestic divestiture plans proposed by the government to be unworkable but also noted that the industry had in the meantime acquired two substantial new competitors in primary-aluminum production, "thousands of firms which fabricate aluminum products," and about 50 firms engaged in the production of secondary aluminum out of aluminum scrap.

In the National Lead case, the government proposed that National Lead and duPont each be required to dispose of one of its two principal titanium-pigment plants. But the Supreme Court pointed out that compulsory-patent-licensing terms in the decree seemed likely to create two new competitors and saw in the record no showing that the plants to be divested were adapted for independent operation. Nor was there any showing, for that matter, the Court went on, that four major competing units would be preferable to two. "Assuming, as is justified, that violation of the Sherman Act in this case has consisted primarily of the misuse of patent rights," the Supreme Court affirmed a decree directing nonexclusive licensing of the patents at a uniform, reasonable royalty.

Grinnell Case

Divestiture relief separating the Grinnell Corporation from three subsidiaries found to give it an illegal alarm-service monopoly was awarded the government in the district court (236 F.Supp. 244 (D. R.I.), pp. A-1, X-1, ATRR No. 177, 12/1/64). But the Supreme Court agreed with the government that it was entitled to further divestiture breaking up one of the subsidiaries, which was found to have a complete monopoly of burglar-protection and fire-protection central-station services in 92 of the 115 cities in which it was doing business. Again the Supreme Court stressed "that adequate relief in a monopolization case should put an end to the combination and deprive the defendants of any of the benefits of the illegal conduct, and break up or render im-potent the monopoly power found to be in violation of the Act." The decree entered on remand (p. A-8, ATRR No. 315, 7/25/67) also directed that subsidiary to reduce its five-year service contracts to two-year contracts. And all the defendant companies were ordered to make their products available for purchase on nondiscriminatory terms.

United Shoe Case

The district court, in U.S. v. United Shoe Machinery Corp., 110 F. Supp., 295 (D. Mass. 1953), did not grant the government's request that United Shoe Machinery Corp. be dis-solved into three separate shoe-machinery-manufacturing companies. The proposal was la-beled "unrealistic," since United did all its manufacturing at one plant that "cannot be cut into three equal and viable parts." (Indeed, the district judge indicated he did not think the govern-ment itself really took the proposal seriously.) Instead, the decree enjoined United Shoe from further monopolization, ordered it to offer its machines for sale instead of exclusively for leasing, limited the leases to five-year terms, banned certain restrictive lease conditions, required nonexclusive licensing of patents on reasonable nondiscriminatory royalty terms, restricted the acquisition of further patents, and prohibited the acquisition of any shoe-machiner manufacturer or any second-hand shoe machinery. The government took no appeal from the de-cree, and, when United Shoe took an appeal, the order was affirmed per curiam (347 U.S. 521 (1954)).

The decree in United Shoe went on to provide, however, that in ten years "both parties shall report to this court the effect of this decree, and may then petition for its modification, in view of its effect in establishing workable competition." At the time, the district judge seems to have regarded his decree as a tentative one, for he remarked that the more severe relief sought by the government "would be undesirable, at least until milder remedies have been tried" (110 F.Supp. at 349). The defendant was "forewarned by the decree itself that if it abuses this flexibility, the court after the entry of this decree may modify it. Thus the decree invokes the precedent not of Draco, but of Damocles and Dionysius" (110 F.Supp. at 351).

Pursuant to the ten-year trial clause, the government reported on January 1, 1965, that United Shoe continued to dominate the shoe-machinery market and that additional relief was accordingly necessary. The court was asked to order United Shoe to submit a plan for dividing its business into two fully competing companies but decided it had no power to modify the original decree except on a clear showing of grievous wrong "evoked by new and unforeseen circumstances" (266 F.Supp. 328, 334, p. A-23, ATRR No. 301, 4/18/67).

According to the Supreme Court, the district judge misread U.S. v. Swift & Co., 286 U.S. 106 (1932), in his delineation of his power to modify a decree. The Swift opinion rejected a plea by major meat packers that a 1920 Sherman Act consent decree be modified to readmit them to the businesses of meat retailing, stockyard operation, grocery manufacturing, and milk distribution. While the Court did not doubt "the power of a court of equity to modify an injunction in adaptation to changed conditions, though it was entered by consent," it found the packers' powerful economic position had not changed enough to warrant modification of the decree.

If the government can prove its allegations that United Shoe still dominates its market and that "workable competition" has not been restored by the decree, "the present case is the obverse of the situation in Swift." Even if the district court had omitted from its decree the provision for a later report and petition for modification, Mr. Justice Fortas declared, it would still have been the court's duty to modify the decree on a showing that it had not achieved adequate relief. "The duty of the court to modify the decree so as to assure the complete extirpation of the illegal monopoly *** is implicit in the findings of violations of Section 2 and in the decisions of this Court as to the type of remedy which must be prescribed.

Although Mr. Justice Fortas again stressed the necessity of writing a decree that will both terminate the illegal monopoly and deny to the defendants the fruits of the violation and insure that there remain no practices likely to result in future monopolization, divestiture was not mandated for all monopolization cases. The district judge "may, if circumstances warrant, accept a formula for achieving the result by means less drastic than immediate dissolution or divestiture."

Trial Court Discretion

In neither Grinnell nor United Shoe did the Supreme Court dictate the terms of the decree to be issued. Rather it left the details and precise scope to the district judge, merely directing "reconsideration" of certain government requests that appear to have been rejected for invalid reasons and at one point taking pains to merely "suggest" an additional injunctive term. Outwardly, at least, the Supreme Court has wavered in the deference it has shown the district court's choice of remedies. In some Sherman Act decisions, the Court has stressed that "the fashioning of a decree in an antitrust case in such way as to prevent future violations and eradicate existing evils, is a matter which rests largely in the discretion of the court." Associated Press v. United States, 326 U.S. 1, 22 (1945). See also, International Salt Co. v. U.S., 332 U.S. 392, 400-401 (1947); U.S. v. duPont, 353 U.S. 586, 607-8 (1957). In others, though, the Court simply ordered modification of district court judgments without discussing the weight to be assigned the trial judge's selection of the form of relief -- action that was criticized in the dissenting opinion of Mr. Justice Frankfurter in the Paramount case. See also Standard Oil Co. v. U.S., 221 U.S. 1 (1911); U.S. v. American Tobacco Co., 221 U.S. 106 (1911); Timken Roller Bearing Co. v. U.S., 341 U.S. 593 (1951); and especially Hartford-Empire Co. v. U.S., 323 U.S. 386 (1945).

In U.S. v. United States Gypsum Co., 340 U.S. 76, 89 (1950), after citing the statement quoted above from the Associated Press case, the Court said: "We have never treated that power as one of discretion, subject only to reversal for gross abuse. Rather we have felt an obligation to intervene in this most significant phase of the case when we concluded there were inappropriate provisions in the decree." And in its subsequent opinion on relief in the duPont-General Motors case, 366 U.S. 316, 323 (1961), the Court said: "In sum, we assign to the district courts the responsibility initially to fashion the remedy, but recognize that while we accord due regard and respect to the conclusion of the district court, we have a duty ourselves to be sure that a decree is fashioned which will effectively redress proved violations of the antitrust laws." (Emphasis in original.) This time the Court gave a reason for assigning the district court's remedial rulings less weight in antitrust cases than in other litigation. "Our practice reflects the situation created by the congressional authorization, under Section 2 of the Expediting Act, of a direct appeal to this Court from the judgment of relief fashioned by a single judge. Congress has deliberately taken away the shield of intermediate appellate review by a Court of Appeals, and left with us alone the responsibility of affording the parties a review of his determination. This circumstance imposes a special burden upon us, for, as Mr. Justice Roberts said for the court, ' *** It is unthinkable that Congress has entrusted the enforcement of a statute of such far-reaching importance to the judgment of a single judge, without review of the relief granted or denied by him,' Hartford-Empire Co. v. United States, 1945, 324 U.S. 570, 571."

Conclusions

Regardless of the words the Supreme Court uses to define the scope of its review of the relief granted in Sherman Act cases, it is clear that the district courts have had, and probably will continue to have, the more important voice in framing decrees. Although the decrees in the really significant cases are generally challenged on appeal by one side or the other, appeals as a rule attack only some parts of the relief awarded. And it has been the district judges who, with the benefit of knowledge gained through the "painstaking process of adjudication" Mr. Justice Frankfurter referred to in the Paramount case, have developed such ingenious remedies as compulsory licensing of patents. In fact, even divestiture is a remedy that originated in the district courts. See Standard Oil Co. v. U.S., 221 U.S. 1, 78 (1911).

Nevertheless, the emphasis the Supreme Court has repeatedly placed on divestiture or dissolution suggests to some antitrust experts that a decree like Judge Wyzanski's in United Shoe should be regarded as establishing, not a ten-year set of curbs on the defendant's commercial practices, but a ten-year moratorium on divestiture, while less drastic remedies are tested -- i.e., while the defendant is given an opportunity to restore competitive conditions without drastic intervention by the court. That view of the decree is supported by the observation in the Supreme Court's opinion that the district court's reservation of jurisdiction was immaterial -- that the district judge would have been bound to modify the decree in any event if ten years' experience showed it had not achieved adequate relief.

While the Sherman Act on its face does not seem to add anything to the traditional remedial powers of a court of equity, some lawyers maintain that the courts can properly be regarded as having broader injunctive powers in Sherman Act cases than in other equity proceedings. They point out that Congress took unusual action when, having already made the Sherman Act a criminal law, it added enforcement powers based on the broad authority of a court of equity. Congress went even further to stress its reliance on antitrust injunctions when, in Section 6(c) of the FTC Act, it assigned the Federal Trade Commission responsibility to investigate compliance with the Antitrust Division's decrees and report its findings to the Attorney General. And Section 7 suggests that the Commission be used "as a master in chancery, to ascertain and report an appropriate form of decree" in suits brought by the Justice Department.

The United Shoe opinion has been read in some circles as contributing an important new weapon to the arsenal of the antitrust enforcement agencies. According to Business Week, May 25, 1968, the Justice Department acquired "a hefty fist," for it can now go back to court for additional relief in "a previously settled monopoly case." Some antitrust lawyers see, in Mr. Justice Fortas' discussion of the Swift case, a significant failure to distinguish between orders entered by consent and those entered after full litigation. He described Swift as teaching "that a decree may be changed upon an appropriate showing." While the absence of a record, of findings of fact, or even of an adjudication that a violation occurred would seem to be an insurmountable barrier to enlargement of a consent decree in the way Judge Wyzanski is being asked to modify the United Shoe judgment, this is not the first time the Supreme Court has lumped consent judgments with litigated judgments in discussing subsequent modification. The Swift opinion itself said: "The result is all one whether the decree has been entered after litigation or by consent. American Press Ass'n v. United States 245 Fed. 91. In either event, a court does not abdicate its power to revoke or modify its mandate, if satisfied that what it has been doing has been turned through changing circumstances into an instrument of wrong. We reject the argument for the intervenors that a decree entered upon consent is to be treated as a contract and not as a judicial act."

- 0 -

Question

To what extent do existing consent decrees inhibit antitrust enforcement?

Reference

"Antitrust Consent Decrees: Some Basic Policy Questions," address by Assistant
Attorney General Donald F. Turner (pp. A-14, X-1, ATRR No. 336, 12/19/67)

Background

Almost three fourths of the civil antitrust actions filed by the Justice Department have
been terminated by decrees formulated through agreement of the parties without a trial. In addition, the government and the defendants sometimes agree upon the form and content of a decree after a trial and an adjudication of a violation. While judgments agreed to after trial are
sometimes called consent decrees, the present discussion relates only to consent decrees entered without trial. Probably the most important distinction between the two types of negotiated
decrees is that one represents an adjudication of a violation and the other does not. In fact,
decrees entered without trial ordinarily recite that they are entered without findings or adjudication that the defendants have in fact violated the antitrust laws. But see U.S. v. Lake Asphalt
& Petroleum Co., 1959 Trade Cases 69,835 (D. Mass.).

The advantages to the government of settling cases without trial were recognized by
Congress in the Clayton Act. It was to avoid any deterrent to consent settlements that Congress
added to Section 5 the proviso that the authorization for using government judgments as "prima
facie evidence" in private damage actions does not apply to consent judgments.

From the Antitrust Division's point of view, the consent-settlement procedure offers
possibilities for quick disposition of cases and more effective allocation of personnel and funds.
It also affords the Antitrust Division a continuing opportunity to appraise both factual and legal
considerations in the light of additional information made available during negotiations. Sometimes the government seeks through negotiations to obtain quick relief, or some particular
form of relief, when it otherwise might be difficult to obtain. In other situations, the Division,
to get effective relief as to some parts of the litigation, bypasses problems of lesser importance, areas where its proof is weak, or areas where it discovers that its original conception
of relief would work unnecessary hardship or possible injury to third parties. Consequently,
the negotiated consent settlement can involve concessions by the Antitrust Division to obtain
those objectives the Division regards as significant.

Since there is no public legal or factual record against which a consent judgment can be
evaluated, the decree is viewed publicly against only the typically broad allegations of the
government's complaint. Under these circumstances, even when no real concession is made,
it may well appear that the Antitrust Division has settled for a consent decree less restrictive
than it might have obtained after full litigation.

In any event, some of the consent judgments entered into by the government have been
criticized to the extent that questions have been raised as to the value of the consent judgment
as an effective instrument of antitrust policy. For example, in 1958 the House Antitrust Subcommittee conducted an investigation of the Justice Department's consent-decree program
after receiving complaints that "consent decree procedures essentially amounted to a compromise of the government's interest" and that consent decrees "often deprived the government of
relief it could have obtained if it had litigated its case." In its printed report, the Subcommittee examined two decrees in detail -- U.S. v. Western Electric Co., 1956 Trade Cases 71,134
(D. N.J.), known as "the AT&T case"; and U.S. v. Atlantic Refining Co., December 23, 1941
(D. Dist. Col.), known as the Oil Pipe Line decree -- and found each of those decrees to have
"little value as instruments of antitrust policy." "In addition to the compromise of adequate
relief," the report went on, "consent settlements of antitrust cases result in a substantial
lessening, if not the virtual elimination, of the deterrent effect the antitrust laws have on

business operations." Report of Subcommittee No. 5, House Judiciary Committee, 86th Congress, on Consent Decree Program of the Department of Justice, January 30, 1959.

Injunctive provisions, whether formulated by consent or litigation, are generally of indefinite duration, and the passage of time often brings economic or market changes that render the prohibitions ineffective or meaningless. Occasionally special provisions have been added in an effort to make the decree a more flexible device. For example, provision has been made for termination of the decree or some of its provisions on the occurrence of a specific event or the development of certain conditions. U.S. v. International Nickel Co., 1948-49 Trade Cases 62,280 (S.D. N.Y. 1948); U.S. v. American Lead Pencil Co., 1954 Trade Cases 67,676 (D. N.J.)

A number of other consent decrees have included provisions for later modification upon proof of specified circumstances -- e.g., U.S. v. General Motors Corp., 1965 Trade Cases 81,802 (E.D. Mich.) (pp. A-2, X-3, ATRR No. 230, 12/7/65); U.S. v. American Lead Pencil Co., 1954 Trade Cases 69,173 (D. N.J.); U.S. v. Libbey-Owens-Ford Glass Co., 1948-49 Trade Cases 62,802 (N.D. Ohio 1948); U.S. v. International Harvester Co., 274 U.S. 693, 697 (1927); U.S. v. Columbia Artists Management, Inc., 1955 Trade Cases 68,173. Following its defeat in the International Harvester case, the government did not seek additional relief under a modification clause until U.S. v. United Shoe Machinery Corp., 226 F.Supp. 328 (p. A-23, ATRR No. 301, 4/18/67), probable jurisdiction noted, 36 LW 3226 (p. A-2, ATRR No. 334, 12/5/67).

More typically, a consent order contains merely a "retention of jurisdiction" clause: "Jurisdiction is retained for the purpose of enabling any party to this Final Judgment to apply to this Court at any time for such further orders and directions as may be necessary or appropriate for the construction or carrying out of this Final Judgment, [or] for the modification of any of the provisions thereof." Petitions for modification under that clause have almost always failed (e.g., U.S. v. Swift & Co., 286 U.S. 106 (1932); U.S. v. Swift & Co., 189 F.Supp. 885 (N.D. Ill. 1960), affirmed 367 U.S. 909 (1961)), although language in some Supreme Court opinions suggests that modification may be more easily obtainable by the government than by defendants (Chrysler Corp. v. U.S., 316 U.S. 556 (1942); Hughes v. U.S., 342 U.S. 353, 357 (1952)).

In any event, inclusion of the standard clause would not seem to change anything. "Whether the decree has been entered after litigation or by consent * * *, a court does not abdicate its power to revoke or modify its mandate if satisfied that what it has been doing has been turned through changing circumstances into an instrument of wrong." U.S. v. Swift & Co., 286 U.S. at 114-115. Except in the Chrysler case, however, the government has never succeeded in obtaining modification of an antitrust consent judgment over the defendant's opposition. For example, an unsuccessful attempt was made in Ford Motor Co. v. U.S., 335 U.S. 303 (1948).

In U.S. v. RCA, 46 F.Supp. 654 (D. Del. 1942), the government moved to vacate a set of ten-year-old consent decrees so it could sue for stronger decrees. The motion was denied on the theory that the consent decrees conferred a benefit on the defendants and are "a bar to any attempt by the government to relitigate the issues raised in the suit or to seek relief with respect thereto additional to that given by the consent decrees." Nevertheless, the government filed a new action against RCA in 1954. The complaint's allegations of antitrust violations were limited to activities post-dating the filing of the consent decree. The complaint apparently resulted from the discovery of evidence during a grand jury proceeding in which RCA pleaded the consent decree as a bar to the grand jury's subpoena. The Federal District Court for Southern New York refused to quash the subpoena, holding that the consent decree did not bar a subsequent grand jury investigation. Application of Radio Corp. of America, 13 F.R.D. 167 (S.D. N.Y. 1952).

Another attempt to bar a government antitrust action against a defendant already subject to a broad consent decree was challenged in U.S. v. Aluminum Co. of America, 20 F.Supp. 608 (W.D. Pa. 1937). The second suit was allowed to continue because 62 additional defendants were named in the second complaint, a different legal theory was being advanced, and a different relief was being sought. Both the rule applied by the district court and its analysis of the consent decree and the pleadings were upheld by the Supreme Court (302 U.S. 230 (1937)).

In the 1959 report of the House Antitrust Subcommittee, cited above, one of the reasons given for the report's expressions of concern about the consent decree program was the apparent finality of the decrees. "Although antitrust consent decrees are not adjudications that defendants in fact and law have violated the antitrust statutes, they nonetheless have been held to provide, as do other civil judgments, a basis for invoking the doctrine of res judicata and the concept of estoppel associated therewith. Thus, defendants are precluded from collaterally attacking a consent decree on the ground that there are errors contained therein, and the Government is foreclosed from litigating the matters previously concluded by consent." At page 3.) Yet, in U.S. v. International Building Co., 345 U.S. 502 (1953), the Supreme Court said the doctrine of res judicata or estoppel by judgment should not "become a device by which a decision not shown to be on the merits would forever foreclose inquiry into the merits."

In any event, the present head of the Antitrust Division thinks the government can sue for greater relief than that afforded by an existing consent decree. In his December 13 address to the Association of the Bar of the City of New York, he said: "Whatever may be the proper dimensions of the Government's right to secure substantial new relief without adjudication of liability, I believe that the Government should have a considerably broader right to secure further relief when it is prepared to go to trial on issues of liability, either in a reopened earlier proceeding or on the basis of a new complaint. In my view, a consent decree is no 'legal' bar at all, to, say, a new antitrust complaint by the Government, even if the new complaint contains precisely the same charges as those in the original suit. This is not to say that the Government's right to institute and proceed with a new suit is untrammeled; the propriety of permitting the renewed attack is subject to some equitable limitations imposed by the courts. But the limitations imposed by what we might call 'equitable estoppel' should be less demanding than the limitations imposed when the Government seeks modification of a consent decree without litigation of the issues of liability. Specifically, I believe that in appropriate cases the Government should not be precluded from prosecuting a new suit, seeking new relief, merely because there has been no substantial change in circumstances or because the proposed relief goes beyond the 'purpose' of the original consent decree. The public interest in the effective enforcement of the antitrust laws makes it essential that the Government be reasonably free to cure anticompetitive practices or anticompetitive conditions which an earlier consent decree -- for whatever reason -- failed to cure."

On the day before Mr. Turner made his address, the Antitrust Division had filed in the Supreme Court a memorandum defending one of its consent decrees against a charge that it sanctions antitrust violations. Addressing the court as amicus curiae in K-91, Inc., v. Gershwin Publishing Corp., No. 147 (p. A-4, ATRR No. 337, 12/26/67), the government said: "We do not understand the court below to have held that the consent decree now in force against ASCAP of itself makes lawful what would otherwise be unlawful * * *. To the extent that ASCAP's activities, whether under the consent decree or unregulated, violate the antitrust laws, both the United States and private parties have a continuing remedy under the Sherman Act. * * * As conditions change or abuses are disclosed, it may become necessary * * * for the government to seek modifications of that decree or to file suit for additional relief."

FTC Orders

Under Section 5(b) of the FTC Act, "The Commission may at any time, after notice and opportunity for hearing, reopen and alter, modify, or set aside, in whole or in part, any report or order made or issued by it under this section, whenever in the opinion of the Commission conditions of fact or of law have so changed as to require such action or if the public interest shall so require."

In Elmo Division v. Dixon, 348 F.2d 342 (pp. A-17, X-1, ATRR No. 188, 2/16/65), the Court of Appeals for the District of Columbia Circuit refused to let the FTC go ahead with a new complaint proceeding on matters covered by a consent order. In such a situation, the court held, the Commission must follow the reopening procedure spelled out in its Rules. Later, the court of appeals upheld the Commission's order reopening the consent order (p. A-6,

ATRR No. 339, 1/9/68). And the court sustained the Commission's contention that, in reopening a proceeding terminated by consent order, the Commission needs no stronger "public interest" finding than it needs when it files a new complaint.

Conclusions

Mr. Turner's statement to the Association of the Bar of the City of New York indicates that there are some markets in which he would like to move but feels frustrated by outstanding consent decrees. Solutions suggested for Mr. Turner's dilemma include the writing of decrees that either expire after a specified term of years (e.g., 12-15 years: Victor H. Kramer, "Modification of Consent Decrees," 1 Hoffmann's Antitrust Laws and Techniques 385) or that expire or add specific new restrictions, upon a showing of designated future market conditions.

While prompt adoption of these techniques might well bring about elimination of the problem at some time in the future, its solution for industries in which important consent decrees now exist depends on success either in modifying old judgments or in prosecuting new suits. When the Assistant Attorney General decides to file a new complaint, he probably needs to be concerned about the effect of an existing consent decree only if he seeks to enjoin conduct attacked in the original complaint but not prohibited by the decree or when he seeks a decree provision proposed during the consent order negotiations but left out of the judgment. The rationale of the Alcoa case discussed above indicates that any conduct post-dating the consent decree or not covered by the original complaint can be attacked in new litigation.

Whether the government proceeds by complaint or petition to reopen, its attempt to resurrect decree provisions abandoned during pre-consent negotiations is in a sense a default on a contractual commitment. A consent decree has many attributes of a contract -- a contract approved by a court and, according to the RCA opinion, "binding on the government." Yet the Supreme Court has explicitly rejected "the argument *** that a decree entered upon consent is to be treated as a contract and not as a judicial act." U.S. v. Swift & Co., 286 U.S. at 115. The question Mr. Turner faced up to and answered in the negative is whether this "judicial act" equitably estops the government from claiming what it once conceded. Surely the courts would not find the government estopped to enjoin an antitrust violation. It has been held that a consent decree cannot be construed as sanctioning an antitrust violation -- that any decree attempting to do so would be void. U.S. v. Columbia Artist Management, Inc., 1963 Trade Cases 70,955 (S.D. N.Y.).

Many antitrust lawyers believe that an existing consent order is never a legal bar to the initiation of new antitrust litigation against a continuing violation. Yet the consent decree does raise what might be called a psychological barrier to further action. That barrier is probably especially strong in merger proceedings, for a consent order that stops short of divestiture could logically be read to represent an express consent by the government to continuation of common ownership as well as a recognition that common ownership and operation would not jeopardize competition in violation of the Clayton Act once the consent order's restrictions become operative. Again, however, it seems doubtful that a court would bar a new government move for divestiture if it turns out that the merger, despite the restrictions of the decree, has produced unfortunate market results. Yet the courts might well distinguish between structural and behavioral violations; they might not be so willing to let the government reopen an abandoned attack on a purely structural violation.

Whether the Antitrust Division acts on its chief's threat to bring new suits or adopts one of the proposals advocated for limiting the term of future consent judgments, neither step is expected by antitrust experts to make defendants less likely to settle antitrust litigation. Today the chief incentive for settlement is usually avoidance of a judgment that can be used by treble-damage plaintiffs.

- 0 -

Subject: Intervention   (Published 4/18/67)

Question

Is the Supreme Court's ruling on intervention in its recent El Paso decision likely to lead to widespread granting of intervention motions in other antitrust suits brought by the Justice Department?

References

Cascade Natural Gas Corp. v. El Paso Natural Gas Co., 385 U.S. 129, 35 LW 4227 (pp. A-18, X-1, ATRR No. 294, 2/28/67)

U.S. v. Aluminum Co. of America, 41 F.R.D. 342 (E.D. Mo. 1967) (p. A-12, ATRR No. 289, 1/24/67)

U.S. v. Bowling Proprietors' Assn. of America, Inc. (S.D. N.Y.) (p. A-12, ATRR No. 297, 3/21/67)

Correspondence on Consent-Decree Procedures Between Assistant Attorney General Donald F. Turner and Representative Emanuel Celler (D-NY) (pp. A-15, X-1, ATRR No. 297, 3/21/67)

Background

In the 85th Congress the House Antitrust Subcommittee recommended that parties who may be affected by the terms of a consent decree in a government antitrust case should be given an opportunity to intervene in the case. The subcommittee further recommended that a consent decree submitted to a court for approval should be accompanied by a statement that sets forth the acts involved, the defendant's position, the meaning of the provisions used in the decree, and the reasons for the Antitrust Division's acceptance of the particular compromise.

In the wake of that report, the Attorney General in mid-1961 (pp. A-1, X-9, ATRR No.1, 7/18/61) established the present consent-decree policy of the Department of Justice. Unless special considerations dictate otherwise, consent decrees are filed in court at least 30 days prior to becoming final. During that 30-day period the Antitrust Division will receive and consider written comments pertaining to the proposed judgment. The Antitrust Division can withdraw its consent any time prior to final entry of the judgment of the court. The right is also reserved "to object to intervention by any party not named as a party by the government."

El Paso Decision

In the recent El Paso decision, the Supreme Court reversed a district court's denial of intervention motions filed by the State of California, a Southern California electrical utility, and an Oregon-Washington natural-gas distributor. All three wanted to participate in formulating the divestiture decree that was ordered by the Supreme Court (376 U.S. 651, pp. A-2, X-5, ATRR No. 143, 4/7/64) when it found that El Paso Natural Gas Co. had violated Section 7 of the Clayton Act by acquiring Pacific Northwest Pipeline Corp. and thereby eliminating a possible future competitor from the California natural-gas market.

The Court ruled that California and the electrical utility are entitled to intervene as a matter of right under Federal Rule of Civil Procedure 24(a) because they are "so situated" geographically as to be "adversely affected" by the merger. As for the natural-gas distributor, the Court thought it unnecessary to decide whether that more geographically remote firm had a right to intervene as of the time the district judge denied the motion. Rule 24(a) has since been amended to allow intervention to protect "an interest relating to the property or transaction which is the subject of the action," if that interest is not "adequately represented by existing parties." Since further proceedings were necessary in any event, the Court decided the new Rule 24(a) language is broad enough to let in the distributor as well. The opinion's only explanation of the distributor's "interest" in the "transaction which is the subject of this action" is a reference to the distributor's contentions that there has been a grossly unfair division of gas reserves between El Paso and the new company, which will be the distributor's sole supplier of natural gas.

Since the Court granted intervention as a matter of right, it did not reach the question of permissive intervention. Rule 24(b) provides: "upon timely application anyone may be permitted to intervene in an action: (1) when a statute of the United States confers a conditional right to intervene, or (2) when an applicant's claim or defense and the main action have a question of law or fact in common. ***In exercising its discretion the court shall consider whether the intervention will unduly delay or prejudice the adjudication of the rights of the original parties."

Celler-Turner Correspondence

After the El Paso decision, House Judiciary Committee Chairman Emanuel Celler (D-NY) urged the Antitrust Division to adopt the Supreme Court's rationale for its consent-decree procedures. He declared that the "Supreme Court underscored a deficiency" in the procedures that are currently utilized in formulating consent decrees. He referred to the recommendation made by the 85th Congress that private parties who may be affected by the terms of the decree "should be given an opportunity to intervene in the government's case." The adoption of the recommendation, he urged, "would go far to minimize the settlement procedures" that led to the Court's criticism in the El Paso case.

The head of the Antitrust Division did not dispute the value of letting those who differ with the government's judgment have an opportunity to make their views known, but he pointed out that the present procedure of filing proposed consent decrees 30 days in advance of formal entry provides such an opportunity. The filing of proposed decrees is well publicized, and the government tries to follow a practice of sending proposed decrees to known complainants.

In his view, private intervenors are looking out for their private interests. Some want to obtain an adjudication of liability in order to bring treble-damage suits; others oppose effective antitrust relief because it would damage their interests as suppliers or customers of the defendant companies.

He explained that the government, on the other hand, must consider not only the scope and effectiveness of the relief set out in the decree but also the strength of its case on the law and the facts, the amount of the government's resources that would be tied up in litigation in the case, the desirability or necessity of obtaining significant relief rapidly, the value of any additional relief as compared to the value of the relief available immediately, and the effect that consent to a particular decree might have on other similar cases.

The Assistant Attorney General pointed out that, while the government consistently opposes efforts at formal intervention, it has regularly acquiesced when private parties have sought to file statements or briefs with the district court or have requested oral argument before the court. (Even in the El Paso case, the district judge, though he denied formal intervention, received written and oral argument from some 20 would-be intervenors. Formal intervention procedures would reduce the number of consent settlements obtained by the government, he insisted. An intervenor cannot force a particular type of decree on an unwilling defendant. If the defendant is not prepared to go beyond what he has agreed to in a proposed consent decree, the intervenor can do no more than force the government to choose between dismissing the case and proceeding to full litigation. Therefore, by forcing on the government and defendants at least some of the burdens of litigation they sought to avoid, "the very process of formal intervention, if that is held to carry with it the full rights of the litigant to present evidence and to appeal, would threaten to eliminate one of the major motivating factors that leads both the government and the defendants to attempt to work out an appropriate decree."

Recent Intervention Motions

In the Alcoa case listed above in the references, the Eastern Missouri Federal District Court denied a motion by Lupton Mfg. Co. to intervene in the government's Section 7 Clayton Act suit against Alcoa's acquisition of Cupples Products Corp. More than two years earlier the court had held Alcoa's acquisition to be unlawful (233 F. Supp. 718, pp. A-3, X-18, ATRR No. 168, 9/29/65) and entered its divestiture decree. The decree had been appealed to the Supreme Court and affirmed without opinion in October 1965 (382 U.S. 12, p. A-6, ATRR No. 222, 10/12/65). Lupton had filed a bid to supply construction materials for New York City's World Trade Center and contended that award of the contract to Alcoa-Cupples would frustrate the antitrust judgment.

Lupton had notified the Antitrust Division of the Alcoa bid and asked the Division to request a court order barring the bid. However, the Division had refused to act. The district judge was satisfied that "the Justice Department has diligently protected the interests of the public in obtaining the goals set out by this court to restore Cupples to a position as an independent entity in the aluminum fabricating business." Moreover, he was convinced that to deprive Cupples of the contract "would further complicate its salability" and therefore interfere with compliance with a divestiture decree. Lupton has filed notice in the district court that the denial of intervention is being appealed to the Supreme Court.

Two associations of bowlers have complained that the proposed consent decree in U.S. v. Bowling Proprietors' Assn. of America (p. A-14, ATRR No. 293, 2/21/67) contains language that will interfere with their legitimate efforts to standardize tournament bowling rules and otherwise promote the sport through "sanctioned" tournaments and national rankings. They filed a motion (p. A-12, ATRR No. 297, 3/21/67) asking the Federal District Court for Southern New York to let them intervene in the lawsuit.

The two associations object to provisions in the decree prohibiting the BPAA from discriminating against any bowler for bowling on nonmember lanes or for lack of membership in "any bowling proprietor association or association of bowlers." They fear that the words "any *** association of bowlers" would forbid the bowling proprietors to request the two associations to conduct sanctioned tournaments, with the effect of returning bowling to its disorganized state of 50 years ago. In line with its policy of cooperating with the informal presentation of objections to consent-decree terms, the Antitrust Division has procured a 30-day extension of the time during which it remains free to withdraw its consent to the proposed judgment.

Similarly, informal objections from other retailers and the State of California have twice blocked entry of proposed consent judgments in the government's suit to separate a group of West Coast grocery chains from their joint trading-stamp subsidiary. (U.S. v. Blue Chip Stamp Co., p. A-7, ATRR No. 284, 12/20/66).

Conclusions

Contrary to Congressman Celler's assertion, the Supreme Court did not underscore a deficiency in the Antitrust Division's consent-decree program. The decree approved by the district court in El Paso was not a consent order but a decree filed by stipulation of the parties and entered after extensive hearings on the form of divestiture to be used and in response to a Supreme Court mandate to order "divestiture without delay." The Supreme Court expressly disclaimed any intention to question the authority of the Attorney General to settle antitrust suits -- before or after appeal. But, the Court declared, the Department of Justice "by stipulation or otherwise has no authority to circumscribe the power of the courts to see that our mandate is carried out. No one, except this Court, has authority to alter or modify our mandate.

Many observers feel the El Paso decision will be limited strictly to its facts. They point out that the case involved not only a Supreme Court mandate but also a regulated industry. Even Mr. Justice Stewart, in dissent, felt that the natural-gas distributor was entitled to protection of its gas supply, although he would have left that protection to the Federal Power Commission. Moreover, the problems involved in unscrambling the El Paso acquisition appear more complicated than those presented by most other mergers. (See Analysis "Divestiture Problems in Merger Cases," p. B-1, ATRR No. 196, 4/13/65, reprinted at p. 118, Antitrust and Trade Regulation Today: 1967.)

On the other hand, the Supreme Court said nothing that would limit the scope of intervention under Rule 24. In fact, the dissent insisted that the gas distributor was allowed to intervene "to vindicate competition in California," a market in which the distributor does not operate.

In addition, Rule 24 is certainly applicable in consent-decree procedures. The Rule provides: "Upon timely application anyone shall be permitted to intervene in an action." Federal Rule of Civil Procedure 3 states that an action is commenced by filing a complaint with the court. Therefore, when the Antitrust Division files its complaint, intervention motions are in order, regardless of whether or when a proposed consent decree is filed.

In his letter to Congressman Celler, Mr. Turner indicated that the Antitrust Division would continue to oppose formal intervention. Justice Department opposition to intervention is likely to carry great weight with a district court, for the consent-decree procedure gives a would-be intervenor an opportunity to raise questions about the proposed decree. Finally, formal intervention would entail evidentiary hearings that the district judge may wish to avoid. Even if he were inclined to hold such hearings, there is little guarantee that the defendant would not withdraw his consent and thereby force a full trial on the government's complaint.

- 0 -

PART VIII – FTC PRACTICE

Subject: Discovery in FTC Proceedings   (Published 9/5/67)

Question

What significant changes, if any, has the 1967 revision of the FTC's Rules of Practice made in pre-trial discovery?

References

Analysis, "Pre-trial Discovery in FTC Proceedings," p. B-1, ATRR No. 295, 3/7/67; reprinted at p. 301, Antitrust & Trade Regulation Today: 1967 Sections 3.21-3.41 & 4.8-4.11, FTC Rules of Practice, effective July 1, 1967 (p. X-22, ATRR No. 309, 6/13/67)

Background

Last June, for the third time in six years, the FTC republished its General Procedures and Rules of Practice. One of the changed circumstances that prompted the revision was the enactment last year of the Freedom of Information Act, Public Law 89-487, July 4, 1966. The theme of that statute is the public's "right to know what its government is doing" (Senate Rept. 813, 89th Cong., 1st Sess., p. 2).

Yet, as in other federal agencies with quasi-judicial functions, procedural rule drafting at the FTC is accomplished within the agency and, in fact, with a good deal of secrecy. There is no exposure of proposed rules for inspection and criticism by outside lawyers who must work with them, and there are no "revisers' notes" such as the Bar is accustomed to rely on in the interpretation of the various sets of federal court rules.

Preparation of the FTC's 1967 rule revisions was assigned to a seven-man committee drawn from the Commission's top-level staff. Its chairman was John V. Buffington, assistant to the Chairman of the Commission, and its other members were the six bureau chiefs. Inquiries concerning the preparation of the rules elicit the response that no further information will be released concerning the committee, its recommendations to the Commission, or changes, if any, made by the Commission itself in the committee's proposals. However, it is known that subordinate bureau staff members did much of the actual drafting of the proposals submitted by the committee.

For the six years preceding this year's revisions, the FTC's procedures for procuring, in advance of trial, the information one's opponent has regarding the matters to be litigated were patterned somewhat after the Federal Rules of Civil Procedure. In the new Rules effective July 1, however, the Commission has completely rewritten its discovery procedures in a style and sequence that makes them appear more unlike the Federal Rules.

Section 3.33, "Depositions," for example, no longer echoes the language of Federal Civil Rule 26. A new set of standards must be met before a deposition may be taken. Under Section 3.33(a), an examiner may order the taking of a deposition only "upon a showing that the deposition is necessary for the purposes of the discovery, and that such discovery could not be accomplished by voluntary methods." He may also order the taking of a deposition "in extraordinary circumstances to preserve relevant evidence that could not be presented through a witness at the hearing." Apparently, therefore, a deposition may no longer be taken for use in contradicting or impeaching a Commission witness.

Section 3.33 also still differs from the Federal Rules in its requirements that the examiner order the taking of the deposition and that first an application be made for such an order. The last sentence of Section 3.33(a) now makes it clear that "depositions may be taken *** upon written interrogatories."

117

Section 3.31, "Admissions as to Facts and Documents," on the other hand, borrows even more heavily now from Federal Civil Rule 36. After providing for requests "for the admission *** of the genuineness of any relevant documents," Section 3.31 goes on to provide for the admission of facts "set forth in such request." Prior to this year's changes, Section 3.13 of the old Rules provided only for admission of facts "set forth in such documents."

Prehearing Conferences

The old Section 3.8's provisions for prehearing conferences are set out in a new Section 3.21 without substantial change except for the addition of a paragraph on subpoenas. Section 3.21(b) is now explicit in authorizing prehearing conferences "for the purpose of accepting returns on the subpoenas duces tecum issued pursuant to the provisions of Section 3.34(b)." Section 3.34(b)(2) permits either party to subpoena before trial any "nonprivileged documents *** which constitute or contain evidence." By that language, hearing examiners are, for the first time, given express authority to grant prehearing access to evidentiary materials in the possession of complaint counsel.

In a decision handed down since publication of the March ATRR analysis referenced above, the Commission has again stressed the importance of its hearing examiners' functions at a prehearing conference. Suburban Propane Gas Corp., Docket 8672 (p. A-10, ATRR No. 308, 6/6/67). The Commission decided that the hearing examiner had an obligation, in a Robinson-Patman Act proceeding against a buyer for knowing receipt of discriminatory discounts, to respond to the buyer's request for a pretrial definition of complaint counsel's burden of proof on the issue whether the buyer knew the discounts could not be cost-justified. "It is his responsibility to properly regulate the course of the hearing and to rule upon, as justice may require, procedural and other motions. This means that at times he may have to construe case law precedents so that the parties will know how to proceed."

Section 3.34, "Subpoenas"; Section 3.36, "Applications for Confidential Records of the Commission and Appearance of Commission Employees"; and Section 4.11, "Release of Confidential Information," supplant the old Section 3.11's provisions for "Production of Documents." They are obviously the rules to be used most frequently to obtain information about the Commission's case or information in the Commission's hands that might serve as a defense. Read together, they provide for access to "documents, papers, books, physical exhibits, or other material in the confidential records of the Commission" whenever (1) such information is required by law to be made available or (2) its disclosure is necessary in the interest of justice.

Under Sections 3.36 and 4.11, an application for production of confidential documents or disclosure of confidential information is to be made in the form of a motion specifying "the material to be produced, the nature of the information to be disclosed, or the expected testimony of the Commission official or employee." The motion must also explain the general relevancy of the information sought, the reasonableness of the scope of the application, and the unavailability of the information from other sources. Unlike an application for a subpoena under Section 3.34, this motion is not to be ruled on by the examiner but is to be certified to the Commission with his recommendation.

Subpoenas

If the confidential information or material sought is something "to which a party is entitled by law," he is to follow the procedure set out in Section 3.34, "Subpoenas." The first two paragraphs of the new subpoena provisions do not substantially change those in Section 3.17(a) and (b) of the old Rules, but Section 3.34(b)(2) now makes it clear that subpoenas can be used for pre-hearing discovery. And there is a new provision in Section 3.35 that applications for compulsory process and rulings on them "may be made ex parte." According to Mr. Buffington, the purpose of the new language is to remove any doubt that subpoenas can be issued ex parte; some examiners had been unwilling to follow that procedure.

In Section 4.8 through 4.11, the Commission spells out general principles as to the availability of its records and files to the public and to litigants. Here, too, the Commission completely rewrites its Rules, apparently in an effort to comply with the Freedom of

Information Act of 1966. Whereas Section 1.133 of the Commission's old General Procedures stated that, with certain exceptions, "the records and files of the Commission *** are confidential," the new Rules start with the proposition that "the records of the Commission are available for public inspection and copying with exceptions set out in Section 4.10, "Confidential Information." Under that category Section 4.10 lists: (1) records related solely to the internal personnel rules and practices of the Commission; (2) trade secrets and commercial or financial information that is customarily privileged or is received in confidence; (3) the minutes of Commission meetings; (4) interagency or intra-agency communications "which would not be available by law to a private party in litigation with the Commission"; (5) personnel and medical files and similar files involving personal privacy; (6) law-enforcement investigatory files "except to the extent available by law"; and (7) "such other files and records *** as may be exempted from disclosure by statute or executive order." Under Section 4.11, confidential information is to be released only "upon good cause shown" -- a requirement that prevailed also under the old Rules.

This "good cause" requirement was construed by the Commission in an interlocutory opinion handed down shortly before the new Rules took effect. In School Services, Inc., Docket 8729 (p. A-2, ATRR No. 311, 6/27/67), the Commission turned down an application for production of documents and the taking of the depositions of FTC officials for the purpose of establishing a respondent's claims that a Section 5 FTC Act complaint was issued without a determination either that it was in the "public interest" or that it was based on "reason to believe" that the Act had been violated. The information sought was treated as confidential because it was both the "work product" of the Commission's lawyers and "an integral part" of its decision-making process. The Commission saw in the discovery application "an attempt to probe the mental processes of this agency in investigating respondents."

There is a change in the Commission's first "Hearings" rule -- Section 3.41 -- that may have great significance for discovery purposes. In Section 3.41(b), the Commission has retreated a bit from its continuous-hearing policy and authorized its examiners "to order brief intervals to permit discovery necessarily deferred during the prehearing procedures."

Conclusions

In the analysis published March 7, ATRR concluded: "It is common knowledge that interlocutory appeals and other procedures for litigating discovery issues are sometimes used by respondents' counsel as a means of delaying the proceeding and postponing a decision on the merits. Easy discovery at the FTC might turn out to be at best a mixed blessing for respondents and, on the other hand, an important boost to the Commission's efforts to simplify and shorten its adjudicative proceedings."

More recently, the Commission has been criticized by one of its own members for taking an approach to discovery "which provides a continuing source of unnecessary friction and delay," and "is clearly contrary to the spirit if not the letter of the recently enacted Freedom of Information Act." (Commissioner Elman, dissenting in Interstate Builders, Inc., Docket 8642, p. A-15, ATRR No. 319, 8/22/67.)

Yet the Commission's Rules of Practice, its largely unpublished interlocutory rulings, and the attitude of its trial staff reflect the view that easy discovery for respondents is not in the public interest. In addition to any litigant's instinctive propensity for secrecy, increased here by the FTC Act's admonitions against certain disclosures, FTC practitioners report that they detect feelings on the part of FTC trial lawyers (1) that respondents' counsel generally have the advantage in terms of experience, time, and financial resources, (2) that some respondents are not above influencing witnesses if they get information in advance about the Commission's case, and (3) that their supervisors at the Commission judge their skills on the basis of the number of cases they win. As long as these views prevail, some members of the private bar seem to think, the "sporting theory" of litigation is not likely to die out at the Commission, no matter what changes are made in the Rules.

To some degree, the actual effect this staff attitude will have on preparation for a particular hearing will vary with the preferences of the presiding examiner. Some examiners, more inclined than others to the Federal Rules approach, require full prehearing disclosure of complaint counsel's case as a matter of course. When access is sought to something in the Commissioner's confidential files that is not to be used in evidence, though, the examiner's role is merely advisory, for he is directed by Section 3.36(c) of the Rules to certify such a motion to the Commission with his recommendation.

There are lawyers who see in the rule changes themselves the influence of the secretive attitude of the Commission's staff. One example is the requirement in Sections 3.33(a) of the Rules that the hearing examiner, before ordering the taking of a deposition, find that "such discovery could not be accomplished by voluntary methods." It is seen by some lawyers as a codification of a requirement complaint counsel have frequently sought to have imposed by the examiner. The context in which complaint counsel have most often pressed that contention is Robinson-Patman Act cases in which the company charged under Section 2(f) of the Clayton Act with receiving discriminatory discounts is trying to get evidence that its suppliers' pricing practices do not violate Section 2(a) of the Act. Another codification of a position argued repeatedly in the past by complaint counsel is seen in Section 3.33(a)'s requirement that a deposition "should not be ordered to obtain evidence from a person relating to matters with regard to which he expected to testify at the hearing."

As for the Commission's revision of its "confidential information" rules in response to the Freedom of Information Act, the attitude of some members of the FTC bar is that the Commission made merely a gesture. They feel that the rewriting of the Rules to make everything available that is not designated confidential instead of making everything confidential that is not designated available makes no substantive change. Lawyers attempting to get information from complaint counsel's file on the case they must try say they are apt to be simply referred to the Legal Records Division and then told that everything else is confidential.

Although the Commission's new rules do not seem to make any significant progress toward the type of discovery allowed in the federal courts, some discovery-liberalizing changes were made. Under Section 3.33(a), depositions can be taken for more purposes than were set out in the earlier rules. And the hearing examiner's new authority to order brief intervals between hearings to permit additional discovery could be applied in a manner that would ease the discovery problems of respondents' counsel.

- 0 -

Subject: The Jencks Act at the FTC   (Published 11/14/67)

Question

What rule is being applied by the FTC to govern access to witnesses' pre-trial statements for use in cross-examination?

References

Jencks v. U.S., 353 U.S. 657 (1957)
Jencks Act, 18 U.S. Code 3500
Inter-State Builders, Inc., FTC Docket 8624 (p. A-15, ATRR No. 319, 8/22/67;
    p. A-8, ATRR No. 252, 5/10/66)

Background

Jencks v. U.S. established the right of a defendant in a federal criminal proceeding to production of any pretrial statements the government received from a witness concerning matters as to which the witness has testified on direct examination at the trial. A defendant is entitled to use such information for the purpose of cross-examining the witness, even if the defendant cannot show any inconsistency between the testimony and the pretrial statements. The trial judge is not to inspect the pretrial statements for inconsistencies with testimony but is to let defense counsel inspect them and decide what use might be made of them.

The doctrine of that case was codified shortly thereafter in what is known as the Jencks Act. In the statute, the discovery right was limited to (1) a written statement made and signed or otherwise adopted by the witness or (2) "a stenographical, mechanical, electrical, or other recording, or a transcription thereof, which is a substantially verbatim recital" of an oral statement "recorded contemporaneously." In the event of a government claim that a portion of the statement to be produced bears no relationship to the witness' testimony, the trial judge is to inspect the document initially and excise the irrelevant portions.

The Jencks Rule has been held applicable to administrative proceedings as "one of the fundamentals of fair play required in an administrative proceeding." Communist Party v. SACB, 254 F.2d 314, 327-8 (D.C. Cir. 1958). See also NLRB v. Adhesive Products Corp., 258 F.2d 403, 408 (2d Cir. 1958), and Great Lakes Airline v. CAB, 291 F.2d 354, 364 (9th Cir. 1961). In these cases, the courts applied "the underlying principle" of the Jencks opinion and statute. In Ernest Mark High, 56 FTC 625 (1959), the FTC decided it would apply the Jencks Act to its hearings. It specifically rejected, though, a suggestion that it apply a broader discovery rule said to be defined in the Supreme Court's Jencks opinion. The Commission pointed out that the Supreme Court itself in the meantime had declared the statute to be the exclusive means of compelling, for cross-examination purposes at criminal trials, the production of statements of a government witness to an agent of the government. Palermo v. U.S., 360 U.S. 343 (1959); Rosenberg v. U.S., 360 U.S. 367 (1959). The Court has not yet expressed itself on the applicability of the "principle," opinion, or statute to administrative proceedings.

At the FTC, the most common manner of recording the prehearing statements of witnesses is the "interview report" prepared by an attorney-examiner when he interviews prospective witnesses. In the High case, the Commission refused to allow access to such reports, although it did let the respondent see signed statements the witnesses had supplied its staff. "Commission interview reports ordinarily are in the category of agents' summarizations," the Commission found, and therefore cannot be considered a "substantially verbatim recital" of the witness' statement. If there is any doubt about the report's "substantially verbatim character," the opinion went on, "the examiner should inspect it and make a determination." In three earlier cases, the Commission had denied discovery of interview reports without ruling on the applicability of the Jencks Act: Pure Oil Co., 54 FTC 1892, 1894-95 (1958) (the report was not "used in any way during the course of the hearings" and was "hearsay"); Basic Books, Inc., 56 FTC 69, 85-86 (1959) (there was no evidence that a written statement existed); Bakers Franchise Corp., 56 FTC 1636 (1959) (interview reports are privileged as "work product," and the investigating attorney fully described the substance of his interviews during the hearing).

In R.H. Macy & Co., Inc., FTC Docket 8650 (p. A-4, ATRR No. 244, 3/15/66), the Commission applied the Jencks Act to reports prepared by one of its investigators who was himself called as a witness. Because the reports were used to refresh his recollection, the hearing examiner was directed to order complaint counsel to hand them over to the examiner for inspection and excision of the portions unrelated to the investigator's actual testimony. But the Commission went on to inform its staff that complaint counsel can elect not to comply with such production orders. The price he must pay for such a choice is removal of the witness' testimony from the record.

Commissioner Elman refused to concur in the Macy opinion and promised to develop his views later. He filed his dissent in the first of the two Inter-State Builders opinions cited in the references. In the interlocutory decision, the Commission reaffirmed its adoption of the rule of the Jencks Act, which it characterized as a mere codification of the doctrine established by the Supreme Court. It instructed a hearing examiner to determine whether the interview reports requested in that case represent "a substantially verbatim transcription of the witness' oral words as recorded by the government investigator," applying the criteria laid down by the Supreme Court in the Palermo case and in Campbell v. U.S., 373 U.S. 487 (1963).

In the Campbell case, the Supreme Court reinstated a district's order requiring production under the Jencks Act of an "interview report" prepared by an FBI agent. The Court felt the district judge "was entitled to infer that an agent of the Federal Bureau of Investigation of some fifteen years' experience would record a potential witness' statement with sufficient accuracy as to obviate any need for the courts to consider whether it would be 'grossly unfair to allow the defense to use statements to impeach a witness which could not fairly be said to be the witness' own.' Palermo v. United States, supra." The FTC, however, did not choose to consider its attorneys' interview reports in that light. Rather, it distinguished the result reached in the Campbell case by noting the additional finding there that the witness had adopted the interview report as an accurate reproduction of his statement.

Although the Commission's majority in Interstate Builders explicitly classified the interview reports as confidential information protected by both the "attorney's work product rule" and the normal privilege accorded government informants, it rejected a suggestion that defense counsel must follow the formal demand requirements in Section 1.134 (now Section 4.11) of the Commission's Rules of Practice. "Jencks statements," the Commission reasoned, are within Section 1.133(a)'s (now Section 4.10(c)'s) exemption of documents whose "use may become necessary in connection with adjudicative proceedings." The only requirements are that the production request be made after the witness has testified on direct examination and that some showing be made that he in fact made a written statement or that an interview report was prepared.

The chief point of Commissioner Elman's dissent is that the "Jencks Rule" the Commission should apply is not that set out in the Jencks Act but a more liberal rule he derived from the Supreme Court's decision. Without focusing specifically on procedural deficiencies in the Commission's rule he nevertheless broadly condemned the ex-parte examination of the reports by the hearing examiner. He insisted the approach taken by the Commission means that interview reports will never be available for use in cross-examination, even though "they will undoubtedly continue, for every other purpose to be treated by the Commission and its staff as accurate and reliable documents used in our day-to-day work."

So far the dissent's prediction seems to be borne out. In the Inter-State case, the examiner did find the interview reports involved there did not qualify as "substantially verbatim recitals." And the Commission affirmed his holding when it entered its final order earlier this year.

Conclusions

Despite statements by the courts of appeals that it is "the underlying principle" of the Jencks case and statute that is applicable in administrative proceedings, it is clear from the FTC's two opinions in the Inter-State Builders case that it intends to stick closely to the statute. And, since the Commission's majority recognized in a companion opinion (Balfour Co., Docket 8435) that "the interview reports in the Commission's files ordinarily are agents' summarizations," it also seems clear that Commissioner Elman is correct when he says no interview reports will be made available under the Commission's interpretation of the Jencks statute. Even if the Commission's instruction manual for its attorneys (which it treats as confidential) leaves them free to prepare substantially verbatim interview reports, the staff attitude towards disclosures to respondents is such that the Commission's interpretation of Jencks is likely to discourage the preparation of verbatim reports. (See Analysis, "Discovery in FTC Proceedings," immediately preceding this article.)

Many attorneys experienced in FTC litigation feel, however, that the ban on access to interview reports will be of significance in a very small percentage of cases. Access to them is vital, they feel, in any case where the key to the defense lies in cross-examination. But such cases arise relatively infrequently. After all, the truth-finding value of cross-examination in a hearing before a tribunal of experts is much less than it is when there is a jury to impress.

There is one other difference between jury trials and administrative hearings that may have a bearing on eventual court resolution of the question raised by Commissioner Elman's condemnation of the examiner's ex parte examination of the pre-hearing statement. In criminal trials, which the Supreme Court was dealing with in the Jencks and Campbell opinions, the judge who makes the inspection called for by the statute is not the trier of the facts. Would the Supreme Court be just as willing to allow ex parte inspection when it is to be made by an examiner and when it is not provided for by statute?

- 0 -

Subject: Injunctions Against FTC Proceedings   (Published 12/31/68)

Question

Under what circumstances can FTC action be enjoined or directed by a federal district court?

References

FTC v. J. Weingarten, Inc., 336 F.2d 687 (5th Cir.) (pp. A-1, X-1, ATRR No. 167, 9/22/64), review denied, 380 U.S. 908 (1964)

Lehigh Portland Cement Co. v. FTC, 291 F.Supp. 628 (E.D. Va.) (p. A-5, ATRR No. 381, 10/29/68)

Bristol-Myers Co. v. FTC, 284 F.Supp. 745 (D. Dist. Col.) (pp. A-12, X-7, ATRR No. 360, 6/4/68)

Elmo Division of Drive-X Co., Inc. v. Dixon, 348 F.2d 342 (D. C. Cir.) (pp. A-12, X-1, ATRR No. 188, 2/12/65)

Frito-Lay, Inc. v. FTC, 380 F.2d 8 (5th Cir.) (p. A-11, ATRR No. 311, 6/27/67)

Background

It is "the long settled rule of judicial administration that no one is entitled to judicial relief for a supposed or threatened injury until the prescribed administrative remedy has been exhausted." Myers v. Bethlehem Shipbuilding Corp., 303 U.S. 41, 50-51 (1938). In a number of cases, the Supreme Court has made an exception to that rule for threatened administrative action outside the scope of the agency's powers. Allen v. Grand Central Aircraft Co., 347 U.S. 535 (1954); Order of Railway Conductors v. Swan, 329 U.S. 520 (1947); Leedom v. Kyne, 358 U.S. 184 (1958); Leedom v. International Union of Mine Workers, 352 U.S. 145 (1956); Skinner & Eddy Corp. v. U.S., 249 U.S. 557 (1919). These decisions are not entirely consistent with the Myers case, though, for it was also contended in that case that the National Labor Relations Board lacked jurisdiction to take the threatened action. The grounds cited were (1) the absence of interstate commerce involvement and (2) the unconstitutionality of the applicable sections of the Labor-Management Relations Act. Another exception has been made when the agency action is unreasonably delayed in violation of Section 6(a) of the Administrative Procedure Act (now 5 U.S. Code 555(b)). Deering Milliken, Inc. v. Johnston, 295 F.2d 856 (1961).

This general rule requiring exhaustion of administrative remedies has been applied to FTC proceedings; the remedy of the party claiming impropriety in FTC action is review of the Commission's final order in an appropriate court of appeals. Ritholz v. March, 105 F.2d 937 (D.C. Cir. 1939); Crown Zellerbach Corp. v. FTC, 156 F.2d 927 (9th Cir. 1946). Indeed, the jurisdiction of a U.S. court of appeals to review, set aside, or modify final FTC orders does not include power to enjoin an FTC proceeding prior to its conclusion -- even if the Commission is claimed to be acting in excess of its jurisdiction. Chamber of Commerce of Minneapolis v. FTC, 280 Fed. 45 (8th Cir. 1922). (There are, however, circumstances in which the Commission can get preliminary injunctive relief in the courts of appeals. FTC v. Dean Foods Co., 384 U.S. 597 (1966); see analysis, p. 127, Antitrust and Trade Regulation Today: 1967.) Nor does a federal district court have jurisdiction to enjoin an FTC examiner from holding hearings that are said to have been scheduled in an arbitrary and capricious abuse of the examiner's discretion. The respondent before the Commission must first exhaust administrative appeal remedies. Holland Furnace Co. v. Purcell, 125 F.Supp. 74 (W.D. Mich. 1954).

Until 1962, suits to enjoin most federal officials had to be brought in the District of Columbia where the officials could be served with process. In that year, Congress enacted Section 1391(e) of the Judicial Code, permitting suits against federal officials to be brought in any district where the cause of action arose, where any real property involved in the action is located, or where the plaintiff resides, if no real property is involved. Since then, the number of suits for injunctions against FTC activities has increased, and the courts have sometimes asserted jurisdiction to enjoin specific Commission action.

Administrative Delays

The first significant case brought against the FTC under the new venue statute was the Weingarten case cited in the references. By winning an injunction in the Federal District Court for Southern Texas (1963 Trade Cases para. 70,790), J. Weingarten, Inc., delayed for two years issuance of a Section 5 FTC Act order against its knowing receipt of discriminatory advertising allowances. The district court's injunction was based on the Administrative Procedure Act's admonition against administrative delay, for the district judge found that almost three and a half years after issuance of its complaint the Commission had remanded the case to its hearing examiner for the taking of additional evidence in an area where complaint counsel's evidence had been found deficient. The Commission was given thirty days to dispose of the case on its own without remand. On appeal, the Fifth Circuit found that "This case not only proceeded at a rate comparable to that normally experienced in cases of its kind, it also proceeded at a rate satisfactory to Weingarten." An argument that the Commission's remand order shows an arbitrary prejudgment of the case was rejected with an observation that appellate courts often remand cases for "shoring up." The court of appeals "assum[ed], without deciding, that the district court had jurisdiction to enjoin the remand proceedings."

In Lehigh Portland Cement Co. v. FTC, listed in the references, the court denied a request for an injunction directing the Commission to transfer a Section 7 Clayton Act antimerger proceeding to the Justice Department, but it rejected an FTC assertion that a district judge lacks jurisdiction over such a suit. The basis for the suit was a claim that the FTC had evidenced prejudgment of the case in a statement of enforcement policy involving the type of merger under attack. The opinion merely declared that the court "has jurisdiction to hear and determine this matter under 28 U.S.C. 1361 and 5 U.S.C. 702, 706 (formerly Administrative Procedure Act 10). See Amos Treat & Co. v. SEC, 306 F.2d 260 (D.C. Cir. 1962); Deering Milliken v. Johnston, 295 F.2d 856 (4th Cir. 1961); Abbott Laboratories v. Gardner, 387 U.S. 136 (1967); Gardner v. Toilet Goods Assn., 387 U.S. 167 (1967)."

The Commission's practice of issuing press releases announcing its enforcement actions was the subject of complaint in FTC v. Cinderella Career & Finishing School, Inc. (pp. A-1, X-1, ATRR No. 349, 3/19/68). Without discussing the scope of its own power to halt FTC action, a federal district court had enjoined the Commission's issuance of news releases, declaring that these releases give "the appearance of constituting a prejudgment of the issues." The court of appeals found the issuance of releases to be within the Commission's authority but it too failed to discuss the scope of the district courts' jurisdiction to issue injunctions against the Commission.

Rule Making

In the Bristol-Myers case listed in the references, a drug company sought an injunction against the Commission's issuance of a proposed trade regulation rule. The court was told that the Commission has no power to conduct rule-making proceedings but may conduct only adjudicatory proceedings. The district judge declared the injunction suit "premature" since "no one can tell today what type of rule, if any, will eventually be adopted by the Commission. When one is adopted, if it is adopted at all, will be the proper time to seek court review." The same opinion rejected a request for an injunction against press releases. "The courts may no more enjoin government departments from issuing statements or making statements to the public than they can enjoin a public official from making a speech."

Although the Supreme Court has ruled that the Commission cannot be enjoined from conducting an investigation (FTC v. Claire Furnace Co., 274 U.S. 160 (1927)), it has indicated that the validity of an FTC investigation can be tested in a suit under the Declaratory Judgment Act. U.S. v. St. Regis Paper Co., 368 U.S. 972 (1961). In St. Regis, a company under investigation sought to avoid penalties imposed upon it under Section 10 of the FTC Act for failing to comply with Commission orders for production of its file copies of census reports. It termed the penalties unfair because it had no way of testing in advance the validity of the Commission's orders. In the Supreme Court's eyes, the Declaratory Judgment Act "appears sufficient to meet petitioner's needs." This language appears to endorse the holding of the Court of Appeals for the Second Circuit in that case that a suit could have been brought under the Declaratory Judgment Act to challenge the Commission's orders. 285 F.2d 607 (1960).

A complaint about the procedural route followed by the Commission in reopening a matter once settled by consent order was held to be within a district court's jurisdiction in the Elmo Division case cited above. The district court was directed to entertain a suit for an injunction barring prosecution of a new complaint and requiring the Commission to proceed instead by reopening the original case, as provided for in the consent order and the Commission's Rules of Practice. Once the Commission had promulgated the rule and incorporated it into the consent order, the court of appeals reasoned, action at odds with the rule is indistinguishable from the ultra vires administrative actions held enjoinable in Leedom v. Kyne, Skinner & Eddy Corp. v. U.S., and B.F. Goodrich Co. v. FTC, 208 F.2d 829 (D.C. Cir. 1953). In its Goodrich opinion, the Court of Appeals for the District of Columbia Circuit sustained the jurisdiction of a district court to enjoin enforcement of a quantity-limit rule the Commission had promulgated under the Robinson-Patman Act for the tire industry without meeting the statute's fact-finding requirements.

Subsequently, however, in Frito-Lay, Inc. v. FTC, 380 F.2d 8 (5th Cir.)(p. A-11, ATRR No. 311, 6/27/67), the Court of Appeals for the Fifth Circuit held that a district court does not have jurisdiction of a declaratory-judgment suit attacking an FTC Section 7 Clayton Act complaint as having been brought against a meat packer exempt from FTC jurisdiction. The Fifth Circuit's "per curiam" opinion states that only in extraordinary cases can there be deviation from the ordinary rule that only courts of appeals have jurisdiction to review Commission orders. "The writings of the Supreme Court are unsettled as to when a showing of jurisdictional defect will be considered as justification for such a deviation. Judicial intervention without exhaustion of administrative remedies is not justified, however, where, as here, the merit of appellant's jurisdictional attack is far from clear, the administrative body may be more qualified than the court to initially consider the jurisdictional question, and the injury sought to be avoided is merely the normal cost of administrative litigation. See Davis, Administrative Law Text §§ 20.01-.03 (1959)." 380 F. 2d at 10.

Similarly, the courts have insisted that a challenge to the existence of an interstate-commerce basis for FTC jurisdiction be litigated first before the Commission. Lone Star Cement Corp. v. FTC, 339 F.2d 505 (9th Cir. 1964); Stewart Concrete & Material Co. v. FTC, 1967 Trade Cases, Para. 72,098 (S.D. Ohio) (p. A-5, ATRR No. 307, 5/30/67).

Conclusions

The legal standards for enjoining threatened actions by the FTC seem to have crystalized around the test set out in the Frito-Lay opinion. When they decide pending and future suits to enjoin FTC action, the courts are likely to be resolving merely the issue whether the threatened administrative action is a sufficiently grave dereliction of duty to make inadequate the remedy provided by eventual review of the Commission's final order. In the light of the Cinderella case discussed above and of Sperry & Hutchinson Co. v. FTC, 256 F.Supp. 136 (S.D. N.Y.) (p. A-4, ATRR No. 259, 6/28/66), some experts feel that complaints about evidentiary, discovery, or purely procedural matters will be given short shrift -- that only particularly adventuresome efforts of the Commission to expand either its subject-matter jurisdiction or the force and effect of its cease-and-desist orders are likely to cause the courts to resort to the doctrine of the two Leedom cases.

Some lawyers practicing before the Commission attribute the trend away from the issuance of injunctions curbing Commission action to reforms instituted years ago in the Commission's own internal procedures. Since the era years ago when a hearing examiner's findings and order might have been written by the Commission's trial attorneys, the FTC has progressed to a point where it is difficult to find excesses serious enough to warrant pre-order intervention by injunction. Some FTC practitioners report that the Commission's litigating staff still takes unreasonable positions sometimes. But, when complaint counsel won't conform to recognized rules, it is now generally possible to get corrective action from his division chief or his bureau director, or even by means of an informal appeal to the Commission itself.

One area that may still have unresolved issues as to the availability of injunctive relief relates to the Commission's rule-making processes. The Commission's authority to promulgate trade regulation rules, for example, was challenged while the Commission was considering its cigarette labeling and advertising rule (see Analysis, "Trade Regulation Rules," p. 290, Antitrust and Trade Regulation Today: 1967), although as a result of subsequent developments the matter was not taken to court in that context. Abbott Laboratory v. Gardner, 387 U.S. 136 (1967), suggests greater hospitality in the courts for injunction suits against rule making, but there the administrative rule-making process had been completed, and the only question was whether someone subject to the rule could claim to be aggrieved before any action had been taken to enforce the rule. It would probably be considerably more difficult to get an injunction against rule making before the rule is issued, Pharmaceutical Manufacturers Association v. Gardner, 381 F.2d 271 (D.C. Cir. 1967).

- 0 -

Subject: FTC Press Releases   (Published 3/26/68)

Question

What measures can a businessman take to protect himself from the adverse business consequences of the FTC's public announcement of its charges before their accuracy is finally determined?

References

FTC v. Cinderella Career & Finishing Schools, Inc., 1968 Trade Cases Para. 72,385
   (D.C. Cir.) (pp. A-1, X-1, ATRR No. 349, 3/19/68)
S. 924 (p. A-9, ATRR No. 292, 2/14/67)

Background

The FTC prepares and distributes press releases publicizing every one of its litigated complaint proceedings at never fewer than four stages: complaint, answer, initial decision, and final order. Copies of releases are mailed to some 900 publications and about 1500 other addressees, including many law firms. Another 200 or so are picked up at the Commission's Public Information Division by messenger services employed by news agencies, law firms, and business enterprises. A consent order used to be publicized only once, when it and the complaint were issued. But, now that the Commission has adopted a 30-day waiting period for proposed consent orders, two press releases are distributed: a full-dress announcement of the proposed order and, at the end of the 30-day period, an abbreviated press notice of final adoption of the order, with a reference, for the details, to the original press release.

According to the Senate Subcommittee on Administrative Practice and Procedure, Congress has received many complaints that the Commission issues damning press releases while the existence and lawfulness of the conduct about which it is complaining are still matters to be determined. Senator Edward E. Long (D-Mo), Chairman of the Subcommittee, reported these complaints when he and Senator Everett Dirksen (R-Ill) introduced S. 924. That bill would amend Section 9 of the Administrative Procedure Act to require that administrative agencies give corporations and individuals "an equal opportunity" to answer charges made in press releases. The Senate passed such a bill (S. 1336) in 1966, but it was not acted on by the House. When he introduced the new bill, Senator Long acknowledged that the public has a right to know about the issuance of an FTC complaint, "but the press release too often leaves the impression that the subject of the complaint has already been found guilty."

Less than a month after the two senators made their move, the Commission found itself embroiled in litigation over its press-release policy. About to be proceeded against for false advertising, the Cinderella Career & Finishing School, Washington, D.C., sued to prevent the Commission from distributing a press release publicizing the complaint (p. A-10, ATRR No. 296, 3/14/67). On the day the injunction complaint was filed, the Federal District Court for the District of Columbia denied a temporary restraining order, and the next day the Commission issued its complaint, along with the regular press release. The School then amended its complaint to seek an order barring a press announcement of its answer to the Commission's charges (p. A-3, ATRR No. 298, 3/28/67) and this time was able to persuade another judge to issue a preliminary injunction (p. A-9, ATRR No. 300, 4/11/67). In a subsequent opinion explaining his action (p. A-6, ATRR No. 303, 5/2/67), the district judge declared that the Commission's issuance of news releases prior to final adjudication in a formal complaint proceeding gives "the appearance of constituting a prejudgment of the issues." The releases were described by the opinion as "public statements appearing to support the allegations of the complaint." He said the inevitable result of any Commission news release prior to final adjudication is to "spread throughout the public and business community the impression that the respondents were guilty of unlawful and deceptive practices and were not honorable or ethical persons with whom to be doing business." He had serious doubts "that the Commission has power under Section 6(f) of the FTC Act to issue any news releases in a quasi-judicial proceeding unless and until the matter has been fully adjudicated." While an appeal from that decision was pending, an FTC examiner decided (p. A-20, ATRR No. 345, 2/20/68) that there is insufficient evidence to support the Commission's charges -- a holding still to be reviewed by the full Commission.

On Appeal

Nevertheless, the Court of Appeals for the District of Columbia Circuit vacated the preliminary injunction and instructed the district court to dismiss Cinderella's complaint. The court of appeals did not deny that an FTC press release "in this or any other complaint proceeding, is undoubtedly deleterious to the respondents' economic, business and community status." But the appellate court was convinced that the FTC Act gives the Commission authority to publicize its enforcement activities on its own initiative, and "'in the discharge by Congress of a dominant trust for the benefit of the public, the possibility of incidental loss to the individual is sometimes unavoidable.' American Sumatra Tobacco Corporation v. SEC, 71 App. D.C. 259, 262-63, 110 F.2d 117, 120-21 (1940)." In fact, the court of appeals saw in the FTC Act "authority in the Commission, acting in the public interest, to alert the public to suspected violations of the law by factual press releases whenever the Commission shall have reason to believe that a respondent is engaged in activities made unlawful by the Act which have resulted in the initiation of action by the Commission." But the court made a point of saying that it is not ruling on the sufficiency of a complaint containing an allegation that the Commission's charges are knowingly false, that the Commission discriminated against the plaintiff, or that the news release did not fairly and accurately summarize the Commission's complaint.

Soon after the Cinderella suit was brought, the Commission began adding to each press release announcing a complaint, immediately below the lead paragraph, a "NOTE" stating: "A complaint is issued whenever the Commission has found 'reason to believe' that the law has been violated and that a proceeding is in the public interest. It is emphasized that the issuance of a complaint simply marks the initiation of a formal proceeding in which the charges in the complaint will be ruled upon after a hearing and on the record. The issuance of a complaint does not indicate or reflect any adjudication of the matters charged." The Court of Appeals for the District of Columbia Circuit found this added warning "well intended" and "commendable" but found "its practical value in minimizing the derogatory inferences *** at best minimal."

Antitrust Division

The Justice Department, too, issues press releases on every new court proceeding the Antitrust Division initiates, every proposed consent order it negotiates, and every voluntary termination or withdrawal of one of its court actions. The Department does not ordinarily circularize the press, though, when a court decides a contested case or when a proposed consent order is entered as final. Its press releases are also usually shorter than the Commission's and seem generally to stick more closely to the language of the complaint or indictment. But a Justice Department announcement of a complaint or indictment contains no caveat or "NOTE," such as the FTC adds, to specifically disclaim a finding of guilt. And the Department's announcement of consent decrees, unlike the Commission's releases on consent orders, do not add the reminder that the consent is not an admission or finding of guilt.

When the Justice Department first started issuing announcements of its cases in May of 1938, it submitted its policy to the American Bar Association for an opinion as to propriety under Canon 20 of the ABA's Canons of Professional Ethics: "Newspaper publications by a lawyer as to pending or anticipated litigation may interfere with a fair trial in the courts and otherwise prejudice the new administration of justice. Generally they are to be condemned." The ABA Committee on Professional Ethics, in Opinion No. 199, decided that "Canon 20 does not prohibit issuance of statements by public officials." But the opinion went on to state: "While we see no objection to statements reflecting departmental policy, nor to statements of fact relating to past proceedings in a nature of reports, where, as here, the statements relate to prospective or pending criminal or civil proceedings, they shall omit any assertion of fact likely to create an adverse attitude in the public mind respecting the alleged actions of the defendants to such proceedings."

Apparently the only subsequent statement of news release policy by the Justice Department is an April 16, 1965, statement by the Attorney General that appears at 28 C.F.R. 50.2. That statement spells out the limits on Justice Department releases that announce the initiation of criminal proceedings. The announcement is to give only (1) the defendant's name, age, residence, employment, marital status, and "similar background information;" (2) "the substance or text of the charge;" (3) the identity of the investigating and arresting agency and length of the investigation; and (4) "the circumstances immediately surrounding an arrest." "Only incontrovertible, factual matters" and not "subjective observations" are to be disclosed, and even ordinary background information on the arrest is to be withheld if its release would serve no law-enforcement function and would be prejudicial. The release -- and Justice Department personnel -- must avoid (1) observations about a defendant's character or prior criminal record (although the criminal record "may be made available upon specific inquiry"); (2) statements, confessions, or alibis attributable to a defendant; (3) references to investigative procedures; (4) statements about the identity, credibility or testimony of prospective witnesses; and (5) statements concerning evidence or argument in the case.

Conclusions

No one seems to question the proposition that FTC and all other administrative proceedings must be conducted in public, especially in view of the Freedom of Information Act of 1966, 5 U.S.C. 1002. But that statute merely prohibits federal agencies from concealing the records of their proceedings from persons who come looking for them. Nothing in its phraseology can be read as requiring or encouraging agencies to take the initiative in publicizing the charges they bring. On the other hand, as the D.C. Court of Appeals noted, Section 6(f) of the FTC Act does authorize the Commission "to make public *** information obtained by it." Indeed the Commission was originally conceived as an agency for collecting and disseminating data about the business community.

The practice of issuing press releases is a common one among federal agencies, and the FTC goes no further than the others. In fact, the Commission's releases on respondents' answers are unique, and it is just as thorough in publicizing the dismissal of charges as it is in publicizing a cease-and-desist order. In addition, an FTC respondent usually has advance notice of what is coming: he has been served with a draft of a complaint and has rejected a proposed consent order. Sections 2.31-4, FTC Rules of Practice (p. X-20, ATRR No. 309, 6/13/67). He therefore can have an answering statement ready for the press -- an advantage some lawyers would like to see enhanced by the Commission's advance service of a proposed press release along with the complaint.

It is the nature of the charges involved, not the particular press-release policy followed, that has caused the FTC to be the first agency to get involved in litigation over public announcements. The decisions of the Interstate Commerce Commission, Securities and Exchange Commission, and Federal Power Commission, for examples, make headlines in the daily press only when they resolve major public issues or affect huge corporations whose names are news. But a typical FTC proceeding, while small in economic scope and geographical area of interest, involves the marketing practices of a business whose customers and potential customers make up a significant portion of some local newspaper's readership. The FTC's addition of the precautionary "NOTE" to its news releases is a tacit recognition of merit in Cinderella's complaint that its business would be hurt even if the charges turned out to be unfounded. In practice, however, the "NOTE" serves as a warning to only the newspaper editors: as a rule, it is left out of the story the public sees.

Nor will a court injunction always solve the problem. Most newspapers keep a close watch on local court dockets, so filing of an injunction suit may simply mean that the public's attention will be called to the Commission's action earlier and more often. In many instances, moreover, an officially sanctioned press release will promote accuracy and prevent the publication of an exaggerated or emotional description of the charges. It also frequently forestalls direct questioning of the attorneys involved by reporters and thereby promotes observance of Canon 20. It may well be, therefore, that the innocent respondent would have gained little protection from an opposite holding by the D. C. Court of Appeals.

If a respondent can't persuade the FTC in pre-complaint negotiations that he is innocent or that the matter should be disposed of on the basis of his assurance of voluntary compliance, then he may have no choice but to submit to whatever adverse results flow from the publicity accompanying issuance of a consent order or a complaint. It seems doubtful that it would often pay to counter with an answering publicity campaign. That tactic would probably serve in most situations to call the FTC's action to the attention of additional potential customers who might otherwise have overlooked it.

- 0 -

PART IX – PRIVATE ENFORCEMENT

Subject: Proof of the Fact of Injury and "Causation" in a Damage Suit   (Published 5/16/67)

Question

What problems are encountered by antitrust damage claimants in proving that they were in fact injured as a result of the antitrust violation?

References

Analysis, "Measure and Proof of Damages in Private Suits," (p. 308, Antitrust and Trade Regulation Today: 1967)

Analysis, "The 'Business or Property' Requirement for Damage Actions," (p. 312, Antitrust and Trade Regulation Today: 1967)

Analysis, "Standing to Sue for Treble Damages," (p. 305, Antitrust and Trade Regulation Today: 1967)

Continental Ore Co. v. Union Carbide & Carbon Corp., 370 U.S. 690 (pp. A-24, X-13, ATRR No. 50, 6/26/62)

Monticello Tobacco Co. v. American Tobacco Co., 197 F.2d 629 (2d Cir. 1952)

Wolfe v. National Lead Co., 225 F.2d 427 (9th Cir. 1955)

Background

Section 4 of the Clayton Act allows an award of treble damages only to "any person injured in his business or property by reason of anything forbidden in the antitrust laws." Therefore, the private plaintiff must establish, not only a violation, but two additional elements: "Injury" to his business or property; and a causal connection between the violation and the "injury." In the analysis cited above on proof of the amount of damages, it was pointed out that the Supreme Court has been easy to please in testing the sufficiency of evidence supporting the amount of damages awarded by a jury. Story Parchment Co. v. Patterson Parchment Paper Co., 282 U.S. 555 (1931), was cited for that proposition. But that opinion endorsed a requirement of certainty in proof of both the occurrence of injury and the causal connection between the antitrust violation and the injury.

In the ordinary tort action, the existence of an injury and its causal relationship to the defendant's negligence are easy to separate. In most antitrust litigation, on the other hand, they are closely linked together. The damage claimant is usually trying to establish that he would have received more income or incurred lower costs "but for" the defendant's antitrust violation. The evidence he presents to show that he was hurt serves also to establish that what hurt him was the antitrust violation. Consequently, many of the court opinions dealing with these problems treat them as a single issue without revealing the specific requirements applied to either standing alone.

An example of a fact situation in which the courts tend to consider injury and causation together is Bigelow v. RKO Radio Pictures, 327 U.S. 251 (1946). The suit was brought by a theater operator complaining about a conspiracy to discriminate against him in the distribution of first-run motion-picture films. To show his damages, he compared his theater's earnings with those of a comparable theater able to secure first-run films and compared his net receipts during a period when the conspiracy was fully operative with his receipts during a period when he had been able to procure first-run films. The court of appeals reversed a jury verdict for the theater operator holding, that neither of these lines of proof established what the theater's earnings would have been in the absence of the conspiracy. But the Supreme Court reversed, applying the rule that "the wrongdoer may not object to the plaintiff's reasonable estimate of the cause of injury *** because not based on more accurate data which the wrongdoer's misconduct has rendered unavailable."

133

The Supreme Court's Continental Ore opinion listed in the references seems to deal only with the problem of causation, for the injury claimed was the complete destruction of the damage claimant's business, the actual occurrence of which was apparently not contested. It was claimed that failure of the claimant's business was caused by a conspiracy controlling the supply of a vital raw material. The court of appeals held that the damage claimant had to show not only the conspiracy and a failure of his business for lack of the material but also that he had made timely demands for the raw material from the defendants and that he had exhausted all other possible sources of the material. Again the Supreme Court found "sufficient evidence for a jury to infer the necessary causal connection between respondent's antitrust violations and petitioners' injury." The Court quotes its statement in Bigelow that "in the absence of more precise proof, the jury could conclude as a matter of just and reasonable inference from the proof of defendants' wrongful acts and their tendency to injure plaintiff's business, and from the evidence of the decline in prices, profits, and values, not shown to be attributable to other causes, that defendants' wrongful acts had caused damage to the plaintiffs."

Tying Arrangements

Not always do the U.S. courts of appeals have to be reminded by the Supreme Court to give effect to the doctrine of the Bigelow Case. In Richfield Oil Corp. v. Karseal Corp., 271 F.2d 709 (1959), the Ninth Circuit agreed with a damage claimant's assertion that, "having shown the illegal restraint applied to its product" by a competing seller, "it had proved the causal connection between the defendant's wrongful act and the loss of revenue." The Section 1 Sherman Act restraint was an exclusive-dealing arrangement under which Richfield Oil Corp. supplied all its service stations with their requirements of tires, batteries, and accessories. Later in another TBA case -- Lessig v. Tidewater Oil Co., 327 F.2d 459 (p. A-10, ATRR No. 132, 1/21/64) -- the Ninth Circuit pointed to an additional item of evidence as proving that the exclusive-dealing requirement hurt the complaining retailer. "Evidence that a merchant has been required to pay more for goods which he resells is sufficient to establish, prima facie, that he has been damaged; tested by common experience, such proof is adequate to 'establish with reasonable probability' that profits on resale were less." To the oil company's argument that higher costs of sponsored TBA would not necessarily mean lower retailer profits, the court responded that the oil company's illegal activity made production of such evidence impossible by preventing the retailer from dealing in a competing line of TBA.

Another example of a Sherman Act conspiracy whose intended and natural result was the injury complained of by the damage claimant can be found in Emich Motors Corp. v. General Motors Corp., 340 U.S. 558 (1951). The damage claimant had no trouble proving a Sherman Act violation; he used a criminal conviction of General Motors for coercing its automobile dealers into exclusive use of General Motors' financing subsidiary and for terminating the franchises of those dealers who did not comply. But the Court of Appeals for the Seventh Circuit had held (181 F.2d 70 (1950)) that the criminal judgment could not be used as evidence that the conspiracy of which General Motors had been convicted occasioned the franchise cancellation complained of in the damage suit. The Supreme Court reversed, treating the criminal judgment as prima facie evidence of not only the general conspiracy to monopolize automobile financing but also of the effectuation of the conspiracy by coercing dealers to use General Motors financing. "It therefore was necessary for petitioners only to introduce, in addition to the criminal judgment, evidence of the impact of the conspiracy on them, such as the cancellation of their franchises and the purpose of General Motors in cancelling them, and evidence of any resulting damages."

Monopolization

The Emich case was distinguished by the Court of Appeals for the Second Circuit when it held, in Monticello Tobacco Co. v. American Tobacco Co., 197 F.2d 629 (1952), that the criminal conviction affirmed in American Tobacco Co. v. U.S., 147 F.2d. 93 (6th Cir.), and 328 U.S. 781, could not be used as evidence that a would-be cigarette marketer's failure was caused by the restraint of trade and monopolization attempt of which the major tobacco companies had been convicted. It was the Second Circuit's view that "the mere fact of conviction cannot make the major tobacco manufacturers liable for every business casualty in the cigarette field." The major manufacturers' control of their market was found to have no impact on the damage claimant, since he always had ready access to cigarettes and had never sought to buy leaf tobacco for his own manufacturing purposes. And the major manufacturers' price-fixing activities could not have affected the damage claimant, since there was no suggestion that the major manufacturers had dictated the prices to be charged by nonparticipants in their conspiracy.

The issue of the sufficiency of proof of the fact of damage seems to have been considered independently of causation by the Ninth Circuit in Wolfe v. National Lead Co. As in the Continental Ore Case discussed above, a manufacturing enterprise was complaining about a conspiracy that deprived it of an essential raw material. The district judge dismissed the suit for failure to show any injury, pointing to evidence (1) that the years of shortage were profitable for the damage claimants, (2) that a later year was less profitable even though they had an abundance of the raw material, (3) that the damage claimants were newcomers to the industry, (4) that all members of the industry had been limited in their supplies of the critical raw material during the period of the alleged conspiracy, and (5) that the damage claimants had received their share of the short material. The Court of Appeals for the Ninth Circuit agreed with the district judge that these circumstances were illustrative "of the completely speculative nature of the evidence as to any hurt or damage claimed to have been suffered."

Conclusions

Decisions like those in the Monticello and Wolfe cases make it clear that, despite some of the courts' broad language suggesting that juries can infer the fact of damage from proof of the violation, the burden of proving that he was hurt and that his injury was the result of the antitrust violation remains on the damage claimant in every suit. The Ninth Circuit's statement in Fox West Coast Theaters Corp. v. Paradise T. Building Corp., 264 F.2d 602 (1958), that "the mere unlawful combination over a period of time to eliminate competition is proof of damage" was made in a context of clear evidence of injury and causation.

More typical, perhaps, is the Eighth Circuit's language in McCleneghan v. Union Stock Yards of Omaha, 349 F.2d 53 (p. A-17, ATRR No. 211, 7/27/65): "Proof of monopoly or restraint of trade and evidence that plaintiff was a customer or competitor of the wrongdoer is not sufficient in itself to support a recovery. Proof of damage to the public or to others will not without more support a finding of fact of damage caused by the defendants' wrongful acts."

The weight of the burden of proving a causal relationship between a proven violation and a proven loss or injury seems to vary from one type of antitrust violation to another. It is probably easier, for example, to establish that a price-fixing conspiracy was the cause of a higher price paid by a complaining customer during the period of the conspiracy than it is to show that a monopolization attempt by a few large producers in an industry caused the failure of one of their competitors. When damage suits are based on the price discrimination provisions in Section 2(a) of the Clayton Act, the task of proving a causal connection between the violation and the claimed damage will often be easier when the complaint comes from a buyer who was discriminated against than when the complaint comes from a competitor of the seller who discriminated. One of the elements the damage claimant has to prove to establish a violation is probable injury to competition. Consequently, a buyer suing because he was discriminated against will have furnished most of his "causation" proof by the time he finishes his proof of the violation. A competing seller, on the other hand, can often prove the competitive-injury element of a Section 2(a) violation without evidence of matters that directly affect him. See Utah Pie Co. v. Continental Baking Co., 386 U.S. 685, 35 LW 4373 (p. A-16, X-17, ATRR No. 302, 4/25/67). In any type of case, one of the best means of showing "causation" is proof of the violators' intent to cause the injury complained of.

Although the Supreme Court's opinion in the Utah Pie case deals with the threshold problem of proving probable competitive injury as an element of a Section 2(a) violation, there is language in it demonstrating that a treble-damage claimant need not prove that his profit-and-loss statement shows a minus figure. A business enterprise can be in good economic shape and still prove losses recoverable under the antitrust laws -- by proving it would have made larger profits but for the antitrust violation. See Mechanical Contractors Bid Depository v. Christiansen, 352 F.2d 817 (10th Cir.)(p. A-6, ATRR No. 229, 11/30/65).

Even after he has presented prima facie proof of injury and causation, the damage claimant is not always home free. The defendant can -- often does -- counter with evidence that the damages claimed were the results of economic factors other than his conduct. He can point to such factors as the damage claimant's inefficiency, poor management decisions, or inferior product, to special conditions prevailing in the market at the time the injury was suffered, to cost increases that would have boosted prices as much as the price-fixing conspiracy proven by the damage claimant, or to a new technological development that made the plaintiff's product obsolete.

Some antitrust experts feel, however, that alternative explanations supplied by a defendant for the plaintiff's losses are effective only when they completely eliminate the antitrust violation as a possible reason for the losses. If the damage claimant is able to show clearly that he was hurt and that the antitrust violation was at least one of the causes, federal judges tend to allow recovery.

The electrical-equipment cases are often cited to illustrate this point, for the manufacturers seemed to have little success with their contentions that such factors as higher costs and limited production capacity would have pushed prices to at least the level they reached during the price-fixing conspiracy even if there had been no conspiracy. The opinion in Ohio Valley Electric Corp. v. General Electric Co., 244 F.Supp. 914 (S.D. N.Y. 1965), describes the attempt of one federal district judge to separate the portion of the price increase attributable to the conspiracy from that attributable to changed economic conditions. But even he allocated less than one sixth of the price increase to the factors relied on by the defendant manufacturers.

Of course, the defendant is also entitled to present rebuttal evidence showing that the damage claimant in fact suffered no economic loss at all. The most common type of defense attempted in this area is proof that the losses or added costs were passed on to customers in the form of higher prices. The law on whether and when the "passing-on" defense can be used is sufficiently complex to warrant separate treatment in a subsequent ATRR ANALYSIS (see p. 153, infra).

- 0 -

Subject: The Public-Injury Requirement   (Published 4/2/68)

Question

Must an antitrust treble-damage plaintiff allege and prove public injury as a separate and distinct element of his cause of action?

References

Klor's, Inc., v. Broadway-Hale Stores, 359 U.S. 207 (1959)
Radiant Burners, Inc., v. People's Gas, Light & Coke Co., 364 U.S. 656 (1961)
Syracuse Broadcasting Corp. v. Newhouse, 295 F.2d 269 (2d Cir. 1961)
Switzer Bros., Inc., v. Locklin, 297 F.2d 39 (7th Cir. 1961)
Atlantic Heel Co. v. Allied Heel Co., 284 F.2d 879 (1st Cir. 1960)
Donlan v. Carvel, 209 F.Supp. 829 (D. Md. 1962)
Epstein v. Dennison Mfg. Co., 1966 Trade Cases, Para. 71,852 (S.D. N.Y.) (p. A-4,
    ATRR No. 267, 8/23/66)

Background

Contrary to a number of earlier decisions by lower federal courts, the Supreme Court ruled in the Klor's case that a private antitrust treble-damage claimant complaining about a boycott violating Sections 1 and 2 of the Sherman Act need not allege or offer proof that the boycott caused injury to the public. Placing boycotts among those "classes of restraints which from their 'nature or character' were unduly restrictive, and hence forbidden," the Court declared: "As to these classes of restraints, *** Congress had determined its own criteria of public harm and it was not for the courts to decide whether in an individual case injury had actually occurred."

The first appellate court to consider the scope of the Klor's doctrine was the Court of Appeals for the First Circuit in Atlantic Heel Co. v. Allied Heel Co. The court declared "the question for our decision is whether or not the allegation of a conspiracy to destroy a competitor *** is a per se violation of Section 1 so that the rationale of the Klor's case applies, and, thus, no allegations of further facts showing the basis of public harm and consequent unreasonableness of the restraint are necessary." The First Circuit eliminated the requirement of alleging and proving public injury only after it had concluded that the damage complaint had alleged a per se violation of the Sherman Act.

Then in the Radiant Burners case, the Supreme Court, although again dealing with a boycott in per se violation of Section 1 of the Sherman Act, stated the rule as follows: "To state a claim upon which relief can be granted under that section, allegations adequate to show a violation and, in a private treble-damage action, that plaintiff was damaged thereby are all the law requires." That language was read by both the Second and Seventh Circuits in the Syracuse Broadcasting and Switzer Bros. cases as eliminating public injury as a separate element in private damage suits based on conduct that does not violate the antitrust laws unless its unreasonableness or anticompetitive effect is proven. In In re McConnell, 370 U.S. 230, 231 (1962), the Supreme Court itself interpreted Klor's and Radiant Burners as holding "that the right of recovery *** in a treble damage antitrust case does not depend at all on proving an economic injury to the public." In Donlan v. Carvel, however, the Maryland Federal District Court went back to the proposition that specific allegation and proof of public injury is necessary for anything but a per se antitrust violation. The court went on to find that public injury had been sufficiently alleged in the complaint it had been asked to dismiss. The court made no reference to Radiant Burners, Syracuse Broadcasting, or Switzer Bros. but relied entirely on its reading of Klor's as applicable only to per se violations.

The latest opinion to deal with the subject is Epstein v. Dennison Mfg. Co., 1966 Trade Cases Para. 71,852. Without mentioning any distinction between per se and other Sherman Act violations, the Southern New York Federal District Court simply found a treble-damage complaint "fatally defective since it does not allege any facts which show injury to the public."

Conclusions

The Epstein and Donlan opinions do not reflect prevailing law on the point.

Epstein is the only surviving precedent for requiring separate allegation and proof of public injury in any private antitrust action. The statements in the Atlantic Heel and Donlan cases limiting the Klor's doctrine to per se violations were not necessary to the decisions reached there. In Atlantic Heel, a per se violation was found to be alleged, and in Donlan there were found to be separate allegations of public injury. Epstein is the only reported decision since Klor's and Radiant Burners in which a court has actually dismissed a treble-damage complaint for lack of a separate allegation of public injury.

On the other hand, the appellate court decisions in Syracuse Broadcasting and Switzer Bros. stand as precedents in which separate public-injury evidence was held unnecessary to show violations of the Sherman Act in conduct that was not unlawful per se. Unfortunately, those opinions do not contain an exposition of the rule applied. Nevertheless, the logic of the court of appeals' holdings seems clear: If, as the Supreme Court has said, Congress has determined there is public injury in every violation of the Sherman Act, then every allegation of a Sherman Act violation necessarily encompasses an allegation of injury to the public. It makes no difference whether the conduct in question is alleged to violate the Act because such conduct is, by its very nature, always in unreasonable restraint of trade or is alleged to violate the Act because it is unreasonable in the particular economic and motivational context in which it occurred. Similarly, evidence sufficient to establish a violation necessarily establishes public harm under the theory that Congress has determined that public injury is inherent in every antitrust violation.

Moreover, this is a theory as applicable to the Clayton Act as to the Sherman Act, although all the reported decisions dealing with the public-injury issue have been Sherman Act cases.

- 0 -

Subject: Evidence from Government Cases   (Published 4/22/69)

Question

What evidence can treble-damage claimants get from Justice Department antitrust cases terminated by consent decrees or nolo contendere pleas?

References

Harper & Row Publishers, Inc. v. Decker, 7th Cir., January 9, 1969; review denied, April 1, 1969 (p. A-35, ATRR No. 403, 4/1/69)

Hancock Bros., Inc., v. Jones, 1969 Trade Cases para. 72,677 (N.D. Calif. 1968)

Standard Fruit & Steamship Co. v. Lynne, 393 U.S. 974 (p. A-5, ATRR No. 387, 12/10/68)

U.S. Industries, Inc. v. U.S. District Court, 345 F.2d 18 (9th Cir.) (p. A-17, ATRR No. 198, 4/27/65)

Background

Under Section 5(a) of the Clayton Act, the "final judgment or decree" obtained by the United States in an antitrust proceeding is admissible as "prima facie evidence," in a subsequent treble-damage suit against the same defendant, "as to all matters respecting which said judgment *** would be an estoppel as between the parties thereto." In Twentieth Century-Fox Film Corp. v. Brookside Theatre Corp., 194 F.2d 846 (8th Cir. 1952), the plaintiff was permitted to introduce in evidence not only the government's decree but also its complaint, the bill of particulars, and the court's findings of fact and conclusions of law.

The Supreme Court sometimes has encouraged trial courts to allow damage-suit plaintiffs broad access to the evidence procured by the government for its antitrust cases. The Court has seen in Section 5(b) of the Clayton Act a congressional intent "to assist private litigants in utilizing any benefits they might cull from government antitrust actions." Minnesota Mining & Mfg. Co. v. New Jersey Wood Finishing Co., 381 U.S. 311, 317 (1965). Noting that in most instances the pleadings, transcripts of testimony, exhibits, and other documents of the government's case are available to a damage plaintiff, the Court described government cases "as a major source of evidence for private parties." 381 U.S. at 319.

Congress has expressed a view that government antitrust litigation is not to be conducted in secrecy. The Publicity in Taking Evidence Act of March 3, 1913, 15 U.S. Code 30, provides that the taking of depositions in government Sherman Act injunction suits "shall be open to the public as freely as are trials in open court; and no order excluding the public from attendance on any such proceedings shall be valid or enforceable." This statute may not have been repealed by Federal Rule of Civil Procedure 30(b), which authorizes a trial court to order "that the examination shall be held with no one present except the parties to the action and their officers or counsel." See 4 Moore's Federal Practice para. 30.10.

A general intention to keep the activities of administrative and executive agencies open to the public was also expressed by Congress in the Freedom of Information Act, 5 U.S. Code 552. But there is an exception in the Act that makes it largely inapplicable to the law-enforcement activities of the Justice Department and its Antitrust Division. Subsection (b)(7) of the Act preserves the secrecy of "investigatory files compiled for law enforcement purposes." This exemption is not limited to criminal investigations. Clement Brothers Co. v. NLRB, 282 F.Supp. 540 (N.D. Ga. 1968).

"Investigatory files" secrecy was also protected when in 1962, the Justice Department's investigatory powers in antitrust cases were significantly broadened by enactment of the Antitrust Civil Process Act, 15 U.S. Code 1311-1314, authorizing the issuance of civil investigative demands. Section 4(c) of that statute provides that "no material so produced shall be available for examination, without the consent of the person who produces such material, by an individual other than a duly authorized officer, member, or employee of the Department of Justice."

Civil Litigation

Defendants in government antitrust litigation try to make as little evidence as possible available in the public record. If the government's case, whether civil or criminal, is tried, not only is a judgment for the government available as "prima facie evidence" of an antitrust violation, but the entire record of the proceeding is available to prove the precise scope and nature of the violation. A treble-damage claimant will usually find there everything he needs except proof of the fact and amount of his damages.

Occasionally, a defendant in a government suit will succeed in convincing the district judge that some of the information furnished the government during discovery proceedings is sufficiently confidential or privileged to be segregated from the public record.

In Olympic Refining Co. v. Carter, 332 F.2d 260 (9th Cir. 1964), a damage claimant wanted to see interrogatory answers that were subject to protective orders. In an effort to cooperate with the plaintiff, the Antitrust Division filed a motion to vacate the protective orders, but the district judge had denied the motion and quashed the damage plaintiff's subpoena. In the district court's view it was the protective orders that had enabled the government to obtain "full and complete disclosure" in the first place. The Court of Appeals for the Ninth Circuit reversed the district judge, finding nothing in the Federal Rules of Civil Procedure that would authorize a court to protect trade secrets and sensitive competitive information "from such disclosure as is relevant to the subject matter involved in a pending action. All that may be done is to afford such protection from disclosure as is practicable, consistent with the right of access thereto for purposes of litigation." Therefore, the district court was directed to modify the protective orders to give the damage-suit plaintiff access to the interrogatory answers "subject to such reasonable restrictions as may be necessary and practicable to prevent unnecessary disclosure."

Fear of developing a record for use by damage claimants is often a strong motivating factor in a defendant's election to accede to a consent decree rather than litigate the government's charges. Recognizing this to be a factor in settlement negotiations, Congress added to Section 5(a) of the Clayton Act a proviso "that this section shall not apply to consent judgments *** entered before any testimony has been taken." Like its investigations, the Antitrust Division's consent-decree negotiations are treated as strictly confidential.

That rule of confidentiality has not been applied, though, to documents exchanged by the parties in the post-decree mechanics of compliance with the decree. Shortly after entry of the consent decree in U.S. v. United Fruit Co., 1958 Trade Cases para. 68,941 (E.D. La), the Federal District Court for Eastern Louisiana granted United Fruit's motion for a protective order prohibiting inspection by outsiders of "any document submitted by either party in this case," apparently because the court feared that disclosure of the documents would create problems in the foreign relations of the United States. A request by a United Fruit competitor for leave to inspect and copy compliance programs and reports was denied in Standard Fruit & Steamship Co. v. Lynne, cited in the references. In a petition to the Supreme Court for a writ of mandamus (p. A-1, ATRR No. 375, 9/17/68), the competitor alleged the government was interested in obtaining the competitor's view as to the compliance program. The Supreme Court denied mandamus without comment and subsequently (p. A-7, ATRR No. 393, 1/21/69) dismissed an appeal citing Shenandoah Valley Broadcasting, Inc. v. ASCAP, 375 U.S. 39 (1963), which rejected direct appeals in private controversies outside the "mainstream" of government litigation.

Criminal Prosecutions

In criminal antitrust cases, nolo contendere pleas are accepted as "consent judgments" falling within the Section 5(a) proviso, but the status of guilty pleas is not entirely clear (see analysis, "Use of Prior Antitrust Judgments Against Defendants in Treble-Damage Actions," p. B-1, ATRR No. 74, 12/11/62; reprinted, p. 318, Antitrust and Trade Regulation Today: 1967. The Section 5(a) status of a criminal judgment based on a guilty plea may not be significant, since the plea is surely admissible in any event as an admission or statement against interest.

When a defendant is convicted and sentenced on the basis of a nolo contendere plea, there is often a great deal of information developed before entry and acceptance of the plea, as well as subsequently in the determination of the sentence to be imposed. Federal Rule of Criminal Procedure 6(e) forbids disclosure of matters occurring before the grand jury except "to the attorneys for the government for use in the performance of their duties." Any further disclosure may be made only when "directed by the court preliminarily to or in connection with a judicial proceeding." In the electrical-equipment cases, damage claimants were accorded access to substantial portions of the transcripts of testimony elicited by the grand jury that had indicted the manufacturers. The Federal District Court for Eastern Pennsylvania, where the grand jury sat, promulgated a standard operating procedure for nationwide use in procuring the grand jury testimony of any witness whose deposition was to be taken for a damage suit. Philadelphia v. Westinghouse Electric Corp., 211 F.Supp. 486(1962). That procedure was upheld later by the Court of Appeals for the Fifth Circuit in Allis-Chalmers Mfg. v. Fort Pierce, 323 F.2d 233 (1963).

Documents subpoenaed by several grand juries during an antitrust investigation of the publishing industry were ordered produced for inspection by treble-damage plaintiffs in the Harper & Row case listed in the references. The production order was entered by the Federal District Court for Northern Illinois, in which the Judicial Panel on Multi-District Litigation had consolidated, for pre-trial purposes, 21 treble-damage suits filed against publishers and wholesalers of library editions of children's books. In their petition for Supreme Court review of the order, the defendants asserted that there is nothing in the record before the district court to support a finding of "good cause" or "particularized need" for production of the documents, that there has never been an appropriate hearing on the existence of those prerequisites, and that the lower court issued its order with no Rule 34 motion pending before it.

When a damage claimant is denied access to the grand jury transcript and documents procured by the grand jury, he may be able to find a less direct route to the information he wants through identification of the witnesses who appeared before the grand jury. A list of the names of the grand jury witnesses may be obtained in several ways. The returns to the subpoenas served on the witnesses should be available in the office of the clerk of the district court, since they are public records. While some courts seem to impede access to those returns, there does not appear to be any reason why the names of the grand jury witnesses known to the defendant cannot be obtained through interrogatories under Federal Civil Rule 33.

After indictment, if there are discovery and other pre-trial proceedings before nolo pleas are tendered, information helpful to damage claimants may get into the public record of the case or the defendants themselves may come into possession of evidence that is subject to discovery in a suit for damages. Before the nolo contendere pleas were accepted in U.S. v. Union Camp Corp. (p. A-12, ATRR No. 353, 4/16/68), there were several statements by the defendants that they were admitting the allegations of the indictment "in open court." However, admissions of guilt made in connection with entry of a nolo plea have sometimes been treated as "part and parcel of the plea" and therefore not usable in subsequent damage litigation. Polychrome Corp. v. Minnesota Mining & Mfg. Co., 263 F.Supp. 101 (S.D. N.Y. 1966) (p. A-8, ATRR No. 287, 1/10/67).

Even after a nolo contendere plea has been tendered to the court, government counsel often makes statements helpful to potential damage claimants in open court either at the time of acceptance of the plea or later at time of sentencing. Indeed, the government often files a sentencing memorandum with the court or with the probation officer for inclusion in his presentence report. Under Rule 32(c) of the Federal Rules of Criminal Procedure, as amended in 1966, the court "may disclose to the defendant or his counsel all or part of the material contained in" the "pre-sentence investigation and report by the probation service of the court." While this language indicates that the report is not to become part of the public record of the case, there are no decisions whether portions of it are subject to discovery from a defendant who obtains a copy of it.

In U.S. Industries, Inc. v. U.S. District Court, 345 F.2d 18(9th Cir. 1965), the government admitted that its pre-sentencing memorandum to the probation officer contained information that related to the grand jury proceedings and was protected by Rule 6(e) of the Criminal Rules. Therefore, when damage plaintiffs sought access to the government memorandum, the Court of Appeals for the Ninth Circuit first deleted those portions whose exclusion it considered necessary to respect "the policy considerations behind the rule of secrecy of grand jury investigations." Having done so, the Court ordered the document unsealed and made available to the damage plaintiffs.

Because the U.S. Industries case was decided before the 1966 amendment adding the Federal Criminal Rule 32(c) language quoted above, it was distinguished by the district judge who decided the Hancock Bros. case cited in the references. The Antitrust Division was willing there to have its pre-sentencing reports made part of the public record so they could be disclosed to treble-damage claimants. But one of the convicted defendants in the criminal case sued for a declaratory judgment, and the district judge decided that the pre-sentencing reports "should remain under the seal of confidentiality." Again much of the information contained in the pre-sentencing reports was procured in the grand jury proceedings, and the district court declared: "it is a firmly established policy of the law that acts of the grand jury and evidence taken before it are to be protected from public scrutiny." Since the only reason given by the damage-suit plaintiffs for disclosure was that they would be able to avoid expense and additional work, the district judge could not see the "compelling necessity" that must be shown for disclosure of grand jury records.

Conclusions

Despite all the rules of secrecy protecting criminal investigations and proceedings, a criminal prosecution terminated by nolo pleas often offers a damage claimant more avenues of access to evidentiary materials than a civil case producing a consent order. One antitrust lawyer has suggested that the advantages of a nolo contendere plea over a guilty plea "can be overrated at least insofar as the consequences in subsequent treble-damage actions are concerned." Victor H. Kramer, "Subsequent Use of the Record and Proceedings," 38 ABA Antitrust L. J. ___ (Spring Meeting, 1969).

Certainly an antitrust defendant who is not convinced of his innocence and wants to get the maximum benefit out of a nolo contendere plea should submit that plea to the court at the earliest possible moment. Demands for bills of particulars and efforts at discovery of the government's case too often bring into the defendant's possession information or documents that are easier to get from the defendant by Rule 34 motion or Rule 33 interrogatories than they would be to get from the government or the court. In addition, government counsel is, more often than not, sympathetic to the needs of private damage claimants and therefore less than reluctant to take advantage of opportunities in open court or in memoranda to make revelations that can be used by damage claimants. The generally cooperative attitude of government counsel, antitrust lawyers also report, often makes it possible for damage plaintiffs to derive valuable information from direct conversations with government counsel. While the Antitrust Division's policy in this regard is not entirely clear, its attorneys do seem to be given considerable leeway in cooperating with state and local agencies that file treble-damage actions. Experiences reported by plaintiffs' lawyers indicate that the amount of cooperation varies from lawyer to lawyer.

- 0 -

Subject: Class Actions   (Published 6/20/67)

Question

What impact are recent changes in the federal "class action" rule likely to have in antitrust damage litigation?

References

Federal Rule of Civil Procedure 23, as amended February 28, 1966, 383 U.S. 1047

Symposium, "Amended Federal Rule 23," 31 ABA Antitrust Law Journal 251

Eisen v. Carlisle & Jacquelin, 41 F.R.D. 147 (S.D. N.Y.) (p. A-1, ATRR No. 274, 10/11/66)

School District of Philadelphia v. Harper & Row Publishers, 267 F.Supp. 1001 (E.D. Pa.) (p. A-1, ATRR No. 303, 5/2/67)

Background

Few types of litigation produce a larger percentage of multi-plaintiff lawsuits than do private antitrust damage actions. And in no other field of litigation can greater significance be assigned the federal courts' rule governing "class actions" -- suits by one or a few representative plaintiffs on behalf of a larger group of claimants and suits against one or a few representative defendants to establish rights against a larger group of persons.

The circumstances under which class actions may be brought in the federal courts and the special procedures to be followed in handling them are set out in Rule 23 of the Federal Rules of Civil Procedure. Until July of 1966, when amendments promulgated by the Supreme Court in February of that year became effective, Rule 23 contemplated three types of class actions for which the federal courts had developed three different standards as to jurisdiction and scope. Claims by or against a class of persons "so numerous as to make it impracticable to bring them all before the court" could be asserted by representative plaintiffs if the claims (1) were "joint, or common, or secondary" to a primary right whose owner refused to enforce it (a "true" class action); (2) were "several" and related to specific property (a "hybrid" class action); or were "several" but involved "a common question of law or fact" and "common relief" (a "spurious" class action).

All antitrust actions brought in reliance on that rule were "spurious" class actions. Few were allowed to proceed as class actions during the first decade of the post-World War II surge in antitrust litigation. Yet, in Weeks v. Bareco Oil Co., 125 F.2d 84 (1941), the Court of Appeals for the Seventh Circuit saw "strong and persuasive reasons" for extending the class-suit theory to antitrust conspiracies, which have "a singleness of object" and an "integral core." The turning point seemed to come in 1952 with the Seventh Circuit's decision in Kainz v. Anheuser-Busch, 194 F.2d 737. Relying on the principle established in the Weeks case, the Seventh Circuit this time recognized as a legitimate class a group of retailers complaining about prices said to discriminate against them. Finally, in Nagler v. Admiral Corp., 248 F.2d 319 (1957), the Court of Appeals for the Second Circuit established quite lenient standards for antitrust plaintiffs claiming to be acting for a "spurious" class.

1966 Amendments

With the recent amendment of Rule 23, however, determination of the propriety of a purported "class action" assumed an entirely different complexion. "The amended rule describes in more practical terms the occasions for maintaining class actions; provides that all class actions maintained to the end as such will resolve in judgments including those whom the court finds to be members of the class, whether or not the judgment is favorable to the class; and refers to the measures which can be taken to assure the fair conduct of these actions." Advisory Committee's Notes, Proposed Rules of Civil Procedure, 39 F.R.D. 69, 99.

No longer does the rule recognize three types of class actions; nor does it concern itself with the sort of rights -- "joint" or "several" -- to be enforced. Rather it simply lists the circumstances under which a class action may be brought. In fact, its provision for judgments binding on all members of the class in effect wipes out the concept of "spurious" class actions. Under the old rule, judgments in such suits were effective only as to such parties as actually participated in the litigation. "Spurious" class actions were therefore frequently characterized as mere devices for permissive joinder of additional plaintiffs or additional defendants.

The new rule sets out six prerequisites to the type of class action that arises in the antitrust field. First, the rule retains the old requirement that the class must be "so numerous that joinder of all members is impracticable." In such pre-amendment cases as Harris v. Palm Spring Alpine Estate, Inc., 329 F.2d 909 (9th Cir. 1964), and Advertising Specialty National Assn. v. FTC, 238 F.2d 108 (1st Cir. 1956), the courts said that "impracticable" does not mean impossible but merely extremely difficult or inconvenient.

Second, there must be "questions of law or fact common to the class." The old rule spoke of "question, " rather than "questions, " of law or fact, "but the Advisors' Notes make no comment on the change."

Third, "the claims or defenses of the representative parties" must be typical of the claims or defenses of the class.

Fourth, the "representative parties" who sue must be such as "fairly and adequately protect the interests of the class." This requirement, too, seems to be in substance a carryover from the old rule, although it may now assume a great deal more importance. Since the old rule provided, in "spurious" class actions, for judgments bonding only on those who actually appeared as parties and intervened in the action, the courts often passed up any inquiry into the adequacy of the representation of the class. An extensive inquiry is now likely to be regarded as necessary, however, in view of the new rule's provisions making the judgment binding on all members of the class.

Fifth, the court must find that "the questions of law or fact common to the members of the class predominate over any questions affecting only individual members." And, sixth, the court must find "that a class action is superior to other available methods for the fair and efficient adjudication of the controversy." Each of these last two requirements is new. In making these two findings, the court is to consider: "(A) the interest of members of the class in individually controlling the prosecution or defense of separate actions; (B) the extent and nature of any litigation concerning the controversy already commenced by or against members of the class; (C) the desirability or undesirability of concentrating the litigation of the claims in the particular forum; (D) the difficulties likely to be encountered in the management of a class action."

One requirement plaintiffs had to meet under the old rule has been eliminated. It is no longer necessary to establish that "a common relief is sought."

The court is to determine the propriety of the class action "as soon as practicable after the commencement of an action." But the court's order allowing the class action "may be conditional, and may be altered or amended before the decision on the merits."

Class Notification

Once it has been determined that the court is entertaining a proper class action, "the court shall direct to the members of the class the best notice practicable under the circumstances, including individual notice to all members who can be identified through reasonable effort." In that notice, each member of the class is to be told, first, that the court will exclude him from the class if he so requests by a specified date; second, that the judgment will be binding on all members who do not request exclusion; and, third, that any member of the class who does not request exclusion may enter an appearance through counsel.

These notice provisions embody the changes that undoubtedly have the greatest significance for antitrust litigation. The "spurious" class action is no longer an invitation to other members of the "class" to come in and participate in the litigation. Now each is told that he is a party to the lawsuit unless he takes affirmative action to stay out. Although some doubt has been expressed on the point, it would appear that any person who receives notice and demands that the court exclude him from the class affected remains free to bring a separate lawsuit to enforce his own claim. One who receives notice and does not object, on the other hand, apparently gets the benefit of the earlier filing of the complaint, even if he had neglected to file suit himself within the period of time allowed him by the statute of limitations.

The last few paragraphs of the rule give the federal district judges broad powers in the administration of class actions. The court can issue orders "determining the course of proceedings or prescribing measures to prevent undue repetition or complication," requiring notice to each member of the class of any particular development in the litigation, imposing conditions on the original plaintiffs or on intervenors, requiring amendment of pleadings to eliminate allegations as to representation of absent persons, and "dealing with similar procedural matters." Finally, a class action cannot be dismissed or compromised without the court's approval and advance notice to all members of the class.

The new rules were not promulgated without dispute. Mr. Justice Black dissented. "It seems to me that they place too much power in the hands of the trial judges and that the rules might also as well simply provide that 'class suits can be maintained for or against particular groups whenever in the discretion of a judge he thinks it is wise.' The power given to the judge to dismiss such suits or to divide them up into groups at will subjects members of classes to dangers that could not follow from carefully prescribed legal standards enacted to control class suits."

Post-Amendment Decisions

Since the amendments' effective date, there have been two expositive opinions applying the new provisions to antitrust litigation. In each instance the district judge decided not to treat the lawsuit as a class action within the meaning of the new rule. In Eisen v. Carlisle & Jacquelin, the Federal District Court for Southern New York saw little difference between the requirements spelled out in the amended rule and the old judge-made requirements for a "spurious" class action. Substantially all the new rule's requirements were found to have existed under the old rule.

Specifically, the district judge's reason for striking "class action" allegations from a complaint attacking the brokerage differential charged on odd-lot transactions on the New York Stock Exchange was the lack of a showing that the complaining trader will adequately protect the interests of all other odd-lot traders. Because the amended rule purports to abandon the old distinctions between "true," "hybrid," and "spurious" class actions, the district judge took the position that it is more important than ever to make sure the plaintiff will be able to represent adequately all members of his class. After all, he explained, under the old rule only the original plaintiff and intervenors were bound by the judgment, whereas under the new Rule 23 all members of the class are bound by the judgment unless they expressly ask to be excluded. Yet the papers filed in the case gave "no compelling reasons" why the complaining odd-lot trader could adequately protect the interests of "possibly hundreds of thousands" of odd-lot traders. Certainly it was not enough, the court declared, to assert that the complaining trader's lawyers are well qualified antitrust specialists -- a factor that would not serve as a basis for a class action even under the old rule. Austin v. Warner Bros., 19 F.R.D. 93 (S.D. N.Y. 1953).

The district judge seemed even more concerned about the problems that would arise in complying with Rule 23(c)'s requirement that the best notice practicable must be furnished to all members of the class. The complaining trader had not suggested, he pointed out, that a single other person has expressed any interest in the lawsuit. And the judge rejected a suggestion of plaintiff's counsel that press advertisements plus notices to stock-exchange files would constitute satisfactory notice to the class. In fact, the suggestion raised the "suspicion" that the complaining trader "is more interested in notice for the sake of undesirable solicitation of claims than for proper protection of the interests of the other members of the class."

The Eisen decision is now pending on appeal in the Court of Appeals for the Second Circuit, following a holding by the court that an order dismissing the "class action" aspect of the litigation is final and appealable. (370 F.2d 119, p. A-1, ATRR No. 288, 1/17/67; review denied, 35 LW 3392, p. A-2, ATRR No. 304, 5/9/67).

In School District of Philadelphia v. Harper & Row, all "class actions" references were stricken from a price-fixing treble-damage complaint filed by the State of Pennsylvania and the City of Philadelphia against 17 book publishers on behalf of more than 1300 public school systems and public libraries. Not persuaded that questions of law and fact common to all members of the asserted class of claimants predominate over questions affecting individual members, the court treated the lawsuit "as an ordinary civil action, with liberal allowance of permissive joinder and intervention under Federal Rules 20 and 24."

Having thus disposed of the "class action," the district judge went on to express doubts about the "propriety" of several aspects of the new rule. One of the changes at which the court looked askance is Rule 23(c)(2)'s provision for "the best notice practicable under the circumstances" to all members of the class, "including individual notice to all members who can be identified through reasonable effort." This "onerous task" plus "the ensuing detail of the consequent record keeping" are functions the court was "loath to impose on the already overburdened clerical facilities of this court."

Although the damage claimants' counsel offered to undertake the task of sending notices to all members of the class, the court rejected that suggestion as one that would seriously impair the court's "appearance of detached impartiality." Service of notice upon all the hundreds of school districts in other library-operating public agencies that might have claims against the book publishers "is more likely to be the beginning, rather than the end of frustrating complexities." Inquiries would inevitably come in, and the answers would involve the court in direct correspondence with prospective litigants in a pending case, "a very questionable judicial undertaking."

Criticism was also directed at the provision that a class-action judgment is binding on every member of the class who receives individual notice of the action even if he simply ignores the notice. Clearly this provision extends the court's jurisdiction to persons not previously within the court's power, the opinion observed. "Such a radical extension of this court's jurisdiction by the mere inaction of the nonappearing, nonresident citizen is, in our view, unprecedented. By its silence, a proposed class member not only forfeits its previously unfettered right to choose its own forum and to initiate its own litigation, but apparently waives any objections it might have concerning the lack of personal jurisdiction and venue of this court."

The court also had doubts "of the propriety of a rule which extends the binding, substantive effect of a judgment to absent, but 'described,' class members as well as to 'identified' class members. Conceivably, after trial, unsuccessful antitrust defendants could find themselves liable to unidentified, but 'described,' class members, against whom they had no fair opportunity to pursue pre-trial discovery, to define and refine issues in pre-trial conference or to cross-examine upon trial."

Another problem the courts see in the new Rule 23 was discussed in Kronenberg v. Hotel Governor Clinton, Inc., 41 F.R.D. 42 (S.D. N.Y. 1966), a securities-fraud suit brought for the benefit of a class consisting of all purchasers of the securities who relied on the fraudulent misrepresentations. "The court is handicapped somewhat by having to decide 'as soon as practicable after the commencement of the action brought as a class action *** ' whether it may be maintained as such." Forced to make the decision on a motion to dismiss the suit's "class" aspects before any discovery had been had and with only the motion papers for guidance, the district judge denied the motion but made his order conditional, as permitted by Rule 23(c)(1). He reserved the right to reverse his decision later if it turns out the fraudulent representations were so varied as to render the action unmanageable.

Advantages

The new rule's advantages and disadvantages for both the parties and the courts were discussed in some detail at the American Bar Association symposium listed in the references. While there was a great deal of speculation, both optimistic and pessimistic, about what can be done with the new rule, there do seem to be a number of clear-cut advantages for plaintiffs. First of all, the notice provisions promise to develop financial backing for the plaintiff not only in the initial litigation but also in any subsequent appeal. Similarly, this mandatory device for soliciting additional participants in the litigation will make it easier to gather intelligence about the transactions complained of and, presumably, build up the volume of evidence available against the defendant. Third, members of the class who do not elect at the outset to be excluded from the litigation, will have to stick with the suit and will be less likely to lose interest when and if the outcome becomes doubtful.

While each of these advantages for plaintiffs can be considered disadvantages for defendants, the rule could have its benefits for some defendants. Hereafter it will be possible more often to get all antitrust claims of the same sort determined in a single big lawsuit instead of dozens or hundreds of smaller ones. Determination of a multitude of claims in this fashion avoids the possibility of a defendant's being burdened with incompatible standards of conduct in his dealings with the various plaintiffs.

Nor is the new rule an unmixed blessing for antitrust damage claimants. Counsel who decides to file his client's suit as a class action must be prepared to give up much of the control he would otherwise be able to exercise over the litigation. He is inviting the participation not only of other plaintiffs but also of other plaintiffs' counsel. The loss of control is likely to be most noticeable when serious settlement negotiations near a satisfactory conclusion. And a federal district judge pointed out at the ABA symposium that the very specificity with which the new rule spells out the prerequisites for maintenance of a class action may create "potentially significant obstacles" to such actions.

The revisors of Rule 23 probably had uppermost in their minds not the interests of litigants but advantages that might accrue in the administration of justice. Their basic purpose was to promote the public interest by avoiding duplication of effort on the part of the judiciary and facilitating disposition of litigation. While the new rule works toward that goal by providing for concentration of all the litigation in one court, it does not really stick entirely to its concept of a class action as a "representative" suit. After requiring in paragraph (a) that the class must be "so numerous that joinder of all members is impracticable," in paragraph (c)(2) it invites the actual participation, with counsel, of all members of the class.

Actually, purely representative actions may have been possible under the old rule in a "spurious" class suit. In Union Carbide & Carbon Corp. v. Nisley, 300 F.2d 561 (10th Cir. 1962), antitrust damage claimants were permitted to intervene after rendition of a verdict in favor of the named plaintiffs and to claim the benefits of the favorable judgment, even though they would not have been bound by an unfavorable judgment rendered against the named plaintiffs.

Conclusions

The symposium conducted by the ABA Antitrust Section makes it clear that the experts are divided into three camps in their assessments of the impact of the amended Rule 23 on antitrust litigation: Some express enthusiasm about the amount of additional antitrust business there will be for antitrust lawyers; some see the class-action future as a house of horrors for antitrust defendants; but others are relaxing in the thought that nothing much is really going to happen. So far, the opinions handed down from the few courts that have dealt with the amended rule seem to lend support to the third view. Those courts saw many problems in application of the new provisions for spurious class actions and manifested an inclination to use caution in applying the new rule.

It is too early to determine whether amended Rule 23 will operate as a practicable means of consolidating and simplifying multi-claimant antitrust litigation such as the heavy-electrical-equipment cases, the asphalt cases, and the rock-salt cases by coalescing all related claims into a single proceeding before one judge. Despite the holding in the Harper & Row case, some antitrust lawyers believe the rule still has this potential. Since the initiating plaintiff's counsel originally determines the class encompassed by the suit and chooses the forum, the new rule may tend to concentrate important multi-plaintiff private antitrust claims before judges who are sympathetic to them.

There may be a solution, moreover, for the difficulties the Eastern Pennsylvania Federal district Court foresaw in the chore of sending notices to all members of the class. It has been suggested that this "onerous task" could be handled by a master, so that the court would neither become involved in the "very questionable judicial undertaking" of corresponding with parties nor lose "its appearance of detached impartiality" by allowing plaintiff's counsel to send the notices.

It does seem clear that the degree to which the new rule is put to use in antitrust litigation will depend largely on the willingness of the federal judges to give it application. Perhaps the most significant feature of the amended rule is the extent to which control of the litigation is placed in the hands of the district judge. There are two portions of the amended rule that will undoubtedly cause the judges to act with a great deal of restraint in allowing antitrust suits to be maintained as class actions. First, the Kronenberg case demonstrates that the courts will be troubled by the necessity for making the "class action" determination so early in the litigation. Second, their concern at that stage of the proceeding will be heightened by the thought that the judgment eventually rendered will be binding not only on class members who brought suit or subsequently intervene but also all those who receive notice of the action but do not affirmatively elect to be excluded from the judgment.

Some judges are therefore going to be tempted to follow the lead of the Eastern Pennsylvania Federal District Court in the Harper & Row case and make liberal use of Rule 20, "Permissive-Joinder of Parties," and Rule 24, "Permissive Intervention," to protect the rights of nonparty members of a class of antitrust damage claimants. And those judges who are willing to apply the new Rule 23 can be expected to make extensive use of their power under paragraph (c)(1) to add conditions to any order allowing a class action and to make subsequent changes in that order at any time prior to a decision of the merits.

Nevertheless, the climate in the federal courts has improved so significantly for antitrust plaintiffs in the last decade that the number of class actions is sure to grow. In large part, the actual impact of the amended rule will depend upon the answers the courts eventually provide to a number of questions raised by the amendments. One question still to be answered is whether the pendency of a class action serves to toll the running of the statute of limitations against members of the class who are not participating and have not intervened. Presumably, the statute would be tolled as to persons who had been notified and have taken no action to exclude themselves from the judgment. And it would seem not to be tolled for the person who receives notice and does elect to be excluded. But it is not clear what happens to the claimant who for some reason has no notice of the litigation.

Suppose a damage claimant learns of the litigation only after it has been decided. Will he be permitted to come into court and recover in reliance on the judgment already obtained? More significantly, perhaps, how will the courts administer settlement as to class members who are not named plaintiffs and have not participated in the litigation but have not made the affirmative choice to be excluded?

- 0 -

Subject: Class Actions — Recent Decisions   (Published 5/28/68)

Question

What questions raised by antitrust class actions by the 1966 amendment to
Federal Civil Rule 23 have been answered by recent decisions under the Rule?

References

Analysis, "Class Actions for Treble Damages," next preceding item
Eisen v. Carlyle & Jacquelin, 391 F.2d 555 (2d Cir.)(pp. A-26, X-17, ATRR No. 349,
      3/19/68)
Knuth v. Erie-Crawford Dairy Coop. Assn., 395 F.2d 420 (3d Cir.) 1968 Trade Cases
      para. 72,435 (p. A-10, ATRR No. 357, 5/14/68)
Iowa v. Union Asphalt and Roadoils, Inc., 281 F.Supp. 391 (S.D. Iowa) (p. A-13,
      ATRR No. 350, 3/26/68)
Philadelphia Electric Co. v. Anaconda American Brass Co., 43 F.R.D. 452 (E.D. Pa.)
      (pp. A-24, X-1, ATRR No. 342, 1/30/68)
Siegel v. Chicken Delight, Inc., 271 F.Supp. 722 (N.D. Calif.) (p. A-12, ATRR
      No. 319, 8/22/67)

Background

Since the publication of ATRR's analysis on the impact of amended Federal Rule of
Civil Procedure 23 on private antitrust litigation, two appellate court opinions on that subject
and a number of significant district court opinions interpreting the new rule have been written.
The Federal district court decisions -- not all of them in antitrust cases -- have answered
some of the questions raised in the analysis and either taken issue with or endorsed some of
the early Rule 23 holdings described there.

Recognizing that the changes made in Rule 23 "received somewhat less than an enthusi-
astic reception" in the early district court decisions, the Court of Appeals for the Second Circuit reversed one of those decisions in Eisen v. Carlyle & Jacquelin and insisted on "a liberal
rather than a restrictive interpretation" of the new rule. The court of appeals agreed with district-court statements that more careful inspection of the adequacy of representation is called
for under the amended rule, in view of the "res judicata effects given to the judgments in those
suits." But it did not agree with statements that a small number of claimants cannot adequately represent a large class. "One of the primary functions of the class suit is to provide 'a
device for vindicating claims which, taken individually, are too small to justify legal action
but which are of significant size if taken as a group.'" Escott v. Barchris Construction Corp.,
340 F.2d 731, 733 (2d Cir. 1965), cert. denied 382 U.S. 816 (1966). "Individual claimants
who may initially be reluctant to commence legal proceedings may later join in a class suit,
once they are assured that a forum has been provided for the litigation of their claims."

The court of appeals was not convinced, as the district judge seemed to be, of the importance that other members of the class of claimants manifest an interest in the litigation by
seeking to intervene. Noting that absent class members will be able to share in the recovery
in the event of a favorable judgment and may for various reasons wish to avoid the binding effect of a possible adverse judgment, the Second Circuit declared: "If we have to rely on one
litigant to assert the rights of a large class then rely we must." See also Mersay v. First
Republic Corp. of America, 43 F.R.D. 465 (S.D. N.Y. 1968); Dolgow v. Anderson, 43 F.R.D.
472 (E.D. N.Y. 1968); Hohmann v. Packard Instrument Co., 43 F.R.D. 192 (N.D. Ill. 1967).

Notice Requirement

One of the reasons given in an early federal district court decision (School District of
Philadelphia v. Harper and Row Publishers, Inc., 267 F.Supp. 1001 (E.D. Pa.) (p. A-1, ATRR
No. 303, 5/2/67), for a reluctance to apply the new Rule 23 was the "onerous task" of giving
notice to all members of the class. That court rejected a suggestion that the job of giving the
notice could be delegated to counsel for the plaintiff seeking to represent a class of claimants.

The Second Circuit, on the other hand, adopts the view that this task "must rest upon the representative party when he is the plaintiff." Indeed, in Richland v. Cheatham, 272 F.Supp. 148 (S.D. N.Y. 1967), the plaintiffs' reluctance to accept the burden of sending notices was one of the reasons the court gave for refusing to allow maintenance of the suit as a class action.

Chief Judge Lumbard dissented from the Second Circuit's holding, maintaining that the amount of individual recoveries were going to be so small and the administrative problems so vast that "obviously the only persons to gain from a class suit are not potential plaintiffs, but the attorneys who will represent them." The suit was brought by a securities dealer alleging a conspiracy to fix the brokerage differential for "odd lots" on the New York Stock Exchange, and he estimated his damages at only $70. The majority, too, was reluctant to permit actions that "are not likely to benefit anyone but the lawyers who bring them." Consequently, it directed the district court, before allowing this suit to proceed, to conduct a further inquiry into the problems of administration of the suit. If the defendants are able "to present data indicating that in analogous situations large sums have been absorbed by paper work, fees of special masters, printing, proceeds and so on," and "if as a practical matter class members are not likely ever to share in an eventual judgment, we would probably not permit the class action to continue."

One of the problems the district judge is to look into in the Eisen case is the feasibility of carrying out Rule 23's direction that all members of the class be given the "best notice practicable." If it is feasible to identify an adequate number of members of the class who may be given individual notice, then the plaintiff must assume the burden of giving them such notice or else suffer dismissal of the class suit. The Second Circuit did not disagree with the dismissal of the class action in School District of Philadelphia v. Harper and Row as one involving "a myriad of complex, frustrating, needless problems in attempted management." Rather, it pointed to the comment in that opinion that, prior to dismissal, there had been "numerous hearings and conferences."

Difficulty in promulgating the notice required by Rule 23(c) was again characterized in Philadelphia Electric Co. v. Anaconda American Brass Co. 43 F.R.D. 452 (E.D. Pa.) (pp. A-24, X-1, ATRR No. 342, 1/30/68) as one of the factors to be considered in weighing the feasibility of managing a proposed class action -- i.e., in determining whether "a class action is superior to other available methods for the fair and efficient adjudication of the controversy," within the meaning of Rule 23(b)(3). That court attempted "to reduce the likely difficulties of management to a tolerable level" by limiting its definition of the class. One form of notice the courts are apparently willing to accept in difficult situations is publication in prominent newspapers. See p. 27, Wall Street Journal, May 20, 1968.

The second appellate-court opinion discussing amended Rule 23 is Knuth v. Erie-Crawford Dairy Coop. The Third Circuit was not so ready as the Second to rely on one litigant to represent a large class of small claimants. But its answer was to instruct the district court to use the Rule's notice procedure to test the interest of other class members. The district judge had dismissed a single dairy farmer's claim to represent 1200 other milk producers after 98 members of the class had filed affidavits saying they do not wish to be represented by the plaintiff. In the Third Circuit's view, this is "an inadequate factual basis" for dismissal. "We think the use of the procedure provided by the new F.R. Civ. P. 23(c) would have been more likely to have provided trustworthy evidence for deciding whether, number-wise at least, the plaintiff could fairly and adequately protect the interests of the class." The district judge was in effect instructed to see that all class members are given notice of the action and an opportunity to respond before any determination is made as to the adequacy of representation by the class plaintiff.

Common Questions

Another class-action requirement that has been the subject of litigation is Rule 23(a)(2)'s provision that there must be "questions of law or fact common to the class." In Iowa v. Union Asphalt (p. A-13, ATRR No. 350, 3/26/68), the Southern Iowa Federal District Court found common issues despite the fact that some members of the purported class purchased directly from the alleged price-fixing conspirators while others employed contractors who made the purchases from the alleged price fixers. In the Eisen case, the Second Circuit made the statement that differences relating only to the computation of damages are not enough, in and of themselves, to justify dismissal of a class action. Variations in application of the statute of limitations, brought about by application of the fraudulent-concealment doctrine, were held not to preclude a finding of common issues of fact in Zeigler v. Gibraltar Life Ins. Co. of America, 43 F.R.D. 169 (D. S.D. 1967).

One of the unanswered questions raised in the earlier ATRR analysis is whether the pendency of a class action serves to toll the running of the statute of limitations against members of the class who are not participating and have not intervened. In Philadelphia Electric Co. v. Anaconda, the Philadelphia Federal District Court handed down a ruling that permitted members of a class of claimants to wait for the court's determination as to the validity of the class action even though the limitations period expired in the meantime. If the court determines that a class action may be maintained, the district judge reasoned, that determination relates back to the date of the filing of the complaint, and all members of the class can participate in the judgment. If the court determines that there are not common questions or there is not a proper class, that determination, too, relates back to the date of the suit, and inactive members of the purported class have lost their rights. If, on the other hand, the reasons for dismissing the class action are matters of "judicial housekeeping," then the determination does not relate back, and members of the class should have an opportunity to prove "reliance upon the pendency of the purported class action sufficient to toll the statute of limitations." Otherwise, every class member would have to file a separate action within the limitation period as a precautionary measure. In that case, having decided that it had a class action, the court went on to announce that it would set a deadline for members of the class who do not elect to be excluded from the suit to come forward and file proof of claim or be forever barred.

Rule 23 (e)'s provision for court approval of any proposed dismissal, compromise, or settlement has been applied to a settlement negotiated with several of the named defendants well in advance of any definition of the class of plaintiffs and of any determination that the suit was in fact a proper class action. Philadelphia Electric Co. v. Anaconda American Brass Co., 42 F.R.D. 324 (pp. A-1, X-1, ATRR No. 313, 7/11/67).

Use of the class-action technique on behalf of franchisees complaining of antitrust violations by their franchisor was given a boost by the decision of the Northern California Federal District Court in Siegel v. Chicken Delight, Inc. (p. A-12, ATRR No. 319, 8/22/67). Five franchisee plaintiffs were held adequate to represent a class of more than 600 "Chicken Delight" franchisees scattered across the country.

Conclusions

If the Second Circuit's attitude toward the new class-action rule is accepted generally, it supplies answers to at least two of the previously unresolved important questions presented in applications of the rule. First, and perhaps most significant for antitrust litigation, it confirmed the willingness of the federal courts to permit the aggregation and representation of a multitude of treble-damage claims by one or a few of the persons asserting the claims. Apparently evidence of apathy on the part of other members of the class is of little or no importance.

Second, the court of appeals' opinion resolves the conflict over the mechanics of serving notice on class members by putting the burden on the plaintiff's shoulders. Other authorities indicate that only the mechanics of notice sending are delegated to the plaintiff; the notice sent is the court's, not any party's. Kronenberg v. Hotel Governor Clinton, Inc., 41 F.R.D. 42 (S.D. N.Y. 1966); Frankel, "some preliminary observations concerning Civil Rule 23," 43 F.R.D. 39 (1967).

While both of these rulings would surely broaden the use of class actions in antitrust litigation, there are other factors to counter such a trend. One such factor is difficulty in giving adequate notice, which apparently was assigned significant weight by the Second Circuit in its directions to the district court regarding the mandated inquiry into the problems of administering a class action. Moreover, a new element has been added to the district judge's determination whether a class action is superior to other available methods of litigating the claims. The recently enacted Multi-District Litigation Act, 28 U.S.C. 1407 (p. X-1, ATRR No. 353, 4/16/68), may well be regarded by the court as an improvement in the "other available methods" and hence reduce the appeal of class actions as a means of court management of multi-claim litigation.

   Nevertheless, some antitrust experts are more convinced than ever that the new Rule 23 is being applied in a manner that could significantly increase the use of class actions in antitrust litigation. Some types of antitrust violations -- particularly those involving the Robinson-Patman Act -- may be ideally suited to class actions because they may inflict harm on a large number of small businessmen, no one of whom suffers damage in an amount approaching that needed to support the always substantial expense of substantiating and litigating a treble-damage claim. And the attitude expressed by the Second Circuit has convinced some lawyers that the threat of treble-damage liability has become so extreme that they must now urge their clients to use even more care in their observance of the antitrust laws. They see a possibility that the new provisions for combining the claims of a host of treble-damage plaintiffs may provide the impetus for extending antitrust into new areas that have been closed to the Antitrust Division and the Federal Trade Commission by reason of budget limitations.

- 0 -

Subject: The "Passing—On" Defense   (Published 11/7/67 and 8/13/68)

Question

What effect is the Supreme Court's decision curtailing use of the passing-on defense likely to have on antitrust treble-damage judgments?

References

Hanover Shoe, Inc., v. United Shoe Machinery Corp., 392 U.S. 481, 36 LW 4643
(pp. A-1, X-24, ATRR No. 362, 6/18/68)
Analysis, "Proof of the Fact of Injury and 'Causation' in a Damage Suit," p. 133, supra.

Background

Section 4 of the Clayton Act allows an award of treble damages to "any person injured in his business or property by reason of anything forbidden in the antitrust laws." Once a private plaintiff has proven an antitrust violation and established standing to sue, the next hurdle he must clear is proof that he was in fact injured in his business or property. Almost every antitrust damage claimant has sought recovery of one or more of three types of economic injury: (1) loss of profits he would have earned in a freely competitive market, including increased cost of doing business; (2) loss of capital or decrease in value of investment; and (3) if he is an ultimate consumer of the product he bought, the excessive price he had to pay for it.

A damage claimant relying on loss of profits or decrease in value of investment obviously has the burden of showing an actual reduction in his net worth. But there has been a great deal of litigation over the questions whether a plaintiff suing for overcharges or increased costs must prove a reduction in net worth and whether, if he does not, the antitrust violator can successfully defend with evidence that the damage claimant passed along his higher costs by charging higher prices.

Rationally, it would seem, a businessman who is able to add cost increases to his selling price without losing sales has not lost anything -- i.e., he has not been "injured in his business or property." In fact, if he can -- again without losing sales -- follow the common practice of setting his price at a fixed percentage above cost, a cost increase will boost his margin and he may actually come out ahead. Of course, the price increase may often cause him to lose sales. If he sues for loss of that business, however, then he is no longer relying on the overcharge or increased-costs theory of damages.

The first time the Supreme Court dealt with the "passing-on" issue in an antitrust case, the above logic proved irresistable. In Keogh v. Chicago & Northwestern Ry., 260 U.S. 156 (1922), a manufacturer who had charged a railroad with conspiring to fix freight rates in violation of the Sherman Act was held to be alleging damages that "are purely speculative." The Court reasoned that the allegedly excessive freight rates "may not have injured Keogh at all," since his competitors presumably had to pay the same freight rate. "Under these circumstances no court or jury could say that, if the rate had been lower, Keogh would have enjoyed the difference between the rates or that any other advantage would have accrued to him. The benefit might have gone to his customers, or conceivably, to the ultimate consumer."

Four years earlier, in Southern Pacific Co. v. Darnell-Taenzer Co., 245 U.S. 531 (1918), the Court had rejected a passing-on defense in a suit to enforce a reparation award made by the Interstate Commerce Commission. But that decision was specifically distinguished by the Supreme Court in its opinion in the Keogh case. An antitrust treble-damage action, the Keogh opinion declared, "is not like those cases where a shipper recovers from the carrier the amount by which its exaction exceeds the legal rate."

Price Discrimination Cases

There is one other antitrust case in which the Supreme Court, while it was not dealing with the passing-on defense, did use language suggesting that the total amount of overcharges

is an appropriate measure of damages. In a suit based on the Robinson-Patman Act, "if petitioner can show [price discrimination], *** it would establish its right to recover three times
the discriminatory difference without proving more than the illegality of the prices. If the
prices are illegally discriminatory, petitioner has been damaged, in the absence of extraordinary circumstances, at least in the amount of that discrimination." Bruce's Juices v. American
Can Co., 330 U.S. 743 (1947). The opinion did not discuss the significance of the deletion from
the Robinson-Patman Act of language in the original bill that would have designated as the "presumed" measure of damages "the pecuniary amount or equivalent of the prohibited discrimination."

Despite the language used by the Bruce's Juices opinion, most of the court of appeals opinions on price-discrimination damages have refused to allow damages in the amount of the prohibited discrimination without proof that the discriminatorily higher price had not been passed
on to the consumer. The Eighth Circuit first allowed recovery of the pecuniary amount of the
discrimination in Elizabeth Arden Sales Corp. v. Gus Blass Co., 150 F.2d 988 (1945), but apparently changed its mind later in American Can Co. v. Russellville Canning Co., 191 F.2d
38 (1951). The Second Circuit has twice held that the discrimination is not a proper measure
of the plaintiff's loss. Sun Cosmetic Shoppe v. Elizabeth Arden Sales Corp., 178 F.2d 150
(1949); Enterprise Industries v. Texas Co., 240 F.2d 457 (1957).

During the 1940's, there was a series of court of appeals decisions, known as the "oil
jobber cases" in which jobbers suing for Section 1 Sherman Act violations were denied recovery
of overcharges that were passed along to their customers. Clark Oil Co. v. Phillips Petroleum
Co., 148 F.2d 580 (8th Cir. 1945); Northwestern Oil Co. v. Socony-Vacuum Oil Co., 138 F.2d
967 (7th Cir. 1943); Twin Ports Oil Co. v. Pure Oil Co., 119 F.2d 747 (8th Cir. 1941). In the
Clark case, the jobber's margin was guaranteed by his supplier. In the Twin Ports and Northwestern cases, it was held that the plaintiff had the burden of showing at the outset that the increase in the price he had to pay was not passed on to his customers. In the absence of such
proof, the Northwestern opinion declared, the inference is that the increase was passed along.
Similar results were reached in Miller Motors, Inc. v. Ford Motor Co., 252 F.2d 441
(4th Cir. 1958), and Wolfe v. National Lead Co., 225 F.2d 427 (9th Cir. 1955). Then, in the
Hanover Shoe case, 185 F.Supp. 826 (1960), affirmed 281 F.2d 481 (1960), the Federal District Court for Middle Pennsylvania rejected a dismissal motion based on evidence that the
complaining shoe manufacturer had passed on the excessive machinery costs to his customers.
The district court declared that "the plaintiff's injury occurred when he was charged too much
for the machinery," citing the Supreme Court's decision in Southern Pacific Co. v. Darnell-
Taenzer Lumber Co. The Hanover decision was affirmed by the Third Circuit on the opinion
of the district court.

Later, in Freedman v. Phila. Terminals Auction Co., 301 F.2d 830 (1962), the Third Circuit backed off somewhat from the rule of the Hanover case. Fruit brokers were denied recovery of excess auction-market charges that had been passed on to customers. The Hanover case
was distinguished on the theory that it was premised on findings that the shoe manufacturer was
a consumer and not a middleman. Implicit in that finding in the Hanover case, the Third Circuit went on, is the "doctrine enunciated in earlier cases that middlemen cannot recover damages when they suffered no injury by reason of their payment of proscribed charges."

Electrical-Equipment Cases

The problem came up again in the Electrical-Equipment Cases. In Commonwealth
Edison Co. v. Allis-Chalmers Mfg. Co., 335 F.2d 203 (1964), the Seventh Circuit applied the
rule of the Darnell-Taenzer case that "the general tendency of the law, in regard to damages,
*** is not to go beyond the first step." Therefore, it decided that "the pass-on doctrine as
enunciated in the oil jobber cases *** should be given limited application and is the exception
rather than the rule." Moreover, it did not believe "that the applicability of the defense should
*** depend entirely on whether plaintiffs are classified as middlemen or consumers." Rather,
the oil jobber cases were distinguished on the theory that the jobbers' service-station customers "or at least the ultimate consumers" had independent rights to recover damages under the
antitrust laws. In the Electrical-Equipment Cases, on the other hand, "the possibility of plaintiffs' present and future customers recovering against defendants are nonexistent." The Seventh
Circuit had already denied the State of Illinois leave to intervene on behalf of consumers.

An even stronger opinion against the passing-on defense was written by the Federal District Court for Southern New York in Atlantic City Electric Co. v. General Electric Co., 1964 Trade Cases 71,015, where the issue was baldly stated as "whether plaintiff may use increased costs as a separate and distinct measure of damages without regard to gain or loss of revenue." After listing the three normal theories of recovery -- loss of profits, increased costs, and decrease in value of investment -- the court insisted that "no two categories of injury are necessarily mutually exclusive" and reasoned that "as a practical matter, recognition of the passing-on doctrine is tantamount to a repudiation of the 'increased costs' measure of damages and a limitation on the extent of recovery primarily to lost profits." For that court, "the most significant consideration is the strong policy in favor of private treble-damage actions, which are intended not only to compensate those injured by violations of the antitrust laws, but also to function as an independent method of enforcing antitrust policy."

In a sense, it was the passing-on theory that was the basis of recovery in Armco Steel Corp. v. North Dakota, 1967 Trade Cases 72,058 (p. A-16, ATRR No. 301, 4/18/67). In a suit charging construction-steel suppliers with a price-fixing conspiracy, the Eighth Circuit allowed the State of North Dakota to recover the amounts by which construction contractors increased their bids to cover the conspiratorial price increase. It made no difference to the court that some of the contractors may actually have paid less for the steel once it was delivered than the price quotations on which they based the bids submitted to state highway authorities. And in Washington v. American Pipe & Constr. Co. (p. A-22, ATRR No. 328, 10/24/67), the Hawaii Federal District Court accorded states standing to sue for overcharges on pipe bought by general contractors for installation in public projects. A suggestion that an injury to "end-users" is too remote to support recovery was rejected.

Because price fixing is the most common charge made in antitrust treble-damage complaints, proof of damages frequently consists of showing the difference between the prices a complaining buyer paid his defendant-supplier and the prices he would have paid but for the antitrust violation. If the complaining buyer is not an ultimate consumer or a public agency representing consumers, he need not always absorb the entire overcharge passively. He may be able to preserve his profit level by increasing his own price, by cutting other costs, or by increasing his sales volume. The pre-1968 decisions described above reveal that the courts have engaged in considerable backing and filling on the issue whether the supplier can disprove damages by showing that the overcharge was passed along to the buyer's customers.

In the Hanover Shoe case, an 8-1 Supreme Court majority declared the passing-on defense inoperative in almost all buyer-supplier situations. "If in the face of the overcharge the buyer does nothing and absorbs the loss, he is entitled to treble damages. This much seems conceded. The reason is that he has paid more than he should and his property has been illegally diminished, for had the price paid been lower his profits would have been higher. It is also clear that if the buyer, responding to the illegal price, maintains his own price but takes steps to increase his volume or to decrease other costs, his right to damages is not destroyed. Though he may manage to maintain his profit level, he would have made more if his purchases from the defendant had cost him less. We hold that the buyer is equally entitled to damages if he raises the price for his own product. As long as the seller continues to charge the illegal price, he takes from the buyer more than the law allows. At whatever price the buyer sells, the price he pays the seller remains illegally high, and his profits would be greater were his costs lower."

The Supreme Court was "not impressed by" a suggestion that sometimes it is the illegal overcharge that makes it possible for the buyer to increase the price he charges his customers -- for example, when the overcharge is imposed equally on all the buyer's competitors and the demand for the buyer's product is so inelastic that the buyers and his competitors are all able to increase their prices by the amount of their cost increase without suffering a sales decline. "A wide range of factors influence a company's pricing policies," the Court observed, and "normally the impact of a single change in the relevant conditions cannot be measured after the fact." It is extremely difficult to determine what effect a change in price will have on total sales and how costs will be affected by a change in sales volume. Even if total sales and unit costs remained unaffected by a buyer price increase matching his supplier's overcharge, there still remains "the nearly insuperable difficulty of demonstrating that the particular plaintiff could not or would not have raised his prices absent the overcharge or maintained the higher price had the overcharge been discontinued."

The Court expressed fear that injection of the passing-on issue into treble-damage litigation would mean that damage actions "would be substantially reduced in effectiveness." Although the task of showing that the particular plaintiff could not or would not have raised his prices in the absence of the overcharge "would normally prove insurmountable," the Court thought it "not unlikely that if the existence of the defense is generally confirmed, antitrust defendants will frequently seek to establish its applicability." As a result, "treble damage actions would often require additional long and complicated proceedings involving massive evidence and complicated theories," and the damage claim would pass along to ultimate consumers with "only a tiny stake in a lawsuit and little interest in attempting a class action."

Fundamentally, the Court went on, it is following a view set forth in Chattanooga Foundry & Pipe Works v. Atlanta, 203 U.S. 390 (1906), and Southern Pacific Co. v. Darnell-Taenzer Lumber Co., 245 U.S. 531 (1918). True, Keogh v. Chicago & N.W. Ry., 260 U.S. 156 (1922), stated a contrary rule, but it did so in a dictum after the Court had already determined that ICC approval of the alleged conspirators' rates gave those rates immunity from antitrust attack. "We ascribe no general significance to the Keogh dictum for cases where the plaintiff is free to prove that he has been charged an illegally high price."

Before leaving the subject, Mr. Justice White's majority opinion recognized that there might be situations where the passing-on defense could succeed — "for instance, when an overcharged buyer has a pre-existing 'cost-plus' contract, thus making it easy to prove that he has not been damaged -- where the considerations requiring that the passing-on defense not be permitted in this case would not be present. We also recognize that where no differential can be proved between the price unlawfully charged and some price that the seller was required by law to charge, establishing damages might require a showing of loss of profits to the buyer. (Some courts appear to have treated price discrimination cases under the Robinson-Patman Act in this category. See, e.g., American Can Co. v. Russellville Canning Co., 191 F.2d 38 (C.A. 8th Cir. 1951); American Can Co. v. Bruce's Juices, 187 F.2d 919, opinion modified, 190 F.2d 73 (C.A. 5th Cir.), cert dismissed, 342 U.S. 875 (1951)."

Conclusions

An important factor in the Hanover Shoe opinion is the Court's outspoken desire to avoid any impairment of the effectiveness of treble-damage actions as an antitrust enforcement tool. The Court's emphasis of this element leaves open the possibility that it may not regard the amount of an illegal overcharge as the exclusive measure of the buyer's lost profits. Conceivably, the buyer could show that the actual economic effects of increased prices went beyond the amount of the overcharge. He might prove, for examples, added carrying charges involved in financing a more expensive inventory, loss of profits on further sales he would have made if he had not had to raise his own prices, or increased selling costs incurred in attempting to prevent a drop in sales.

Yet the opinion says in so many words that in most commercial contexts the seller cannot reduce recovery below the amount of the overcharge -- whether by proof of passing-on, cost reduction, or increased sales volume. It simply makes no difference what happened to the buyer's profit level. Through his overcharge, the seller took "more than the law allows," and the buyer is entitled to full reimbursement plus the full benefit of any measures he took to mitigate his damage. Since he had a right to, and might have, taken those mitigating steps even in the absence of the alleged overcharge, the gains he realized from them are not really related to, and hence do not reduce his damage from, the antitrust violation.

Neither of the Court's two types of exceptional situations that might allow application of the passing-on defense creates a very broad exception. The Court itself recognizes there won't be many instances when it is "easy to prove that [the buyer] has not been damages"; earlier it had called that burden of proof "normally *** insurmountable." And situations "where differential can be proved between the price lawfully charged and some price that the seller was required by law to charge" are rare by definition.

Indeed, it is hard to think of any set of facts that will fit the definition except the price-discrimination example mentioned by the Court. The complaining buyer in a Robinson-Patman Act case is the one who paid the higher of the two discriminatory prices. He complains that one of his competitors was given a discount that enabled his competitor to lure away some of his customers with price cuts. The antitrust violation here does not involve the seller's taking from the complaining buyer of "more than the law allows." There is no overcharge. Dozens of other buyers might have been charged the higher price and yet have no right of action for damages; they may not have had to compete with the favored buyer. Rather, what the seller did was to take less from the favored buyer than the law requires him to take. But this benefit to his competitor can in no sense be regarded as a measure of the damage suffered by the buyer who brought suit. The damage he is ordinarily complaining about is loss of profits on sales he would have made if his competitor had not been given an unfair price advantage. So he must prove that he lost sales and profits. Unfortunately, this analysis may not be reconcilable with the dictum in Bruce's Juices, Inc., v. American Can Co., 330 U.S. 743, 757 (1947) that: "If the prices are illegally discriminatory [plaintiff] has been damaged, in the absence of extraordinary circumstances, at least in the amount of that discrimination."

Even aside from the problem of measuring damages, evidence that a price differential was passed along to the complaining buyer's customers may have a significant role in treble-damage suits based on the Robinson-Patman Act. In a price-discrimination case, proof of passing-on is relevant to an issue other than damages. Surely the defendant seller can rebut proof of competitive injury with evidence that the buyer was able to pass along the price differential to his customer without suffering a loss of profits, even if introduction of this evidence will cause "additional long and complicated proceedings." Once the passing-on evidence is introduced, there would appear to be no reason for not considering it in determining damages. There is authority requiring a buyer to show that he mitigated his damages, by lowering his own resale prices or developing his own promotions, etc., before claiming injury to himself. Sun Cosmetic Shoppe, Inc., v. Elizabeth Arden Sales Corp., 178 F.2d 150 (2d Cir. 1949); Enterprise Industries v. Texas Co., 240 F.2d 457 (2d Cir. 1957). In the Enterprise Industries case, the Second Circuit refused to give literal effect to the dictum, quoted above from the Bruce's Juices opinion, pointing out that a provision making the price differential the measure of damages was eliminated in conference from the Senate bill that became the Robinson-Patman Act.

A question that intrigues many antitrust lawyers is how the Supreme Court's reasoning in Hanover Shoe may affect recovery in a series of treble-damage suits by successive buyers. If Hanover, a shoe manufacturer, is to recover the full amount of excessive rentals for shoe machinery supplied by United Shoe Machinery Co., can Hanover's wholesaler and retail customers sue United Shoe for the amounts by which their costs were increased when Hanover passed on the machinery costs? If it is a "normally *** insurmountable" task to trace an illegal overcharge as the cause of a corresponding price increase by the buyer, then a subsequent buyer may have a "normally *** insurmountable" burden in attempting to prove that the original overcharge -- and hence the antitrust violation -- was the proximate cause of his cost increase. But this time the "additional long and complicated proceedings involving massive evidence and complicated theories" would be introduced at the election of the damage claimant and would be action in furtherance of the damage suit, not something that would substantially reduce the effectiveness of treble-damage actions.

The question is not academic. Pending in the Eastern Pennsylvania Federal District Court is a suit by the City of Philadelphia charging steel-wheel manufacturers with a price-fixing conspiracy alleged to have caused an increase in the cost of railway cars bought by the City from Budd Co. Under the Hanover Shoe doctrine, it seems likely that Budd could recover the full amount of the overcharges it paid for wheels. Similarly, plumbing fixtures manufacturers have been sued for price-fixing overcharges by both the Philadelphia Housing Authority and companies that built houses for the Authority. Are the defendants in these cases, if held liable, to be forced to pay six times the overcharges?

Successive actions of this nature are sure to run into objections against "double recovery." Since they would be tort actions, not litigation over title to a specific fund or res, technically there would be no "double recovery." In theory, however, it is difficult to see how the first buyer could recover the overcharge on the ground that it cannot be traced to his own price increase and then the second buyer recover it as traceable to the same price increase. Yet multiple claims of this sort are likely to come before different juries, so all plaintiffs conceivably could win.

As a practical matter, the "double recovery" problem can be overemphasized. The fact is that few antitrust cases ever get to juries. Most treble-damage actions are settled -- "resolved by attrition rather than by trial . . . decided by calculating minds putting price tags on peace and expense, rather than by triers of fact attempting to price real damage." Hoffman, "Proof of Damages in Private Litigation," 36 ABA Antitrust Law Journal 151 (1967).

- 0 -

Subject: In Pari Delicto   (Published 9/12/67 and 9/10/68)

Question

    To what degree may a businessman acquiesce or participate in an antitrust viola-
tion without losing his right to recover damages the violation inflicts on him?

Reference

    Perma Life Mufflers, Inc., v. International Parts Corp., 392 U.S. 134, 36 LW 4571
        (pp. A-1, X-15, ATRR No. 361, 6/11/68)

Background

    In a treble-damage suit a defendant may assert by way of defense, that the damage
claimant has violated the antitrust laws. If the assertion is that the damage claimant has
participated in the very transaction his suit attacks as an antitrust violation, then the defense
is known as the "in pari delicto" defense -- i.e., an assertion that the damage claimant is
"in pari delicto" or equally at fault. When the defendant, on the other hand, alleges an antitrust violation by the damage claimant that is not the one set forth as the basis of the damage
suit, he is often said to be asserting the "unclean hands" defense.

In Pari Delicto

    The doctrine of "in pari delicto" was established for antitrust litigation in Eastman
Kodak Co. v. Blackmore, 277 Fed. 624 (2nd Cir. 1921). However, there are two situations in
which a treble-damage claimant's participation in the antitrust violation did not foreclose his
recovery: (1) when disparity of economic bargaining power forced him into the participation,
Eastman Kodak Co. v. Southern Photo Co., 273 U.S. 359 (1927), and (2) when he had severed
his relationship with the unlawful scheme and claimed damages sustained only after such
severence, Victor Talking Machine Co. v. Kemeney, 271 Fed. 810 (3rd Cir. 1921).

    In Crest Auto Supplies, Inc., v. Ero Mfg. Co., 246 F.Supp. 224 (1965), affirmed
360 F.2d 896 (7th Cir. 1966), and Perma Life Mufflers, Inc., v. International Parts Corp.,
1966 Trade Cases para. 71,801 (1966), affirmed, 376 F.2d 692 (7th Cir. 1967), the Northern
Illinois Federal District Court, finding the parties equally at fault, denied two groups of
"exclusive franchisees" the right to maintain antitrust suits against their suppliers for losses
they claimed to have suffered as a result of exclusive-dealing provisions in the franchise
agreements. Relying on its own 1964 decision in Rayco Mfg. Co. v. Dunn, 234 F.Supp. 593,
the court said a litigant cannot "complain of injuries which resulted from alleged antitrust
violations to which it was a voluntary party." In distinguishing cases such as Lessig v.
Tidewater Oil Co., 327 F.2d 459 (p. A-10, ATRR No. 132, 1/21/64) and Osborn v. Sinclair
Refining Co., 286 F.2d 832 (4th Cir. 1960) cited by the franchisees, the district judge explained that those cases dealt with the proposition that alleged illegal conduct cannot immunize
the other party against liability to those injured. Decisions disallowing a defense to parties
equally at fault, he went on, have been limited to situations in which the damage claimant has
not violated the antitrust laws in combination with the defendant.

    The U.S. Court of Appeals for the Seventh Circuit affirmed the Crest Auto decision,
rejecting without discussion the dealers' contention that whether they were in pari delicto is
a question of fact and therefore should not be decided without a trial. Satisfied from the pleadings and depositions that the dealers had sought business opportunities in the form of
franchises and had looked into the proposition offered by their supplier, the court concluded
that the district judge properly granted summary judgment to the supplier.

    One judge dissented, though, when the Seventh Circuit affirmed the district court's
decision in Perma Life. The damage claimant had relied on the Supreme Court's decision in
Simpson v. Union Oil Co. of California, 377 U.S. 13 (pp. A-8, X-1, ATRR No. 145, 4/21/64),
which the dissenter pointed out was not discussed by the court of appeals in the Crest opinion.
But the majority observed that the Supreme Court's opinion "does not mention pari delicto and

we think it did not intend to annihilate a principle so long imbedded in the law." The key to the Simpson case, the majority continued, is that Union Oil was in a position, by means of its leasing arrangements, to coerce the complaining dealer into selling at prices fixed by Union Oil. When Union Oil canceled the lease, the dealer was deprived not only of the right to purchase from Union Oil, but also of a place to do business.

The dissenter based his objection on "a close study of the Simpson case, including the briefs filed therein." Simpson, too, had freedom of choice to accept or reject the tendered lease and consignment contract. He went into the deal with his eyes open, just as did the damage claimants in the present case. In Simpson, the Court of Appeals for the Ninth Circuit used the "in pari delicto" doctrine to deny the retailer any recovery. That point was fully briefed in the Supreme Court, and, since the retailer prevailed in the Supreme Court, the dissenter was "forced to conclude that the Supreme Court rejected the in pari delicto defense." The dissenter was also convinced that the public policy justifying the denial of the defense in a case of this sort was stated by the Supreme Court in Kiefer-Stewart Co. v. Jos. E. Seagram & Sons, Inc., 340 U.S. 211 (1951).

Unclean Hands

In Kiefer-Stewart, the Supreme Court held that allegations of horizontal price fixing by liquor wholesalers were no defense to one wholesaler's damage suit charging two distillers with a price-fixing conspiracy. The Court stated that "if [the damage claimant] and others were guilty of infractions of the antitrust laws, they could be held responsible in appropriate proceedings brought against them by the government or by injured private persons. The alleged illegal conduct of [the damage claimant] however, could not legalize the unlawful combination by [defendants] nor immunize them against liability to those injured."

In Florists' Nationwide Telephone Delivery v. Florists' Telephone Delivery Ass'n., 371 F.2d 263 (7th Cir. 1967), the Seventh Circuit reversed a $150,000 jury verdict in favor of one florists' association against another because the district court had refused to instruct the jury on the "unclean hands" defense. The jury verdict sustained allegations that the defendant association's rules on members' advertising were unreasonable trade restraints, and the judge had refused to instruct the jury that it could find the advertising rules to be a reasonable means of self-protection against the plaintiff association's boycott. If the defendant association can establish that its trade-restraining restrictions are reasonable methods of self-protection against the activities of the other association, the court declared, then the second association would be barred from both recovery of damages and injunctive relief.

Recently, a legitimate-theater operator assumed to have had no reasonable business alternative to participating in a booking office's illegal activity was not seen by the Eastern Pennsylvania Federal District Court as being "in pari delicto" with the booking office's unlawful conduct. Goldlawr Inc., v. Shubert, 268 F.Supp. 965 (E.D. Pa. 1967). Several facts admitted by the booking office only for purposes of the defendant's summary judgment motion convinced the district judge that the theater operator was economically compelled to deal with the booking office: (1) It was the only booking office in the United States. (2) It controlled the booking and the playing of first-class attractions across the country. (3) No independent source of theater attractions existed to encourage any "meaningful" competition with the booking office. (4) The booking office has systematically blocked independent theaters from procuring attractions so that many of them have been forced to go out of business.

The district judge thought that the Seventh Circuit in the florists' case confused in pari delicto and unclean hands. "Moreover, the Court of Appeals for the Seventh Circuit *** referred *** to Crest as follows: 'Likewise, although factually distinguishable, Crest Auto Supplies exemplifies an application of the "unclean hands" doctrine which is pertinent here. Both FNTDN's activities and FTD's challenged rules were concerned with the same transactions ***.'" He then went on to state that "whatever label may be properly affixed to the defense, it has been upheld when the plaintiff has participated freely in the very scheme for which he seeks to recover damages."

Perma Life Case

On the next-to-last opinion day of its 1967-68 term, the Supreme Court handed down a decision declaring that "the doctrine of in pari delicto, with its complex scope, contents, and effects, is not to be recognized as a defense to an antitrust action." But the five opinions that accompanied the Court's decision suggest that the doctrine has some definitions that may still be operative in private antitrust damage actions.

The statement that "the doctrine of in pari delicto, with its complex scope, contents, and effects," is not to be applied in antitrust litigation was made in Mr. Justice Black's opinion for a five-justice majority. It followed a statement of the applicable rule in other terms: "Once it is shown that the plaintiff did not aggressively support and further the monopolistic scheme as a necessary part and parcel of it, his understandable attempts to make the best of a bad situation should not be a ground for completely denying him the right to recover which the antitrust acts give him." Earlier, he indicated he was talking about "the common-law pari delicto doctrine" and pointed out that, "although in pari delicto literally means 'of equal fault,' the doctrine has been applied, correctly or incorrectly, in a wide variety of situations in which a plaintiff seeking damages or equitable relief is himself involved in some of the same sort of wrongdoing." But the justices "have often indicated the inappropriateness of invoking broad common-law barriers to relief where a private suit serves important public purposes." Kiefer-Stewart Co. v. Seagram & Sons, 340 U.S. 211 (1951); Simpson v. Union Oil Co., 377 U.S. 13 (1964). "There is nothing in the language of the antitrust acts which indicates that Congress wanted to make the *** doctrine a defense to treble-damage actions."

A later portion of the opinion makes it clear, though, that the Court did not decide whether "truly complete involvement and participation in a monopolistic scheme could ever be a basis, wholly apart from the idea of pari delicto, for barring a plaintiff's cause of action." The facts of the case before the Court make it unnecessary for the Court to go that far. The damage claimants were retail dealers operating "Midas Muffler Shops" under franchise agreements obligating each dealer to purchase all his exhaust system parts from the franchisor, to carry a complete line of the franchisor's products, and to resell Midas Mufflers at prices and locations specified by the franchisor. In return the franchised dealer received permission to use registered trademarks and service marks and was granted an exclusive right to sell "Midas" products within his defined territory. In these circumstances, the majority opinion noted, there could not have been complete involvement by the dealers in the illegal restraints of trade created by the exclusive-dealing and full-line requirements, for neither of those provisions could be in a dealer's self interest. Moreover, there was evidence that the dealers tried to get out from under these two restrictions.

It makes no difference that the complaining dealers sought their franchises enthusiastically; they did not actively seek each and every clause of the agreement. They accepted many of the restraints "solely because their acquiescence was necessary to obtain an otherwise attractive business opportunity." The courts have no power "to undermine the antitrust acts by denying recovery to injured parties merely because they have participated to the extent of utilizing illegal arrangements formulated and carried out by others." Nor is it significant that the territorial restrictions benefited the complaining dealers. "They cannot be blamed for seeking to minimize the disadvantages of the agreement once they had been forced to accept its more onerous terms as a condition of doing business." These "possible beneficial by-products," on the other hand, "can of course be taken into consideration in computing damages."

While Mr. Justice White joined in the majority opinion and in rejecting "the in pari delicto defense in its historic formulation," he filed a special concurring opinion. "I would deny recovery where plaintiff and defendant bear substantial equal responsibility *** but permit recovery in favor of the one least responsible where one is more responsible than the other." He saw the issue before the court as being a causation problem, maintaining that a damage claimant equally responsible with the defendant for the antitrust violation should be denied recovery "for failure of proof that [defendant] was the more substantial cause of the injury."

Mr. Justice Fortas concurred only in the result. He agreed that "private attorneys general" cannot be denied [recovery] on the basis of the doctrine of in pari delicto." But he insisted that the doctrine does have "a significant if limited role in private antitrust law. If the fault of the parties is reasonably within the same scale -- if the 'delicto' is approximately 'pari' -- then the doctrine should bar recovery."

Mr. Justice Marshall, too, concurred only in the result. His reasons for refusing to join the majority opinion "are, perhaps, less related to the public interest in eliminating all forms of anticompetitive business conduct and more related to the equities as between the parties." He would look not only for substantial equality of fault but also for active participation by the complaining party in the formation and implementation of the illegal scheme. He would deny recovery to the claimants who "actually participated in the formulation of the entire agreement, trading off anticompetitive restraints on their own freedom of action (such as the tying and exclusive dealing provisions) for anticompetitive restraints intended for their benefit (such as resale price maintenance or exclusive territories)."

Justices Harlan and Stewart concurred in part and dissented in part. They held out for application of "the true in pari delicto standard" and expressed the view that much of the judicial disagreement that the case has occasioned relates to the definition of "in pari delicto." "Plaintiffs who are truly in pari delicto are those who have themselves violated the law in cooperation with the defendant." They saw the Kiefer-Stewart decision -- that a supplier sued for resale price maintenance cannot defend by proving the complaining buyer's participation in a horizontal price-fixing conspiracy -- as distinguishable from true in pari delicto because there the defendants' illegal actions were taken in reprisal against altogether independent illegal actions by the plaintiff. And they would deal with large supplier-small customer situations like those involved in the Simpson case, Albrecht v. Herald Co., 390 U.S. 145 (pp. A-1, X-1, ATRR No. 347, 3/5/68), and perhaps the present case "on the theory of a 'coercion' exception to the in pari delicto doctrine."

Conclusions

There are at least three indications in the Perma-Life decision that an "in pari delicto" doctrine will continue to function in private antitrust litigation.

First, Mr. Justice Black excluded the in pari delicto doctrine only as it was defined and applied at common law, "with its complex scope, contents, and effects." Like the passing-on defense (see ANALYSIS, "The 'Passing-On' Defense," immediately preceding this one), in pari delicto, as traditionally used, has ramifications that would frustrate antitrust policy. If the plaintiff "aggressively support[s] and further[s] the monopolistic scheme as a necessary part and parcel of it," even Mr. Justice Black would deny him damages.

Second, after disqualifying any plaintiff who "aggressively support[ed] and further[ed] the monopolistic scheme," the majority opinion clears one who merely engages in "understandable attempts to make the best of a bad situation." Between these two degrees of participation by the plaintiff there are conceivable levels of involvement that the Supreme Court majority has not expressed a view on. For plaintiffs in those categories, the best guideline available is that set out, in somewhat different terms, by Mr. Justice White, who would disqualify the "equally responsible" plaintiff; Mr. Justice Fortas, who would apply the "in pari delicto" label to "equality of position"; and Mr. Justice Marshall, who would find the plaintiff "substantially equally at fault" to be in pari delicto. Indeed, since Mr. Justice White joined in the majority opinion, his "equally responsible" test surely must be regarded as consistent with the majority view.

Third, seven of the justices agree the facts of the case before them clearly establish that the franchisees were not real "collaborators" or "co-adventurers" (Mr. Justice Fortas' terms) in the exclusive-dealing requirements they were complaining about. If the Court should ever get a case involving "collaborators" or "co-adventurers" who are "equally responsible" with the defendant for the illegal conduct, then at least five justices will find the "collaborators" to be in pari delicto and deny them damages.

While an "equally responsible" person appears to be as imprecise a concept as the "reasonable man" of negligence law, some antitrust lawyers think they see, in the Supreme Court's antitrust decisions of recent years, clues that a more precise test may be operative. They believe the most persuasive criteria in "pari delicto" or "equal fault" cases will be the relative size of the parties. Franchisees are merely one example of the type of damage claimant who, because dwarfed individually in size by the defendant he sues, will often be able to avoid a finding of "equal responsibility" for restrictions inserted in a contract.

On those less frequent occasions when the defendant is overmatched in size by the plaintiff, the reasoning goes, it will be correspondingly easier to prove "equal responsibility" -- or "in pari delicto," if that term should continue in use, as at least four justices apparently prefer.

It is also important to remember, though, that Perma-Life is a franchise case. It embodies a message to the franchisor of this era when franchising appears so attractive that he is vulnerable to private antitrust litigation. In a franchising context, the problem of relative degree of fault or responsibility becomes immediately pertinent, not as a matter of post-contractual conduct, but more as a matter of the way in which the contractual relationship is established in the first place. In most instances, establishment of the franchise relationship involves promises by the franchisor that are anticompetitively beneficial to the franchisee and are given in exchange for covenants by the franchisee to confer benefits upon the franchisor of similar dignity. While the small reseller will often have similar post-contract claims against a large manufacturer, the frequency of claims such as those asserted by Perma-Life will probably be greatest in the franchise setting.

Perhaps the primary significance of both the Perma-Life opinion and the Court's rejection of the passing-on defense in Hanover Shoe, Inc., v. United Shoe Machinery Corp., 392 U.S. 481, 36 LW 4643 (pp. A-1, X-24, ATRR No. 362, 6/18/68) (see analysis preceding this one), lies in their manifestation of the Supreme Court's continuing lively interest in the effectiveness of private damage actions as an antitrust enforcement tool.

In recent years the Court's opinions have made increasingly warm statements about private antitrust litigation. Leh v. General Petroleum Corp., 382 U.S. 54 (pp. A-4, X-36, ATRR No. 226, 11/9/65); Minnesota Mining and Mfg. Co. v. New Jersey Wood Finishing Co., 381 U.S. 311 (pp. A-6, X-1, ATRR No. 202, 5/25/65); Continental Ore Co. v. Union Carbide & Carbon Corp., 370 U.S. 690 (1962); Poller v. CBS, 368 U.S. 464 (1962); Radiant Burners, Inc., v. Peoples Gas Light & Coke Co., 364 U.S. 656 (1961).

The attitude and trend evident in these decisions may foreshadow the answers to be expected to some of the other damage-suit issues that have not yet reached the Court -- e.g., standing to sue (ANALYSIS, p. B-1, ATRR No. 288, 1/17/67, reprinted at p. 305, Antitrust & Trade Regulation Today: 1967); use of FTC decrees (ANALYSIS, p. B-1, ATRR No. 278, 11/8/66, reprinted at p. 328, Antitrust & Trade Regulation Today: 1967); applicability of the damage provision to Section 7 Clayton Act violations (ANALYSIS, p. B-1, ATRR No. 227, 11/16/65, reprinted at p. 340, Antitrust & Trade Regulation Today: 1967); and the extent to which the new class-action rule can be used to aggregate small antitrust damage claims (pp. 143 and 149, supra).

In any event, Kiefer-Stewart seems to say the unclean hands defense does not apply to antitrust damage actions. It can be argued that an inconsistency exists in allowing a claim of in pari delicto but not one of unclean hands. But Kiefer-Stewart's basis for disallowing unclean hands as a defense is that antitrust violations by a damage claimant don't legalize illegal activities of a defendant, whereas, the theory of the in pari delicto defense is that the damage claimant's injury is as much the result of his own conduct as the defendant's. The judge in the Goldlawr case made it clear that in pari delicto and unclean hands are not interchangeable terms. In pari delicto applies only in the situation in which the plaintiff has participated in the very activity that is the basis of his suit.

Subject: **Allowances for Attorneys' Fees**   (Published 11/19/68)

Question

What factors influence determination of the amount a successful antitrust damage plaintiff is to be allowed for attorneys' fees?

References

Advance Business Systems v. SCM Corp., 287 F.Supp. 143 (D. Md.) (p. A-10, ATRR No. 367, 7/23/68)

Courtesy Chevrolet, Inc., v. Tennessee Walking Horse Breeders, 393 F.2d 75 (9th Cir.) (p. A-8, ATRR No. 355, 4/30/68), review denied, 393 U.S. 938, 37 LW 3177 (p. A-5, ATRR No. 383, 11/12/68)

Hanover Shoe, Inc., v. United Shoe Machinery Corp., 245 F.Supp. 258 (M.D. Pa.) (p. A-2, ATRR No. 200, 5/11/65)

Bal Theatre Corp. v. Paramount Film Distributing Corp., 206 F.Supp. 708 (N.D. Calif. 1962)

Background

Section 4 of the Clayton Act provides that a person injured in his business or property by reason of violations of the antitrust laws may sue therefor "and shall recover threefold the damages by him sustained, and the cost of suit, including a reasonable attorney's fee." Section 7 of the Sherman Act has a similar, but seldom cited, provision, which uses the phrase "costs of suit," instead of "cost of suit." Black's Law Dictionary, fourth edition, p. 415, attributes to "cost" the broad, general meaning of "expense" and defines only "costs" as designating those items traditionally taxed to the unsuccessful litigant and now listed, for the federal courts, in Sections 1920, 1921, and 1923 of the Federal Judicial Code (Title 28, U.S.C.). Apparently, however, Congress had no specific intent in mind when the "s" was dropped in the Clayton Act, for House Report 627, 63rd Cong., 2d Sess. (1914), says the new provision "is supplementary to the existing laws, and extends the remedy under Section 7 of the Sherman Act." In any event, the rule usually applied is that "the only costs recoverable by a successful plaintiff in a private antitrust suit are those which are normally allowable under 28 U.S.C. 1920 and Rule 54(d)." Twentieth Century-Fox Film Corp. v. Goldwyn, 328 F.2d 190, 222 (9th Cir. 1964).

The statement made in Twentieth Century-Fox v. Goldwyn was challenged recently in Advance Business Systems v. SCM Corp. (cited in the references) by a plaintiff who sought to expand the usual categories of taxable costs for Clayton Act purposes by stressing the Act's use of the phrase "cost of suit." It was pointed out that "costs" is the word used in Rule 54(d) of the Federal Rules of Civil Procedure. While the Maryland Federal District Court did not sustain in this argument, it did say that "In a private antitrust suit a court should not exercise * * * niggardly" its "broad discretionary powers in the allowance or disallowance of costs within the category set out in Section 1920" of the Judicial Code.

This concept that "cost" means the full expense of litigation has been rejected by the courts not only in awarding taxable "costs" but also in applying the Clayton Act's provision that "cost" is to be regarded as "including a reasonable attorney's fee." In setting the attorney-fee allowance, the courts make no attempt to reimburse a successful plaintiff for the fee he has contracted to pay his counsel. The plaintiff's fee agreement with his attorney is "wholly immaterial to the issue before the court." Milwaukee Towne Corp. v. Loew's, Inc., 190 F.2d 561, 570 (7th Cir. 1951); see also Twentieth Century-Fox Film Corp. v. Brookside Theatre Corp., 194 F.2d 846, 859 (8th Cir. 1952). Nor does the fee allowance granted by the court limit the fee that plaintiff's attorney can charge his client under their contractual arrangements. In the Milwaukee Towne case, the fee allowance awarded by the court was substantially less than the fee plaintiff had contracted to pay, but nothing was said to relieve the plaintiff of his fee contract.

Another approach was taken in American Federation of Tobacco Growers v. Allen, 186 F.2d 590, 591-92 (4th Cir. 1951). The Court of Appeals for the Fourth Circuit used language indicating that it assumed the right to the "reasonable attorney's fee" under the Clayton Act accrued to the attorney rather than to the plaintiff.

Actual fee arrangements between plaintiffs' attorneys and their clients generally assume that the allowance set by the court bears no relationship to the fee to be paid. Often the fee contract calls for inclusion of the attorney-fee allowance in the amount of damages and for payment to the attorney of a percentage of the total. Sometimes the plaintiff contracts to pay a percentage of damages plus the amount the court allows as "a reasonable attorney's fee."

One treble-damage plaintiff's lawyer does not believe "that there is any basic difference in the financial arrangement between lawyer and client in this field and in any other field. The usual agreement, with variations, involves a retainer within a range of $5,000 to $25,000, a percentage arrangement on damage recovery, and some understanding on the attorney's fee which is ordered by the court to be paid by the defendant. All clients should be given the opportunity to take an arrangement which provides for a straight hourly rate in lieu of the contingency. Costs must always be paid by the client on regular monthly billings. The plaintiff who accepts an hourly rate should still pay the retainer since, more often than not, the plaintiff is accepting the benefits of a good deal of work already done in the same industry by the particular lawyer involved." Alioto, "The Economics of a Treble Damage Case," 32 ABA Antitrust L. J. 87, 93 (1966).

The Supreme Court seems to have spoken only once in this area. In W. W. Montague & Co. v. Lowry, 193 U.S. 38 (1904), the Court sustained an allowance of $750 for a fee to an attorney who had recovered a judgment for trebled damages in the amount of $1,500, stating: "The amount of the attorney's fee was within the discretion of the trial court, reasonably exercised." The Court was dealing with the damage provision in Section 7 of the Sherman Act, but that "discretion of the trial court" theme has carried over into the many federal district court and court of appeals opinions rationalizing attorney-fee allowances under the Clayton Act.

In the Bal Theatre case cited in the references, the district court listed four criteria to be followed in fixing an allowance for an attorney's fee: "1. The nature of the questions involved, their novelty and difficulty, and the skill and competence of counsel required to properly conduct the cause; 2. The customary charges of the bar for similar services; 3. The standing of counsel in the community; and 4. The amount recovered in the controversy and the beneficial result obtained by counsel." A longer list of "factors considered" was set out in the Hanover Shoe opinion listed in the references. Except for "time and labor spent," however, those factors seem to fall within the four general criteria listed in the Bal Theatre case.

Skill Required

In considering the difficulty of the questions involved, the courts have sometimes indicated that antitrust cases should be regarded as requiring greater "variety and rarity of skill" than other types of litigation. "It is doubtful whether any type of legal work requires a higher degree of professional competence and need of ability than the presentation to a jury of complicated economic questions." Cape Cod Food Products, Inc., v. National Cranberry Assn., 119 F.Supp. 242, 244 (D. Mass. 1954). As long ago as Milwaukee Towne Corp. v. Loew's, Inc., 190 F.2d 561 (7th Cir. 1951), however, the Court of Appeals for the Seventh Circuit declared that "the uniqueness which perhaps formerly attached to such a case has been largely dissipated."

The availability or nonavailability of a relevant government antitrust decree has been listed as an important fact bearing on the difficulty of the lawyer's task and hence on the size of a reasonable fee allowance. In Cape Cod Food Products v. National Cranberry Assn., 119 F.Supp. at 244, the absence of a government decree and of concomitant investigatory assistance to the plaintiff was a factor stressed by the court when it pointed to the difficulties of presenting "complicated economic questions" to a jury. In Twentieth Century-Fox Film Corp. v. Brookside Theatre Corp., 194 F.2d 846, 859 (8th Cir. 1952), the existence of a government decree serving as prima facie evidence of an antitrust violation was given prominence as a consideration for reducing the fee allowance.

In looking at "the customary charges of the bar for similar services," the courts tend to compare the size of fee allowances in other cases with the amount of recovery. The results are not very helpful, for the ratios of recovery to fee allowance vary greatly. A table of cases footnoted in the Hanover Shoe opinion contains a list of fee allowances ranging from less than 8% to 33-1/3% of the amount of treble damages recovered. Hanover Shoe, having recovered over $4 million, was allowed $650,000 for attorney's fees. The Bal Theatre opinion, after examining a similar table taken from other cases, allowed $55,000 for fees to attorneys who had obtained a judgment of $438,900. More recently, in Century Chevrolet, Inc., v. Tennessee Walking Horse Breeders (also listed in the references), the Ninth Circuit ordered a fee allowance increased from $5,000 to $10,000, about equal to the $10,200 recovered as trebled damages.

Sometimes other members of the local Bar are called to testify as to the customary charges for the type and amount of services involved in the damage suit. Such testimony has apparently not carried much weight, however. Courtesy Chevrolet, for example, presented testimony of "a highly respected and competent member of the Los Angeles Bar" that a reasonable fee would be from $140,000 to $150,000. Yet the court of appeals increased the fee allowance to only $10,000. In the Milwaukee Towne case, three Chicago lawyers estimated a reasonable fee at $175,000 - $250,000, so the district judge set the fee allowance at $225,000. The Seventh Circuit cut it to $75,000. Darden v. Besser, 147 F.Supp. 376 (E.D. Mich. 1956), provided for a fee allowance of only $10,000 after a "highly respected and competent member of the local bar" testified that $72,000 would be reasonable. On appeal, 257 F.2d 285 (6th Cir. 1958), the allowance was increased to $30,000.

Mention is sometimes made of the hourly rate reflected in the fee allowance. Hanover Shoe's allowance was described by the court as reflecting $74 per hour for partners and $37 for associates in the nonresident law firm that had primary responsibility for the litigation and $50 per hour for the senior partner of a local firm retained to satisfy the court's rule requiring local association. Even when expressed in terms of hourly rates, the "customary" charge is not easily ascertained. In Bal Theatre, the hourly rate averages out to less than $24 and in the Century Chevrolet case the hourly rate comes to an average of only about $4.37 per hour.

As for "the amount recovered," the courts are not even in agreement on how that factor in setting a fee allowance is to be defined. As indicated by the above references to the Hanover Shoe and Bal Theatre opinions, the district judges tend to measure fee allowance against trebled damages. Indeed, the Massachusetts Federal District Court in the Cape Cod Food case specifically held that "ordinary *** reference is made to the total amount in issue between the parties, or to the total amount recovered by one of them." Yet in Twentieth Century-Fox Film Corp. v. Brookside Theatre Corp., 194 F.2d 846, 859 (8th Cir. 1952), the Court of Appeals for the Eighth Circuit declared that single damages are "the only recovery that may be attributed to the services of counsel for plaintiff as it was through no effort of theirs that these damages were trebled." Accord: Milwaukee Towne Corp. v. Loew's, Inc., 190 F.2d at 571.

On at least one occasion, the large size of the damage award was given as a basis for reducing the attorney-fee allowance. "It should not be made more profitable than it is for a person to become the victim of a conspiracy in restraint of trade." Milwaukee Towne Corp. v. Loew's, 190 F.2d at 570.

Seldom do the courts attempt to weigh the skill of counsel, referring rather to his standing in the Bar. They refer to his "reputation" or "experience." Bal Theatre Corp. v. Paramount Film Distributing Corp., 206 F. Supp. at 718. An exception is the impression a lawyer of less than seven years' experience made on the Massachusetts Federal District Court in the Cape Cod Food Products case. Such was counsel's "indefinable distinction which breathes excellence" that even the relatively little time he spent on the case was regarded as proof of "economy of counsel's methods" and hence of his "outstanding talent." 119 F.Supp. at 242, 244.

Other Statutes

Other federal statutes provide for court allowances for attorneys' fees. A few of them, such as the Federal Tort Claims Act, 28 U.S.C. 2678; Section 28 of the Longshoremen's and Harbor Workers Compensation Act, 33 U.S.C. 928; and Section 206(b)(1) of the Social Security

Act, 42 U.S.C. 406(b)(1), are designed solely to prevent exorbitant fees for collecting certain federal statutory claims. These statutes generally set a maximum fee (25% of recovery under the Social Security Act and 10% under the Federal Tort Claims Act) and forbid the collection by the attorney of any amount in excess of that awarded by the court. Among those that, like Section 4 of the Clayton Act, merely authorize the recovery of a "reasonable attorney's fee," are the Packers and Stockyards Act, 7 U.S.C. 210(f); the Copyright Law, 17 U.S.C. 116; the Fair Labor Standards Act, 29 U.S.C. 216(b); the 1934 Communications Act, 47 U.S.C. 206; and the Interstate Commerce Act, 49 U.S.C. 8. The fee determination under those statutes is likewise left to the discretion of the federal district judge, and there is a similar lack of uniformity or consistency in the results.

There is one Fair Labor Standards Act opinion -- Hutchinson v. William C. Barry, Inc., 50 F.Supp. 292, 298 (D. Mass. 1943) -- that declares: "The spirit of the law is that the plaintiff gets as part of his recovery, if he wins, his whole reasonable counsel fees, not some fraction of them." No such rule has been followed in antitrust cases. Indeed, at least two federal district judges have decided it is their function to determine the amount the defendant should be required to pay as a "contribution" toward the fee of plaintiff's counsel. Webster Motor Car Co. v. Packard Motor Car Co., 166 F.Supp. 856, 866 (D. Dist. Col. 1955); Courtesy Chevrolet, Inc., v. Tennessee Walking Horse Breeders, unreported opinion of S.D. Calif., September 13, 1966, reversed by the Ninth Circuit opinion listed in the references.

In antitrust litigation, the right to recover "a reasonable attorney's fee" does not extend to a successful defendant. Byram Concretanks, Inc., v. Warren Concrete Products Co., 374 F.2d 649 (3rd Cir.) (p. A-3, ATRR No. 295, 3/7/67). It has been held, too, that even a successful plaintiff must prove he has been damaged; he cannot recover an attorney's fee if he establishes only that he is entitled to injunctive relief against future injury. Alden-Rochelle, Inc., v. ASCAP, 80 F.Supp. 888, 899 (S.D. N.Y. 1948). When a plaintiff has proved that he has been injured in some amount but fails to prove the amount of damages with sufficient certainty to support the entry of a judgment for damages, the courts have divided over his right to an allowance for attorney's fees. Alden-Rochelle, Inc., v. ASCAP, 80 F.Supp. at 899 (no allowance); Ledge Hill Farms, Inc., v. W.R. Grace & Co., 1964 Trade Cases 71,105 (S.D. N.Y. 1964)(no allowance); Finley v. Music Corp. of America, 66 F.Supp. 569, 571 (S.D. Calif. 1946)(allowance granted). If the plaintiff recovers only a portion of the damages he claimed, he is not entitled to an allowance for the fee he owes his counsel for work on the items of damages unrecovered. Union Leader Corp. v. Newspapers of New England, Inc., 218 F.Supp. 490, 492 (D. Mass. 1963).

In declaring that a successful plaintiff is not entitled to an attorney-fee allowance if he wins only an injunction, the courts are probably speaking only of the scope and effect of Section 4 of the Clayton Act. It is within the traditional powers of a court of equity to allow attorneys' fees and other additional expense items to a successful litigant, although it is done only "in exceptional cases and for dominating reasons of justice." Sprague v. Ticonic National Bank, 307 U.S. 161, 164 (1939).

Conclusions

The precedents suggest many arguments for both sides litigating the amount a successful treble-damage claimant is to be allowed for his attorney's fee. Unfortunately, almost every argument available to one side his its counterpart for the other. Plaintiff's counsel remarks on the difficulties of antitrust litigation in general, and the defense replies that in the last decade antitrust litigation, and especially private damage suits, have become commonplace and that the law of such litigation therefore has become more familiar to counsel and the courts. Emphasis on the special complexities of a particular case can, as often as not, be answered with a reminder that a preexisting government decree greatly eased the task of the plaintiff's lawyer. Lists of cases awarding substantial percentages of recovery or high hourly rates of compensation produce lists of other cases setting much smaller allowances. Plaintiff's lawyer relies on the public interest in encouraging private antitrust suits as important law-enforcement tools, and defense counsel points to the provision for treble damages as already establishing more than ample incentives for the plaintiff, not to mention the enormous penalty thereby imposed on the defendant.

Extreme variations in the degrees to which each of these arguments appeals to federal judges are apparent in the widely fluctuating results they reach. In addition, the lawyer who must prepare a case for or against a fee allowance will not have the assistance of findings, conclusions, or opinions explaining the weight given the various fee-level determinants. Most court opinions in private antitrust suits concentrate on violation and damage issues, leaving the attorney-fee allowance for summary treatment in the last few sentences.

As a practical matter, development of certainty or uniformity in fee allowances may have limited public-interest value. Since fee allowances have not been tied to fees paid or contracted for, the only function of the fee allowance seems to be the encouragement of private antitrust enforcement suits. And most private damage suits are brought with an eye on the Clayton Act's provision for treble recovery.

Only in that minority of private suits brought for little or no damages but for an important injunction is the attorney-fee allowance likely to be a significant incentive to a potential plaintiff. Here, plaintiffs' attorneys can use the contention that the congressional purpose implicit in the Clayton Act's provision for attorney's fees is the "exceptional" circumstance justifying a full allowance for attorneys' fees under the traditional rules of equity. When a potential plaintiff and his attorney are discussing the advisability of filing an antitrust suit for substantial damages, they are likely to be less concerned with eventual reimbursement for expenses than with prejudgment financing of the litigation -- a problem on which Senator Philip A. Hart (D.-Mich) has recently asked the Small Business Administration to lend a hand (p. A-8, ATRR No. 358, 5/21/68).

(For an extensive compilation and review of the cases on this subject, see Note, "The Nature of 'a Reasonable Attorney's Fee' in Private Antitrust Litigation," 1966 Washington University Law Quarterly 102.)

- 0 -

The material reproduced below was published as a Tax Management Memorandum (TMM 68-1) by TAX MANAGEMENT INC., another BNA service. The Memorandum was prepared by Arthur H. Schreiber of Silverstein and Mullens, Attorneys, Washington, D. C., and has been reviewed by the Tax Management Advisory Board.

Subject: Settlement Payments — Tax Consequences on Receipt   (Published 1/9/68)

Question

What is the proper federal income tax treatment of amounts received in settlement of antitrust litigation?

References

Revenue Ruling 67-33, 1967-35 Internal Revenue Ruling 26
Analysis, "Income-Tax Consequences of Antitrust Payments" (p. X-1, ATRR No. 268, 8/30/66), reprinted at p. 343, Antitrust & Trade Regulation Today: 1967

Background

The tax treatment of amounts received in settlement of antitrust litigation is directly related to the nature of the underlying claim in the action and the actual basis of settlement. Raytheon Production Co. v. Comr., 144 F.2d 110 (1st Cir., 1944) The Tax Court has stated the general rule as follows: "The starting point in cases involving the taxability of amounts received as the result of litigation or the settlement thereof is, in general, the answer to the question, 'in lieu of what were the amounts paid under the settlement received?'" Estate of Mabel K. Carter, 35 T.C. 326 (1960), aff'd 298 F.2d 192 (8th Cir., 1962)

This rule applies with respect to the amounts deemed to constitute "compensatory damages," amounts computed by reference to damage sustained or loss from injury suffered. There are several classifications for compensatory damages. Where the underlying claim is determined to be in the nature of a recovery of lost profits, the amounts received in settlement are taxable as ordinary income. Sager Glove Corp. v. Comr., 311 F.2d 210 (7th Cir., 1962), aff'g 36 T.C. 1173 (1962)). This is based on the view that since the lost profits would, if received, have been taxable as ordinary income, the amounts received in compensation for the loss thereof should be taxable in the same manner.

Where the underlying claim is shown to involve loss, destruction, or diminution in value of capital, the amount received in settlement is treated as a nontaxable recovery of capital to the extent that it does not exceed the tax basis of the asset to which the recovery relates. Raytheon Production Corp.; Durkee v. Comr., 162 F.2d 184 (6th Cir., 1947), rev'g 7 T.C. 773 (1946); Comr. v. Pennroad Corp., 228 F.2d 329 (1955), aff'g 21 T.C. 1087 (1957). Where, however, the amounts received as recovery of capital exceed the basis for the capital asset in question, the excess is generally taxable as capital gain. (See, e.g., Telefilm, Inc., v. Comr., 21 T.C. 688 (1954), rev'd on other grounds, 55-1 USTC Par. 9543 (9th Cir., 1955). The "recovery of capital" approach has been applied, for example, where the amounts received in settlement were shown to be for the destruction of goodwill.

In addition to compensatory damages, a portion of the amount received as recovery in or settlement of civil antitrust litigation may be attributable to the claim for "punitive damages," i.e., an amount which is not based on restitution for actual damages sustained or injury suffered but instead is grounded in the nature of the defendant's wrongdoing. In antitrust litigation, the punitive damages take the form of a claim for treble damages. Section 4 of the Clayton Antitrust Act provides that "any person who shall be injured in his business or property by reason of anything forbidden in the antitrust laws may sue therefor *** and shall recover threefold the damages by him sustained." The actual damages are thus tripled and the additional two-thirds is considered as punitive damages.

Prior to 1955, the punitive two-thirds of a treble damages recovery in antitrust litigation was generally understood by the tax bar to be excluded from gross income. However, the Supreme Court in Comr. v. Glenshaw Glass Co., 348 U.S. 426 (1955) held that such punitive damages were not exempt from taxation but were properly includable in gross income. Although the Supreme Court opinion did not expressly require that punitive damages be taxable as ordinary income, the Internal Revenue Service requires ordinary income treatment. The Tax Court has also stated that the punitive damages must be taxed as ordinary income. Ralph Freeman, 33 T.C. 323 (1959).

A difficult problem of proof arises with respect to the receipt of a lump sum in settlement of the litigation. The Internal Revenue Service, relying on the broad language of Section 61 of the 1954 Internal Revenue Code takes the position that, in the absence of a clear showing by the taxpayer to the contrary, the entire amount received in settlement is taxable as ordinary income, whether attributable to compensatory or punitive damages. Thus, the taxpayer has the burden of proving that the entire amount received or a portion thereof should not be so classified. H. Liebes v. Comr., 90 F.2d 932 (9th Cir., 1937) The extent of this burden of proof was indicated by the Seventh Circuit in Sager Glove: "In order to carry the burden of proof the taxpayer must do more than merely claim alternative designations for what it received -- it must prove a designation so that some orderly tax treatment may be accorded it." See, also, Phoenix Coal Co. v. Comr., 231 F.2d 420 (2nd Cir., 1956).

In view of this burden of proof, it is essential that counsel for the damage claimant be aware that the litigation and settlement documents play an important role in determining the ultimate tax classification of the settlement.

First, it is important that the allegations in the complaint be framed with a view to securing favorable tax treatment of the ultimate recovery of the amounts if the action is settled. Thus, if the complaint merely claims lost profits, the amount received in settlement would, in absence of other evidence, be a recovery of lost profits and be taxed as ordinary income.

And the important document is the settlement agreement which is submitted by the parties for court approval. It should contain express provisions as to the basis of settlement, the precise claims that the amounts received are in lieu of, and the portion of the amounts received that is attributable to each of these claims. If possible, from the viewpoint of the damage claimant, those allegations in the complaint seeking the recovery of capital or related items should be utilized as the primary basis for the settlement. The failure to provide an allocation of the amount received in settlement of antitrust litigation often results in the treatment of two-thirds of such amount as punitive damages and thus taxable as ordinary income.

Treatment of Recoveries for Overcharges

In antitrust treble-damage litigation, one classification of compensatory damages may stem from a claim for damages resulting from illegal price fixing on excessive charges arising out of other monopolistic practices.

In Revenue Procedure 67-33, the Service considered the tax treatment by the recipient of amounts received in settlement of treble-damage claims. The stated purpose of Revenue Procedure 67-33 was to "provide general guidelines and procedure to facilitate proper tax accounting for amounts realized by taxpayers in settlement of certain antitrust actions brought under section 4 of the Clayton Act."

The amounts in question were realized in settlement of treble-damage suits instituted by a number of public utilities in the Electrical Equipment cases. The underlying basis for the civil suits was the criminal prosecution of the defendants under section 1 of the Sherman Antitrust Act for conspiring to fix prices. The defendants were convicted in the criminal actions, and their pleas of guilty and nolo contendere resulted in the imposition of fines on the corporate defendants and both fines and prison terms on some of the individual defendants.

Thereafter, the utility-taxpayers filed suits for damages under Section 4 of the Clayton Act for injuries occasioned by the payment of higher prices for property to be used in their businesses than they would have had to pay in the absence of a price fixing conspiracy. Many of the civil suits were settled prior to verdict or judgment by agreements providing for the payment of amounts aggregating less than the amount of actual damages alleged. A portion of the amounts realized in settlement were attributable to the legal fees and expenses incurred by the utility-taxpayers in pursuing their damage claims, which expenses had been deducted in prior years. In some cases, the portion of the settlement paid with respect to such legal expenses was separately stated in the settlement agreement.

In the Revenue Procedure, the Service set forth general rules that govern the determination of the tax treatment of amounts received in settlement of such litigation. The Service first recognized the general rule that an amount realized in settlement of a legal action should be treated, for purposes of the federal income tax, in accordance with the type of claim to which it is attributable. It accepted the principle that in order to determine whether a particular amount realized in settlement of a taxpayer's claim for treble damages is to be included in gross income or is to be considered a return of capital, the first thing to be ascertained is what the amount represents. Under this analysis, the Service indicated that, for example, to the extent that the amount realized represents redress for injury or loss with respect to property held by a taxpayer and used in his trade or business, such amount is considered to represent a restoration of capital interest.

With respect to treble damages, the Service stated that the portion of the amount realized in settlement of a treble-damage action, which is attributable to a taxpayer's claim for the trebling of actual damages, does not represent a restoration of capital but will be included in the taxpayer's gross income. The Service cited Glenshaw Glass to support its position.

With respect to amounts attributable to legal expenses incurred in pursuing the claim, the Service stated that an amount later realized in settlement of the damage claim that is properly attributable to the recovery of such legal expenses generally does not represent a recovery of capital. This position was based on the fact that such legal expenses incurred under Section 4 of the Clayton Act, which is a special statutory action in the nature of an action in tort, are deductible expenses under Section 162(a) of the 1954 Code. Thus, the later recovery of such amount would represent a recovery of an expense previously deducted for federal income tax purposes.

The Service then set forth the manner in which the amounts received by the public utilities could be treated for federal income tax purposes:

1. Where the taxpayer has reasonably established that the actual damages sustained as a result of the price-fixing conspiracy were in excess of the amounts realized in settlement of the action under Section 4 of the Clayton Act, excluding therefore amounts properly attributable to the recovery of the related legal expenses, the Service will presume, in the absence of substantial evidence to the contrary, that no part of such recovery represents the taxpayer's claim for "punitive" or exemplary damages. Otherwise, the Service would apply the rule that the portion of the amounts realized in settlement which are attributable to taxpayer's claim for trebling of actual damages should be included in gross income.

2. The Service will permit the taxpayer to treat as a return of capital that portion of the amounts realized in settlement (a) which is properly attributable to the actual damages sustained; and (b) which is not in excess of the adjusted bases of those assets used in the taxpayer's business which were involved in the suit for damages. However, the Service will require appropriate adjustment to the bases of such assets in the taxable year of the settlement.

3. The taxpayer will be required to include in gross income that portion of the settlement amount that is properly attributable to a recovery of the taxpayer's costs of suit, but only to the extent not included by the application of Section 111 of the 1954 Code pursuant to the regulations thereunder. (Section 111 of the Code provides that gross income does not include income attributable to the recovery during the taxable year of a bad debt, prior tax, or delinquency amount, to the extent of the amount of the "recovery exclusion" is determined in accordance with section 111(b)(4) and Regs. 1.111-1(b).) The Service further provided that if a

portion of the settlement has been separately stated in the settlement agreement to be payable for such recovery costs, the correctness of the amount designated will not be questioned unless it is unreasonable in light of all of the facts.

Analysis of Revenue Procedure 67-33

The effect of Revenue Procedure 67-33 is to indicate with some degree of certainty the Service position concerning amounts received in settlement of antitrust treble-damage litigation. While Revenue Procedure 67-33 considers a situation involving a regulated public utility realizing amounts in settlement of civil antitrust litigation arising out of the price-fixing conspiracy in the Electrical Equipment Cases, the general guidelines and procedures which it sets forth for the tax treatment of settlement amounts would likely be extended to cover other factual situations involving settlement of civil suits for treble damages brought under Section 4 of the Clayton Act.

The general approach of Rev. Proc. 67-33 may indicate a lessening of the tax burden of proof placed upon the plaintiff with respect to allocating settlement amounts. For example, the creation of a presumption, that the excess of actual damages over the amounts realized in settlement causes the recovery to represent something other than "punitive" damages, is a favorable result for taxpayers. The plaintiff taxpayer, however, must first "reasonably establish" that the actual damages sustained were in excess of the amounts realized in settlement (excluding amounts properly attributable to the recovery of the related legal expenses).

Another favorable aspect of Revenue Procedure 67-33 is the approval given by the Service to treating a portion of the amounts realized in settlement as a nontaxable return of capital. The tests for determining the portion of settlement amounts that may be treated as a return of capital provide a clear guideline as to the information which must be presented in order to qualify for such tax treatment. However, there is no indication of the removal by the Service of the judicially developed requirement that the taxpayer must establish the bases for the assets damaged so that this requirement still retains its vitality under the rules set forth in Revenue Procedure 67-33. Thus, no portion of the amounts realized in settlement will be treated as a return of capital if the taxpayer fails to establish the adjusted bases for assets involved in the suit for damages.

Finally, the inclusion in income of a portion of the settlement amount which is attributable to a recovery of the taxpayer's legal expenses, subject to the application of section 111, is consistent with the underlying approach of matching the tax treatment of the settlement proceeds with the appropriate elements for which such amounts were paid. Moreover, Revenue Procedure 67-33 indicates clearly that a specific allocation in the settlement agreement of the portion of the amounts received in settlement which is attributable to the recovery of the taxpayer's legal costs is desirable, since the Service will recognize the correctness of the amount so designated in the settlement agreement unless it is unreasonable in light of all the facts. Thus, a reasonable allocation of a portion of settlement amounts to legal expenses would avoid a dispute with the Internal Revenue Service over the amount allocable to such items.

Consensus Recommendation

1. Revenue Procedure 67-33 illustrates the continued importance of a specific allocation in the settlement agreement as to the items to which the amounts received in settlement are attributable. The settlement agreement submitted by the parties for court approval should contain express provisions as to the basis of settlement, the precise claims that the amounts received are in lieu of, and the portion of the amounts received which is attributable to each of these claims. The treble-damage claimant would be best served if those allegations in the complaint which seek recovery of capital or related items are utilized as the primary bases for settlement.

2. In light of Revenue Procedure 67-33, the settlement agreement should contain a specific allocation of a portion of the amount to be received in settlement to the taxpayer's recovery of its costs of suit. An express statement should also be made in the agreement, if the damage claimant can arrange it, to the effect that no portion of the settlement amounts are attributable to punitive damages.

3. The taxpayer-plaintiff should also establish a supporting record of the settlement negotiations, of all documents pertaining thereto, and of all other facts and circumstances bearing on the settlement. While neither the courts nor the Internal Revenue Service has indicated the extent to which evidence, other than the settlement agreement itself, will be given weight, such evidence gathered by the taxpayer would serve to support the agreement and thereby enhance the taxpayer's position.

Legislative Proposals

In December (p. A-13, ATRR No. 336, 12/19/67), Senator Philip A. Hart (D-Mich) introduced a bill (S. 2804) to make two-thirds of any antitrust damage recovery -- whether by judgment or settlement -- neither taxable to the recipient nor deductible by the payor. The bill would amend Section 162 of the Internal Revenue Code of 1954. Senator Hart had introduced a similar bill during the 89th Congress, but no action was taken on the proposal.

A bill, which also died, was introduced on the House side by Congressman Emmanuel Celler (D-N.Y.). It would have given an income-tax exemption to recipients of treble-damage payments that were in excess of actual losses. The bill took the form of an amendment to Section 4 of the Clayton Act, and also prohibited antitrust defendants from deducting treble-damage payments from their corporate income tax as "ordinary and necessary" business expenses.

- 0 -

Subject: The Antitrust Defense to Breach-of-Contract Suits   (Published 10/8/68)

Question

In what circumstances are antitrust charges an effective defense to a breach-of-contract suit?

References

American Manufacturers Mutual Insurance Co. v. American Broadcasting-Paramount
   Theatres, Inc., 87 S.Ct. 1 (p. A-8, ATRR No. 267, 8/23/66)
Kelly v. Kosuga, 358 U.S. 516 (1959)
Channel Marketing, Inc., v. Telepro Industries, Inc., 1968 Trade Cases 72,535
   (S.D. N.Y.) (p. A-2, ATRR No. 372, 8/27/68)

Background

"Highly debatable, " "to say the least, " is the way Mr. Justice Harlan has characterized the posture of federal law relating to the availability to a defendant in a breach-of-contract action of a defense that enforcement of the contract would sanction or further an antitrust viola- tion. He used that language in the American Manufacturers case listed above in the references.

Actually, the common law on the enforceability generally of an illegal contract is not simple either in exposition or application. "The well-established general rule is that an agree- ment which violates a provision *** of a constitutional statute, or which cannot be performed without violating such a provision, is illegal and void. *** The general rule applies equally where the consideration to be performed or the act to be done is unlawful and where an agree- ment with respect to the subject matter is prohibited. A contract for an object prohibited by a penal law is void." But "the rule that an agreement in violation of law is invalid does not always apply where the existence of the thing in question is due to a violation of law only in the sense that incidentally some law was violated in its production, where it might have been created without such violation." 17 Am. Jur. 2d, Contracts § 165 (1964).

In antitrust litigation, the general rule of voidness has been applied to "inherently illegal" contracts -- that is, contracts that are either unlawful on their face (Bement v. National Harrow Co., 186 U.S. 70, 88 (1902)) or are part and parcel of an unlawful scheme or con- spiracy (Sola Electric Co. v. Jefferson Electric Co., 317 U.S. 173 (1942)).

Nevertheless, "the courts are averse to holding contracts unenforceable on the ground of public policy unless their illegality is clear and certain. Since the right of private contract is no small part of the liberty of the citizen, the usual and most import function of courts of justice is to maintain and enforce contracts rather than to enable parties thereto to escape from their obligations on the pretext of public policy, unless it clearly appears that they will contravene public right or the public welfare." 17 Am.Jur.2d, Contracts §178. This reluctance to let an informed, competent party elude his commitments seems to have been operative in the development of the law on the right of antitrust violators to enforce their contracts. "As a de- fense to an action based on contract, the plea of illegality based on violation of the Sherman Act has not met with much favor in this Court," the Supreme Court observed in Kelly v. Kosuga, cited above.

Severable Contract Terms

One of the devices the courts have used to allow recovery of damages for breach of contracts containing or related to antitrust violations is to find the illegal portions of the transaction to be severable from the portion on which suit has been brought. The courts are particularly apt to find severability when the illegal aspect of the transaction relates to a subsidiary rather than the main purpose of the contract and when the plaintiff has already performed his obligations under the contract. For the applicable general rules, see Sections 600, 602(1), and 605 of the Restatement of Contracts.

Application of these rules on severability is not simple, however, particularly in the antitrust field. For example, the validity of the severability doctrine when antitrust issues are involved has been put in doubt by a series of Supreme Court opinions in actions to collect patent royalties. Although a patent licensee is ordinarily estopped to challenge the validity of the patent, the inclusion in the licensing agreement of a price-fixing provision whose legality under the Sherman Act depends on the validity of the patent has been held by the Court to remove that estoppel and, upon proof of the patent's invalidity, to render the whole contract void, including the obligation to pay royalties. Sola Electric Co. v. Jefferson Electric Co., 317 U.S. 173 (1942); Katzinger Co. v. Chicago Metallic Mfg. Co., 329 U.S. 394 (1947); MacGregor v. Westinghouse Electric & Mfg. Co., 329 U.S. 402 (1947).

Collateral Contracts

Most of the Supreme Court's opinions dealing directly with the antitrust defense to contract damage actions have discussed the problem of distinguishing between a contract that is part of a Sherman Act conspiracy and therefore illegal and a contract that is merely collateral to the illegal conspiracy and therefore enforceable by either party. First, in Connolly v. Union Sewer Pipe Co., 184 U.S. 540 (1902), the Court was asked to bar a suit for the purchase price of delivered goods because the seller was involved in an illegal price-fixing conspiracy. The Court refused, declaring that "the plaintiff, even if part of a combination illegal at common laws, was not for that reason forbidden to sell property it acquired or held for sale. The purchases by the defendant had no necessary or direct connection with the alleged illegal combination." 184 U.S. at 549.

Continental Wall Paper Co. v. Voight & Sons Co., 212 U.S. 227 (1909), was a similar case except that the Supreme Court found the plaintiff had admitted, by its demurrer to the antitrust defense, (1) that the account sued on "has been made up in execution of the agreements" that formed the Sherman Act combination, (2) that the plaintiff itself was the illegal combination of competitors, and (3) that a part of the illegal conspiracy was to compel all jobbers, including defendant, to sign exclusive-dealing agreements. To give judgment for the plaintiff in this case, the Supreme Court reasoned, would "be to give the aid of the court in making effective the illegal agreements that constituted the forbidden combination." The Connolly decision was distinguished as involving a defendant who had no connection with the operations of the illegal combination except for the purchase contract sued on.

Six years later in D.R. Wilder Mfg. Co., v. Corn Products Refining Co., 236 U.S. 165 (1915), another defendant tried to take advantage of the Continental Wall Paper decision by arguing that his supplier had no legal existence but was an illegal combination of competitors charging unreasonably high and noncompetitive prices. The controlling precedent, however, was found to be the Connolly case; Continental Wall Paper was distinguished because here the contract of sale is not inherently unlawful and is not directly related to the alleged illegal organization of the selling corporation. See also A.B. Small Co. v. Lamborn & Co., 267 U.S. 248 (1925).

The "collateral contract" issue has also arisen in a Robinson-Patman Act context. In Bruce's Juices, Inc., v. American Can Co., 330 U.S. 743 (1947), the Supreme Court sustained a judgment for the price of goods sold and delivered, even though the buyer was ready to prove that he was being charged a discriminatorily higher price than his competitors.

Listing the sanctions imposed by the statute -- fine or imprisonment and liability for treble damages -- the Supreme Court pointed out that uncollectability of purchase price is not one of them. Moreover the Court felt that the Robinson-Patman Act must be applied, in contract actions, on an entirely different basis from the Sherman Act, since no single sale can violate the Robinson-Patman Act. At least two transactions must take place, it reasoned, and a court does not approve the sale made at the discriminatorily lower price when it allows recovery of the higher purchase price called for by the other sale.

This test based on whether the court is giving its approval of, or assistance in making effective, the illegal agreement was pronounced in the Continental Wall Paper case and is the basis for the result reached in the Supreme Court's most recent decision in this area.

Kelly v. Kosuga, 358 U.S. 516 (1959). In that case, both the sales contract sued on and the alleged conspiracy in restraint of trade involved the same two groups of parties. A group of onion growers agreed to buy 287 of 600 carloads of onions from two onion marketers who had threatened to dump the onions on the futures market. Both the sellers and the buyers agreed not to deliver any of the 600 carloads on the futures market for the remainder of the season. In the Supreme Court it was decided that giving legal effect to the completed sale of onions at a fair price would not enforce a violation of the Sherman Act. Indeed, by this time the period of market stabilization the parties had bargained for had long since passed.

Calling attention to the observation in the D.R. Wilder case "that the Sherman Act's express remedies could not be added to judicially by including the avoidance of private contracts as a sanction," the Kelly opinion endorsed a statement of a dissent in the Continental Wall Paper case that courts are to be guided by the overriding general policy of "preventing people from getting other people's property for nothing when they purport to be buying it." An attempt to distinguish Connolly, Wilder and Small as involving situations where the defense was asserted by a person who was not party to the unlawful conspiracy was rejected as "paradoxical" and as creating "a very strange class of private attorneys general."

Conclusions

The Supreme Court's repeated refusal to treat the illegal contract defense as an additional antitrust enforcement tool seems to forestall, in the law relevant to that defense in antitrust cases, any trend comparable to the one that has increased recoveries in treble-damage actions. In both the Bruce's Juices and the Kelly case, the Court clearly stated its intent to rely on direct actions, whether private or government, to enforce the antitrust laws. Reliance on this statement can be predicated not only on the above described reluctance of the courts to hand a "windfall" to a buyer who does not want to pay for goods he has already received but also on the natural desire of any court to avoid involvement with antitrust issues in a relatively simple breach-of-contract suit. This reluctance to decide antitrust issues is particularly noticeable in state courts, where, after all, most breach-of-contract suits are litigated. See American Broadcasting-Paramount v. American Mftrs. Mutual Ins. Co., 249 N.Y.S. 2d 481 (1963), affirmed 271 N.Y.S. 2d 284, 218 N.E. 2d 324 (1966).

But the general rule of the common law still applies; if a contract in and of itself (or "inherently") violates antitrust law, it will not be enforced in any kind of litigation. Merchant Suppliers Paper Co. v. Photo-Marker Corp., 1967 Trade Cases 72,325 (N.Y. App. Div. 1967). And, if the issue is raised by a defendant who is not trying to keep something he hasn't paid for, the Supreme Court's lively interest in promoting compliance with antitrust policy seems likely to affect the result. In this area, at least, the applicable criteria have never really been spelled out and remain as uncertain as Mr. Justice Harlan suggested they are.

Furthermore, the court opinions disallowing the illegality-of-contract defense have generally decided suits for damages; quite different considerations come into play in a suit under equity jurisdiction for specific enforcement of a contract. A defendant able to point to illegal conduct on the part of the plaintiff is in a stronger position in a court of equity than he is in a court of law. Indeed, it has been suggested that it is the equitable nature of the proceedings that accounts for the Supreme Court's refusal, in the patent-royalty suits described above, to consider the price-fixing agreements severable from the patent license.

In some damage actions the antitrust defense has failed because of circumstances that cause the court to "suspect that the claim of Sherman Act illegality was an afterthought to justify having broken a contract that turned out sour." American Mftrs. Ins. Co. v. American Broadcasting-Paramount, 388 F.2d 272, 279 n. 9 (2nd Cir.)(p. A-11, ATRR No. 338, 1/2/68). In view of many antitrust experts, the result in Tampa Electric Co. v. Nashville Co., 365 U.S. 320 (1961), is explainable in that way, too.

Nothing said above, however, has any bearing on the right of a defendant in a contract suit for either damages or specific enforcement to counterclaim for treble damages under the antitrust laws. A contract-suit defendant asserting an antitrust counterclaim operates under the same rules as a plaintiff in establishing his standing to sue and injury to his "business or property." See Analyses, p. B-1, ATRR No. 288, 1/17/67; p. B-1, ATRR No. 293, 2/21/67; and p. B-1, ATRR No. 297, 3/21/67 (reprinted at pp. 305 et seq., Antitrust and Trade Regulation Today: 1967) and p. 133, supra.

Conceivably, a contract-suit defendant denied an antitrust defense by reason of the "severance" or "collateral contract" rule could nevertheless prove an antitrust violation plus each of the above prerequisites to damage recovery. If the plaintiff in the D.R. Wilder case, for example, had been able, given a chance, to show the existence of an illegal conspiracy and the amount by which the price of the corn syrup he bought had been increased by the conspiracy, presumably he could have counterclaimed and recovered -- either as an offset or as an affirmative judgment -- three times the amount of the price increase he paid on all corn syrup purchases, including the purchase contract sued on. But cf. American Mftrs. Ins. Co. v. American Broadcasting, 388 F.2d 272, 286 M.21 (2d Cir. 1967).

On the other hand, a defendant with an acceptable antitrust defense to the contract suit does not necessarily have a claim for damages or an injunction. The successful defendant in Continental Wall Paper may have been able to prove that the illegal combination actually caused him injury or "threatened injury" (Section 16, Clayton Act) to his business or property.

Since state courts have no jurisdiction over federal antitrust treble-damage claims, counterclaim matters arise only in contract suits brought in the federal courts. If a federal court is selected by the plaintiff, the defendant's failure to assert a treble-damage claim by counterclaim may foreclose him from ever recovering his damages. See Rule 13(a), Federal Rules of Civil Procedure, and Hancock Oil Co. v. Union Oil Products Co., 115 F.2d 45 (9th Cir. 1940). In Channel Marketing, Inc. v. Telepro Industries, Inc., 1968 Trade Cases 72,535 (S.D. N.Y.)(p. A-2, ATRR No. 372, 8/27/68), a state-court action on the contract was brought after a federal antitrust treble-damage suit had already been filed by the other party to the contract. After the contract action had been removed to the federal courts, the two proceedings were consolidated on the theory that each would be a compulsory counterclaim under Rule 13(a).

- 0 -

TABLE OF CASES

Page

TOPICAL INDEX

A

Acquisition of disturbing or disruptive competitor 28

Advertising allowances
  dual distribution systems (See also Price discrimination, dual distribution systems)
  price discrimination
    dual distribution systems 71 et seq.
    meeting competition defense 69
  private label price differentials 64
  prohibitions set by trade associations 14
  small retailers engaging in common advertising 9

Alienation, rule against restraints on, in franchises 78

Ancillary covenants, joint ventures of government contractors 85

Ancillary restraint doctrine, franchises 77

Antimonopolization decrees 103 et seq.
  (See also Monopolies)
  neutralization of the extension as purpose 103
  number issued 103
  provision for later report and petition for modification 105
  trial court discretion 105
  workable competition, restored by decree 105

Attorney General's National Committee to Study the Antitrust Laws 64, 96, 100

Attorneys' fees in treble-damage suits, allowance for 164 et seq. (See also Treble-damage suits)

Automobile dealers, subject to labor union exemption from antitrust laws 22

B

Bank acquisitions and mergers 38 (See also Regulated industries, bank mergers)

Bathtub conspiracies (See Conspiracies)

Blacklists, trade practices by trade associations 14

Boycotts, as per se violations 17, 137
  major factor in condemning industry procedures for self-regulation 14

Breach-of-contract suits, antitrust defense to 174 et seq.

background of 174

collateral contracts 177
  Robinson-Patman Act, sanctions imposed by 175
  Supreme Court decisions on 175

illegality of contract defense 176

severable contract terms, to allow recovery of damages 174 et seq.

severance rule 177

voidness, general rule of, applied to inherently illegal contracts 174

Brokerage provision, price discrimination cases 59

Buffington, John V., Assistant to the Chairman of the Federal Trade Commission 117, 118

Business Advisory Procedures of Justice Department 30

Buying, competition in, necessary to avoid per se violation 18

C

Cement industry (See also Mergers)
  cement manufacturers, acquisition of ready-mixed concrete companies by, FTC enforcement policies regarding 27, 32
  vertical mergers, results of 32

Chartener, William H., Assistant Secretary of Commerce for Economic Affairs 99

Class actions (See Treble-damage actions)

Clayton Act, provisions of, in regard to exemptions granted to labor unions from antitrust laws 20

Combination pricing in joint ventures of government contractors 85

Combinations (See also Conspiracies)
  compliance or tacit agreement 3
  consent or agreement 2
  conspiracies, compared with 1
    case based on distinction 3
  parties to, identification of 4
  proof of 1
  Sherman Act, provisions of 1

Commerce requirement, price discrimination cases 57 et seq.

Commercial codes of ethics 13 et seq.

Common-buying agencies by groups of competitors held lawful 18